JOINING HANDS AND HEARTS

Interfaith, Intercultural Wedding Celebrations

a practical guide for couples

Reverend Susanna Stefanachi Macomb
with Andrea Thompson

A FIRESIDE BOOK
Published by Simon & Schuster
New York London Toronto Sydney Singapore

FIRESIDE
Rockefeller Center
1230 Avenue of the Americas
New York, NY 10020

FIRESIDE and colophon are registered trademarks
of Simon & Schuster, Inc.

For information regarding special discounts for bulk purchases,
please contact Simon & Schuster Special Sales:
1-800-456-6798 or business@simonandschuster.com

Permissions acknowledgments appear on page 311.

Designed by Chris Welch

Manufactured in the United States of America

10 9 8 7 6 5 4 3 2 1

Library of Congress Cataloging-in-Publication Data
Macomb, Susanna Stefanachi.
   Joining hands and hearts : interfaith, intercultural wedding celebrations : a
practical guide for couples / Susanna Stefanachi Macomb with Andrea Thompson.
      p.   cm.
   "A Fireside book."
   Includes bibliographical references and index.
   1. Interfaith marriage.   2. Interracial marriage.   3. Marriage customs and
rites.   I. Thompson, Andrea.   II. Title.
HQ1031 .M33   2003
306.84'3—dc21   2002028234

ISBN 0-7434-3698-9

The interfaith message comes in many ways.

A four-year-old boy asked, "Mommy, does God have a face?" His mother responded, "Well, for me, God doesn't have a specific face. God is every face, everybody and everything." This independent little boy carefully pondered what his mother had said and replied, "Well, I want my God to have a face!" His mother gently caressed the boy's hair. "Well then, you give God whatever face you want."

Two years passed. The six-year-old came to his mother. "Mommy, I know what face God has for me." "Which face is that?" his mother asked, intrigued. "My face!" the boy replied. "But, Mommy, for you, God has your face." The mother smiled and hugged him. She felt she had given him the freedom to develop his own relationship with God. That boy is my son.

■　■　■

I dedicate this book to all the couples and their families who have given me the privilege of walking by their sides. It has been a sacred walking.

And to Edward and Adam, my heart, my wings.

ACKNOWLEDGMENTS

∎

It is said that it takes many people to write a book. During this process of compiling and writing, I have been blessed with a team for which I am most grateful.

First and foremost, I thank all the couples and their families for their participation. They shared their hearts. They gave of their spirits. There are no greater gifts. I especially want to thank my collaborator, Andrea Thompson, a gentle soul, for her steady, quiet, and reassuring patience. She has taken volumes of my material and helped make them concise and very readable. No easy feat! Kim Kanner, my editor, has been a beacon of light throughout this process. Her understanding, encouragement, and support will never be forgotten. I wish also to acknowledge the infinite number of people who participate in the making of this book and whom I may never meet, including copyeditor, designer, sales representatives, packers, and shippers. All of us are connected. Thanks also to Russ Galen, Anna Ghosh and Gerard Koeppel for their contributions, and to Fred Courtright for his expert help.

The former Catholic priest and pastor Nino La Stella and the Reverend Dallas B. Decker, an Episcopal priest and interfaith minister, kindly and with sensitivity reviewed the section on Christianity. The beloved Rabbi Joseph Gelberman, an iconoclast of a man, has been my practical and spiritual teacher. He has generously reviewed the section on Judaism and delighted me with his approval. It was he who provided me with the mantle by which to serve in an ever greater capacity. It has been a gift he has given to many and from which there have been immortal rippling effects. Rabbi Joel Braude of Providence, Rhode Island, enriched our Judaism section by contributing some wonderful material.

My dear friend Lisa Hochman, a lady of grace, and the Venerable Lama

Pema Wangdak of New York City gave of their time willingly and unconditionally to edit and improve the section on Buddhism. With their efforts, it became a more beautiful melody. I thank Maki Yamamoto, a pure spirit, for magically appearing just as I was having difficulty locating information on Shinto practices. She explained, translated, and volunteered her time. Pandit Harkishin Sharma and AVM S. Lakshminarayanan (AVSM) generously provided information, beautiful Sanskrit prayers, and translations for the Hindu marriage rite. I thank Sambhavi Lakshminarayanan for being a facilitating angel in introducing me to her father. Nandini Bhagwat also gave her efforts in reviewing the Hindu section. Ms. Lynnea Yancy from the Research and Review Office in the Baha'i National Center in Wilmette, Illinois, corrected and improved our Baha'i section. Many others too numerous to list contributed prayers, blessings, or particular rites, and we have credited and acknowledged them throughout this book. They include Reverend Tozan Hardison of the Seidoan Zen Temple in Blowing Rock, North Carolina, Reverend Lee Saisho Rosenthal of the Vista Buddhist Temple, Vista, California, and Reverend Don Castro of the Seattle Betsuin Buddhist Temple in Seattle.

Special thanks to Laura Bauer, Matthew Andersen, Meg W. Joyce, Tracy Brown, and David Tutera—delightful professional people who help make my job so much fun! I also thank all those who have contributed but have asked, for personal reasons, not to be credited.

Many others have profoundly affected my life and my work in one way or another. Huston Smith's *The Religions of Man* was the first book I read, many years ago, on comparative religions. It struck me heart and soul. His influence is felt throughout *Joining Hands and Hearts*. The Very Reverend James Parks Morton spoke at my ordination ceremony. I was mesmerized by the power of his words. He spoke of the fact that interfaith dialogue was not a fad but had sprung up out of an ever growing need. On the following day *The New York Times* announced that he would resign from his post as dean of the Cathedral of St. John the Divine. The next year he founded the Interfaith Center of New York. The teachings and spirit of Joseph Campbell have inspired and continue to inspire me as person, artist, and minister. Two beings whose presence illuminates—Pir Vilayat Inayat Khan, the man who brought Sufism to America, and His Holiness the Dalai Lama, thank you. Hindu teachers such as Swami Muktananda and Mother Meera have left their mystical impact upon my being.

It was through the examples set by my parents that I learned generosity, commitment, and the meaning of undying love and devotion. Finally, I would not, could not do this work without the love and support of my beloved husband of sixteen years. It is the essence of my relationship with him and with my son that provides much of the fuel and inspiration in my work with couples and their families. I cherish them beyond words. Their saintly demonstration of patience as this wife and mother spent many a late night and weekend in front of the computer is highly commendable as well!

And so . . .

By the grace of God, I have been blessed.

CONTENTS

■

Part II
THE MANUAL: Turning Religious, Cultural, and Universal Rituals, Prayers, Vows, and Blessings into Interfaith Celebrations

Part III

IN THEIR OWN WORDS: Eight Interfaith, Intercultural Couples,
Their Love Stories and Wedding Ceremonies

PREFACE

∎

Shortly after I was ordained, a couple came to talk to me about their upcoming wedding. The groom brought a set of vows that he and his fiancée wanted to use. He didn't write them himself, he said, and he couldn't remember where they had come from, but he thought they were lovely. I did too. Over the following years, I have included these simple, elegant, and quite beautiful words among the selection of possible vows I present to engaged couples, from which they often make their choices. Many of those brides and grooms have elected to say these particular vows—and I still have not been able to uncover their origin.

In the pages that follow, you will find many passages—vows, readings, ritual explanations, quotations—that I have culled from a variety of sources. These sources include books, scholarly materials, religious institutions, personal conversations, and programs couples have presented to me of other interfaith ceremonies they have witnessed and admired. Very often the passages have been adapted, modified to accommodate contemporary sensibilities or a particular couple's needs and wishes. Occasionally, their origins are unknown.

We have made every effort to identify accurately the selections we offer. If we have inadvertently used material incorrectly or without proper acknowledgment, we apologize. Please do let us know if you have information that will add to our understanding of the sources or the rich history of these uplifting passages. We thank you, in advance, and we will make any appropriate changes or additions in future editions of *Joining Hands and Hearts*.

Throughout this book, you will read about the experiences of many couples with whom I have worked. Their names and other personal details have been changed in order to preserve their privacy; their stories are true, and rich with information and suggestions that I believe you will find helpful and encouraging as you plan your ceremony.

If you are a same-sex couple, ceremonies—including readings, vows, the pronouncement, and other elements—can be adapted to your needs. For example, you may substitute the word *partner* or *beloved* for *husband* or *wife*. In place of the word *marriage,* you or your celebrant may refer to *a blessed union.*

JOINING HANDS
AND HEARTS

Introduction:
So You're Getting Married!

Hello, and congratulations on your upcoming marriage! What a glorious, life-affirming choice that is, one that must fill you with hope and excitement. Now that the big decision has been made, your attention has naturally turned to planning your wedding, which includes the ceremony.

As an interfaith minister, I have been privileged to officiate at hundreds of wedding ceremonies, for couples coming from an amazing variety of backgrounds. Interacting with people of so many cultures, colors, and creeds has enriched me—for this is work that makes the spirit soar and the heart sing! These couples have inspired me. What I often refer to as a sacred walking with these couples during the preparation and celebration of their weddings forms the soul of this book.

It is my hope that *Joining Hands and Hearts* will help you create the wedding ceremony of your dreams and perhaps beyond what you have imagined—one that will resonate within you throughout your married lives. This book offers an inclusive, embracing approach, one rooted in and permeated by the same essence that brought you together—love. And if yours is an interfaith, intercultural, or interracial union, then your love doesn't know the boundaries of color, creed, or nationality. I cannot think of anything more beautiful.

Our world is becoming smaller by the minute. Advances in technology and communications, changes in the way we work, the ability to travel anywhere—all have created what is truly a global village. People from all countries interact with one another to an ever-increasing extent. Inevitably, individuals of different faiths, backgrounds, and cultures meet, get to know one another, fall in love, decide to marry. There is no doubt: intermarriage is on the rise. Here are some statistics:

God is one, but his names are many.

Religion is one, but its ways are many.

Spirituality is one, but religions are many.

Humanity is one, but human beings are many.

—*poem read at the Sarva-Dharma-Sammelana at Bangalore—Visions of an Interfaith Future*

In the United States alone, 5 million people are married each year.

Over 40 percent of marriage-age Catholics marry outside the Church, a doubling since the 1960s. Marriages between Catholics and Protestants, once frowned upon, are now accepted by the vast majority of those faiths.

Three in ten Mormons are now in interfaith marriages, although they are encouraged by their church to marry within their faith.

One in three Episcopalians and one in four Lutherans have married outside their churches.

The Greek Orthodox Archdiocese of America reports that two-thirds of its sanctioned marriages are interfaith.

The number of Jewish-Christian couples doubled to one million during the 1990s.

Four in ten Muslims, whose religion allows men but not women to intermarry, have chosen non-Muslim spouses.

The intermarriage rate approaches 60 percent for Buddhists, the fastest-growing Eastern religion in the United States.

How do all these "mixed matches" get married? Increasingly, couples who wish their wedding day to be one of harmony, spirituality, and celebration are discovering the interfaith ceremony. It is a bridge. The great strength of the interfaith ceremony is that it is inclusive. If done correctly, it is an enlightening and enriching experience. Each ceremony contains its particular brand of magic, and all involved come away feeling honored and celebrated. No one feels alienated or offended. One family is not more important than the other. The interfaith ceremony is like a sacred dance that goes back and forth, celebrating each tradition in joy, making room so that everyone feels richer and expanded.

I often tell couples that my job is to serve them and their families with the utmost caring and devotion. *Joining Hands and Hearts* is here to serve *you*, to suggest possibilities and solutions. There is no agenda, religious or otherwise. We all participate in the sacred. The solutions, in the broadest sense, are not about conciliation and giving in but about learning, understanding, respecting, and always making the circle wider. That is what creates a memorable interfaith wedding ceremony. And that is what makes for a successful interfaith or intercultural marriage, one in which the love will continue to grow stronger, deeper, and greater.

■ ■ ■

Joining Hands and Hearts will serve as your guide to designing a wedding tailored to both of your needs and wishes; it will lead you through the steps of planning a ceremony that is uniquely yours. A ceremony involves not only your beliefs but those of both your families. It has to do not only with religion but also with cultural and personal elements of significance to you.

Part I includes an introduction to interfaith; a questionnaire to help you identify, express, and focus your feelings, thoughts, and needs; practical considerations to bear in mind as you begin thinking about your wedding ceremony; a discussion of family matters to help you deal with issues as the planning process goes on; and the outline of a core interfaith ceremony, which you may use as a blueprint for your own wedding.

In Part II, you will find the manual, which begins with a description of general traditions and includes a selection of universal words. These pages provide a sourcebook of passages that correspond to the several stages of the ceremony—readings, prayers, vows, blessings. They are words that speak to all hearts. And they can be incorporated into almost any wedding ceremony. Next you will find an overview of the religions of the world and their marriage ceremonies, adapted for an interfaith service. We have taken traditional elements from various ceremonies and presented them in a universal context, so that each is appropriate for an interfaith assembly. You will find the symbolism and meaning of each ritual and element explained.

> One should believe in marriage as in the immortality of the soul.
>
> —*Honoré de Balzac*

When I meet with an engaged couple to talk about their wedding, sometimes one or both are not very knowledgeable about their own religious or cultural traditions, and often they know very little about their partners'. I would suggest to you, as I do to the couples I work with, read about each other's religions and cultures. Be willing to learn from each other. The wedding is one day—a wonderful, transforming, unforgettable day, but just a day within a lifetime of days. Every interfaith couple should enter marriage with eyes and hearts wide open, and know as much as they can about each other's religion, culture, and family heritage. Inevitably, there will be adjustments to come. But to marry in ignorance, or with the notion that any compromises can be worked out later, is troublesome.

This manual will help get you started. For each religion, I offer a brief explanation of the basic tenets and the spiritual essence that have provided comfort and sustenance to so many people over centuries. It is my hope to give you a glimmer of the light that illuminates each tradition. Unfamiliar doctrine may sound strange or uncomfortable, and may separate and divide. But the teachings of the founders of the world's great religions—the words of Moses, Jesus, Muhammad, Lao Tzu, Buddha—are essentially universal. All religions and spiritual paths originate from and lead to the same place—love.

> Now join your hands, and with your hands your hearts.
>
> —*Shakespeare*, King Henry VI, *Part III*

As an interfaith minister (who grew up in a traditional Catholic family), I find that the more I learn, including from all the couples I have worked with over the years, the bigger I become inside. Through my exposure to the various traditions, they have become somehow part of me. I have discovered that in some way I am Christian, I am Jewish, I am Muslim, I am Hindu, I am Buddhist, I am Taoist, I am Sufi, I am Native American, I am African-American. I am one with the beauty and wisdom of all faiths and cultures. God is called by many names. Perhaps as you and your partner learn from each other, you too will find yourself growing in appreciation of each other's theologies, cosmologies, and belief systems. And from this exposure you too will become bigger, richer inside. You or your partner may have spiritual inclinations toward traditions other than the ones you were raised with, and this book will serve you in that regard as well.

The next section of the manual lists wedding rituals and customs from around the world. Many couples wish to celebrate their cultural roots. In these pages, you will read about customs you might find appealing and appropriate for your wedding (the African-American jumping of the broom, for example, or the Spanish and Mexican exchange of coins), what they mean and how they can be incorporated and explained in a ceremony.

Finally, many of the couples whose ceremonies I have conducted have graciously allowed me to tell their stories. These are tender, delightful, and romantic stories—about how the couples met and fell in love, the obstacles they overcame, their spiritual paths, the choices they made, and the weddings that, together, we designed. Standing in the presence of their love, one cannot help but be sprinkled with their stardust. From their love stories (which are interspersed throughout the book) and sample ceremonies (which are presented in Part III), you may gather any number of suggestions or creative solutions for your own wedding. I hope their stories will not only describe how, when, and where particular elements can be incorporated but also spark ideas on how to unite your family and guests in a oneness of spirit and, especially, how to achieve the balance that is the hallmark of an interfaith service. Perhaps you may even see a bit of yourselves in these brides and grooms.

As you read the ceremonies that we describe in *Joining Hands and Hearts,* it may be apparent to you that one has a more Jewish slant, another a more Christian slant, or whatever the interfaith combination may be. These are decisions the bride and groom have made. It was the couples themselves who chose the rituals, prayers, and blessings for their weddings. There may be any number of reasons for their choices: Perhaps the bride feels more deeply committed to her religious heritage than the groom does to his and he is happy to accommodate her wishes; perhaps his family and guests come from a more traditional environment, and the couple hopes to help them feel most comfortable. Sometimes who is paying for the wedding is a deciding factor. The final decisions are theirs—just as your decisions must be yours.

■   ■   ■

For me it is an honor and privilege to perform marriage ceremonies. The Christian marrying a Hindu, the Protestant marrying a Mormon, the Baptist marrying a Jew, a Jewish groom marrying a Japanese Shinto bride, the bride who loves her Greekness and admires her fiancé's Catholicism, an African-American and a Moroccan Frenchman who relish each other's cultures—to me, these individuals, even when they struggle with their plans and questions, are a cause for rejoicing. They are blessings. "Marriage," wrote Joseph Barth, "is our last, best chance to grow up." And an interfaith or intercultural marriage to me represents one of our universal best hopes of moving toward a promised land, where people of all religions, creeds, and colors live side by side, hand in hand, honoring and celebrating both their uniqueness and their commonality. No us versus them. Or me versus you. When I stand before an interfaith couple and look out at their families and guests, I sometimes feel, This is where it starts. This is our hope for peace.

Part I

PLANNING YOUR WEDDING

Chapter One

What Is Interfaith?

A Philosophy of the Heart

The spiritual visions of man confirm and illumine each other. . . . Great
poems in different languages have different values but they all are poetry,
and the spiritual visions of man come all from One Light.
—Juan Mascaro, introduction to the *Bhagavad Gita*

Interfaith is not a religion. It walks among the religions.

Interfaith begins when we create a bridge between one set of beliefs
and traditions and another. We start by listening to one another, and to
the humanity in all of us. Interfaith emphasizes the universal principles and
spiritual compassion taught by all schools of divinity and ethics. Each religion is an instrument for the divine, and together the world's religions form
a glorious symphony. Interfaith is the acceptance and celebration of
humankind in all its magnificent faiths, colors, cultures, and traditions. It is
the acknowledgment that there is but one light that burns brightly through
each faith and within each heart. In its essence, this light is love. Interfaith
does not take sides.

The idea is not new. The interfaith message of Sufism is twelve hundred
years old. Humanism flowered in the Italian Renaissance. The Unitarian
Universalist Association traces its origins to 1793; the Baha'i faith originated
in 1844, the Theosophical Society in 1875, Ethical Culture the following
year. The United Nations is an international, intercultural, interfaith assemblage. Indeed, the list of interfaith organizations in the United States and
around the world grows longer each year.

"We are made for complementarity," says South African Anglican Archbishop Desmond Tutu. "I have gifts you do not; and you have gifts that I do
not. So we need each other to become fully human."

Learning to understand and appreciate our differences brings enrichment
to our lives. It is love, after all, that breaks down the prejudice and fear

between people of different faiths and cultures. That is the eternal, healing, magical presence that brings an interfaith couple together. "Think not that you can direct the course of love," wrote the Lebanese poet Kahlil Gibran, "for love, if it finds you worthy, directs your course."

Such is the case with interfaith couples. Listen to the story of Cecile and Lance:

Cecile is French-born, the Jewish daughter of a Holocaust survivor. She and Lance, a devout German Catholic, were getting married. She is a petite brunette, worldly and outspoken; he is tall, blond, and quietly direct. They had already undergone counseling and agreed that Lance would retain his religion, but their children would be raised Jewish.

As they plan for their wedding, couples who were raised in different religions or denominations, like Cecile and Lance, or even in the same faith but are not religious, often wish for a ceremony that is both personally meaningful and God-centered but without the dogma. A growing number of individuals feel comfortable creating their own personal theology and philosophy, and embracing a universal deity or power connecting all things.

They represent one aspect of what I see as a reshaping of religious life in America. I find that many people, perhaps searching for meaning in a complex world, are either becoming more religiously conservative or moving away from organized religion and toward spirituality in a universal sense. While some yearn for traditional religion and doctrine, others find it constricting. On the one hand, there are now some sixteen hundred religions and denominations in the United States, half of them established since 1965; membership in Evangelical churches, led by the Church of God in Christ and the Assemblies of God, has boomed in recent decades, as has the Muslim population in the United States. On the other hand, some traditional Protestant church memberships are in steep decline, nontheist Buddhism is the fastest growing Eastern religion in America, and spiritual self-help—from Deepak Chopra and Marianne Williamson to *Chicken Soup for the Soul*—is flourishing. At their best, of course, religion and spirituality overlap and reinforce each other.

Interfaith is a way all people can find common ground. It takes no position on any organized religion; rather, it rejoices in all. Interfaith calendars published by the National Conference for Community and Justice, for example, note the holidays and observances of all the world's religions. Interfaith offers freedom of choice, freedom to interpret, to question, to grow, to stay rooted in your own tradition, or to discover another and make it your own. It offers freedom to create something new; it allows you to be as you are. There is a place in God's universe for all God's children.

The Very Reverend James Parks Morton, head of the Interfaith Center of New York and former dean of the Cathedral of St. John the Divine in New York City, says, "Most fundamentally, interfaith is respect. Respect for different traditions, different religions, different faiths. It is coming to understand them. And more, it is coming to love them. The recognition of the oneness in all its diversity of expression, that is the basis of interfaith."

■ ■ ■

Joining Hands and Hearts is devoted to the interfaith wedding ceremony. What is that? It is a ceremony that completely reflects you as a couple—your love, your relationship, your beliefs and values. It is a collaborative creation celebrating the traditions and beliefs of two people in a universal context, a ceremony that emphasizes spirituality over religion.

But an interfaith ceremony does not imply uniformity. "Never instead of, always in addition to" is the motto of Rabbi Joseph Gelberman, founder of the New Seminary and the All Faiths Seminary in New York City. We retain our own beliefs and philosophies and reach out to the beliefs and philosophies of another. In doing so, we expand. We become richer inside. We hear the essence within each of us, the essence that supports and sustains us all.

However, there can be great disparity between what a couple wishes and what the families may want in a ceremony. Even if the bride and groom have worked out their own issues, a wedding is a family affair and a public statement that parents or other relatives often care about deeply. Couples find themselves trying to coordinate their desires with those of their parents. Grandparents, siblings, and friends often become involved as well.

I know the questions that engaged couples ask themselves, for I have heard them many times. You may have some of the same: How do we have a wedding that is a reflection of us, our love and our relationship? How do we remain true to ourselves and still make our families happy? How can we create a ceremony that merges our religious, spiritual, cultural, and personal beliefs? Can we do this without offending anyone? What issues are likely to arise? How do we talk to and work with our parents? Which rituals do we include? Who will officiate at our ceremony? Where will it take place? What will it look like? What will people think? Has this been done before?

Joining Hands and Hearts will help you answer all of these questions. I hope you will be inspired and comforted by the stories of other interfaith couples. You are not alone! You are not the first! You'll read here the wedding traditions—rituals, prayers, vows, blessings—of many religions and cultures, and see how to adapt and combine them within a universal context. You will see how to honor your heritage in a ceremony that will joyously affect everyone present, particularly family members. You will learn how to create a ceremony that will remain alive within you always. Regardless of your backgrounds, the language of love and marriage is universal.

To return to the story of Cecile and Lance:

Cecile had a dream in which she and Lance were kneeling in a church; she woke up crying. I asked her how her family, particularly her father (the Holocaust survivor), felt about Lance. She said her father believed it was difficult enough to find someone you really love and care for; her father cared for Lance and had given his blessing. But Cecile's guilt remained. "Cecile," I asked, "do you feel you are betraying your father?" She began to cry. I asked, "Do you love this man? Do you know this with utter certainty?" Solemnly, she nodded yes. I continued, "Do you know this in the most inner core of your being, in your very cells?" Again, she nodded. I said, "Then God is on your side! Who do you think created this love in the first place?" I told her a Jewish legend that says spouses are chosen in heaven before they are born. It reflects the Jewish concept of *b'shert*. (We used that legend in Cecile and Lance's ceremony.) What is God if not love?

> R ejoice in your
> differences!
>
> —*Rabbi Joseph Gelberman,*
> *Founder of*
> *The New Seminary and*
> *All Faiths Seminary*

We began working on their wedding. Each ritual, prayer, and blessing was up for discussion. Lance wanted the lighting of candles; Cecile felt the symbolism too Christian. I assured her that candles are lit at many Catholic-Jewish weddings and no one gets offended, not even the rabbis. We could accompany the lighting with a rabbinic proverb or with music, or it could be carried out in silence. Cecile was reluctant, so I suggested she speak to her parents about it. Her mother thought it was "a beautiful idea!" When the ritual was explained to her, she loved the notion of lighting the side candle herself, symbolizing her giving life to her child. We had her blessing.

As the wedding date approached, Cecile's father came to me and said, "You have a very important job." I smiled. "Will you do a good job?" he asked. I told him I would try my very best. "Do you know our history?" he continued. I replied, "I do." His eyes were now fixed on mine, probing. "Are you our Rebbe?" I immediately answered, "Yes, I am!" He laughed, and we embraced. He and I were both well aware I was not a rabbi. He was really asking if I was there to serve his needs. At the ceremony, we spoke about the importance of rejoicing in our differences.

While interfaith celebrates our diversity, it also points to our oneness. Love and marriage are universal. Wedding legends spanning culture, era, race, and creed abound. Consider these:

The Jewish legend I described to Cecile says that forty days before a child is born, his or her spouse is selected in heaven. When these two souls are created, an angel cries out: "This man is made for that woman, that woman for this man. Should these two souls meet on earth and recognize one another for who they really are, they will fall in love. From that moment on, they shall become as one and no hardship can alter the strength of their enduring love."

A Chinese legend holds that two people are connected at their births by an invisible thread; the thread shrinks over the years until the two are brought together in marriage.

In Islamic lore, when two people join in marriage, God himself opens wide the heavens and commands legions of angels to go forth and bear witness to the miraculous act: Two people have fallen in love, and the heavens sing and dance in celebration.

In the Hindu Kama Sutra, it is written that when the one man loves the one woman and the one woman loves the one man, the angels abandon heaven and go to sit in that house and sing for joy.

On a visit to the home of a former Catholic priest and nun, I noticed this saying from the Kama Sutra framed on their wall, with no indication of its origin. I asked the ex-priest where he got it. He answered promptly: "At a Catholic marriage encounter." (These are weekend-long programs for married couples sponsored by the Catholic Church.) I asked if he knew the saying's origin. He did not. When I told him that it was the Hindu love classic, the Kama Sutra, he said, "It may not be Christian in origin, but it is certainly Christian in spirit." I said, "It is interfaith. It is universal."

■ ■ ■

As an interfaith minister who has been blessed to have officiated at a wide variety of interfaith, interdenominational, same-faith, and humanist weddings, I have seen again and again how a carefully crafted, lovingly designed interfaith ceremony is the perfect answer for so many couples. Interfaith appeals to all who want a ceremony completely reflective of themselves, their beliefs, their relationship. It attracts intercultural and interracial couples and their families.

An interfaith ceremony is the solution for those couples whose own religions forbid interfaith marriage. Even couples who have decided that their future children will follow one religion may feel their wedding needs to be the expression of both their backgrounds. An interfaith ceremony often is the only solution when divergent and competing families become involved.

Interfaith also appeals to same-faith or interdenominational couples with no active religious affiliation who don't want a very religious ceremony.

These couples may wish for a deeply moving ceremony in which God, love, and family are emphasized with spirituality, not religious dogma. The focus is on our universal spiritual essence, what is in all of us and in all faiths, and on the couple and their relationship, family and friends, love and life, spiritual and ethical values.

Interfaith also draws in humanist, agnostic, and atheist couples. Often when one partner is an atheist or agnostic, the couple decide not to mention God during the ceremony. But where there is love, there is sanctity. Marriage is sacred. These couples want a humanist ceremony with heart. Although use of the word God is uncomfortable for them or simply not relevant to their belief system, their cultural traditions can still be celebrated. After all, many religious practices developed from or have merged with cultural traditions.

Interfaith appeals to those who have either willingly left or been rejected or unsupported by their religion—divorced Catholics, for example, former fundamentalists or orthodoxes, or same-sex couples. Interfaith attracts couples who want an alternative to a civil ceremony, which they may find lacking in warmth and personal meaning.

The results of an interfaith union are deeply inspiring. Dealing with the preparation and creation of the wedding, however, can be quite a challenge. If you are from different faiths or cultures, you may embark on a very delicate navigation through unfamiliar waters. It is my hope that *Joining Hands and Hearts* will help you steer the course.

You will find here numerous examples of interfaith unions. I was privileged to perform their wedding ceremonies; each couple profiled went through extensive meetings with me, and most answered the probing questions in my questionnaire. Many of these brides and grooms confronted personal, cultural, and psychological challenges. You will see how together we worked through them. As they bridged their differences and celebrated their commonality, they enriched themselves and their extended families as well. I tell them, "Two traditions, twice blessed!" One bride and groom from Canada had been raised in three traditions and seven cultures. They were planning to teach their children the full range of their heritage. Ten times blessed!

How does a Born-Again Christian join with a Jew? A Moroccan Muslim with an African-American Protestant? A Greek Orthodox with a Lutheran? An African-American Baptist and a woman raised Protestant and Jewish; a Hindu and a Russian Orthodox; a Japanese Buddhist and a humanist from a Christian-Jewish home; a Mormon and a Catholic; an Iranian and a Jew who love their cultural traditions; divorced Catholics who could not marry in their church? All these stories and more are told in these pages.

■ ■ ■

I have worked to make this a practical book, a how-to book, and a reference source for the interfaith-intercultural wedding. My questionnaire, which you will find in the following chapter, is key to the process. The couples I have worked with have benefited greatly from taking the time to answer the questionnaire, and I am certain it will help you focus on what you want and what is important to you.

I had just finished a wedding ceremony in a pavilion on the top of a mountain in upstate New York, a place of panoramic views and breathtaking beauty. A guest came toward me. He told me how moving the ceremony had been for him, and added, "I agree with your theology." I tilted my head in amusement. Theology? I was not aware that I had expressed any particular theology, especially because this had been a humanist ceremony with no mention of God. Putting my hand on his, I said, "It is a theology of the heart!"

My approach to a wedding falls somewhere between the traditional and the alternative. Couples, their families, and guests comment on how spiritual and personal my ceremonies are, how moving and inspirational. But the inspiration comes from the couples themselves—and from something far greater than our understanding. The interweaving of traditions gives the assembled company a feeling of unity.

As you think about your responses to the questionnaire, and as you begin to give shape to your wedding, it will be helpful to understand what we mean generally by the religious, spiritual, cultural, and personal elements within a ceremony. The kind of ceremony you hope for, according to these broad categories, will guide many of your decisions—from the celebrant you seek out to the readings or blessings you select. Explore the following four elements, and consider the meaning and importance of each to your life.

The Religious

Religion is an organized system of beliefs, rites, and celebrations centered on divine power. The major religions all follow written scripture; Native American and tribal religions follow oral traditions. Most religions have functionaries—priests, ministers, rabbis, imams, or shamans. In most religions there are ruling bodies that dictate codes of behavior and interpret doctrine. Religion provides tradition and order. There can be great fulfillment in being part of a religious community. It can give life meaning and a sense of cohesion.

Religious couples often come to me when they need help. They may be Greek Orthodox and Jewish, and discover that neither the priest nor the rabbi will perform their service. When one partner (or perhaps both) comes from a conservative religious background, the couple find themselves in the heartbreaking situation of not being able to be married in their faith. A civil ceremony is a possibility, but as religious individuals they are likely to find this option unacceptable. Viewing their pending marriage as sacred, they want a sacred event; they want God mentioned, they want blessings and prayers.

Each religion has a rite for marriage. Some are elaborate and ceremonial, such as the Hindu wedding ceremony, and some are reserved and formal, such as the Quaker ceremony. If either you or your partner is strongly religious, it's critical to ask yourselves if you wish to have an essentially religious ceremony. Which religious traditions do you wish to include?

The Spiritual

Like many of the couples I work with, you may say that you have faith and believe in God, in something both greater than and part of yourselves—but you don't consider yourself very religious. You may practice little or no organized religion. For you, a ceremony of a spiritual nature, in which God is acknowledged in a universal, inclusive way, may feel exactly right.

In an interfaith ceremony, it is crucial to focus on spirituality and to honor religious rituals in a universal manner, because the doctrine of one partner's religion may offend the sensibilities of the other. Celebrating our common spirituality, which is the essence of all religion, is the beauty and power of the interfaith ceremony. No one should feel alienated or offended.

Spirituality exists in and connects all religions. When you read about the ecstasies of Catholic or Hindu saints, Jewish or Sufi mystics, the experience described is the same. In his book *The Power of Myth*, Joseph Campbell tells the story of a friend who attended an international meeting in Bangkok of the Roman Catholic meditative orders. While the Catholic and Buddhist clergy, the functionaries, in attendance had problems understanding one another, the contemplative monks from the two religions understood one another perfectly. That is because the mystical experience is the same for all; it is internal, nameless, and timeless, and derives from the source of all being. Those who experience it know it is beyond boundaries.

Mystical spirituality is distinct from everyday spirituality. While the former is transcendent, found by going inward—often through meditation—

everyday spirituality is grounded in compassion for all humankind. This is the experience of God in the everyday life; its effect is kindness.

A friend of mine is a psychologist, a loving and faithful husband, an icon of a father, a brave cancer survivor, Jewish by heritage though completely unobservant, and a firm atheist. He lives by the laws of psychology and human kindness. He once said to me, "I am not a spiritual person at all." I looked directly at him and replied, "Why, Howard, I think of you as one of the most spiritual people I know!" He retorted, "I'm a complete atheist." "But you feel spiritual," I said. "Define spirituality," he demanded. I replied, "Connected to oneself, and therefore able to connect to others and to the world at large."

Howard, though an atheist, though never having had a mystical experience of God, has what I call everyday spirituality. He is rooted in his compassion and in his humanity, with a deep commitment to helping his fellow man. He tries to alleviate human suffering where and when he can. His view on life has much in common with Buddhist philosophy, though he is not knowledgeable of it. I relish that Howard and I, with different beliefs and faiths, can communicate openly and respectfully. I believe it is because we both value kindness and respect towards our fellow men and women; we share the philosophy of Albert Einstein and Bertrand Russell: "Remember your humanity." We listen and learn from each other; we share spirituality.

> Ways of worshipping are not to be ranked as better or worse than one another. . . . It's all praise, and it's all right.
>
> —*Rumi*

The interfaith ceremony is founded on everyday spirituality; depending on the individuals involved, however, it can also mirror the mystical. When speaking of touching the mystical during an interfaith service, I am not referring to something so abstract and mysterious that one feels apart from it and unable to understand it. Rather, I am referring to a sense of the eternal in the present moment. Most of us have had such a feeling sometime in our lives. Some sense it when they are witnessing a glorious sunset; others have felt it upon holding their newborn child for the first time. Some have received the experience through crisis or at a near-death encounter. One groom described to me a time when he climbed an eighteen-thousand-foot mountain; standing at the summit after his arduous journey, he felt a oneness with the entire world. It's the sense of something bigger than yourself, yet grounded in yourself. You feel very much alive and connected.

Here is an example of the mystical in an interfaith ceremony. At the end of one wedding, an elderly woman hurried toward me. She had the face of one who had just experienced something she could not explain. Her eyes were wide open when she began to speak: "I just have to tell you what happened! Four months ago my husband died. In fact, I almost did not come tonight, but I did not want to disappoint Jamie [the groom]. We were married forty years, and everything you spoke about I had in my marriage. I have not been able to feel my husband's presence until now." She broke into tears. "When you were speaking, he was right beside me." She pointed to an empty chair and put her hand to her mouth. In her face I saw a combination of awe and gratitude. She began to thank me over and over. I took her hands in mine and said, "Thank *you*! Now I have something to tell you. Four months ago, my father died of lymphoma. And with each ceremony since, I have cried afterward." Through my own tears, I thanked her for the affirmation that my father was always with me.

I watched as she recounted her experience to others. Later the groom approached me. "You see that lady?" he said, pointing. "She and her husband had an amazing relationship. They were an incredible, unique couple. When her husband first laid eyes on her, he went up to her and said, 'Someday we are going to be married!' They were married a year later. They were an inspiration to all who knew them."

Some of the questions in my questionnaire are: Have you ever had a mystical experience? Do you believe in God? What do you hold sacred? Couples' responses help me understand their spiritual beliefs so that together we can create a ceremony that is relevant for them. In this way the ceremony speaks to their souls. Antonio, a Catholic from Portugal, and Susan, an American Protestant, had taken a trip during their courtship to Fatima in Portugal. In their answers on the questionnaire, each wrote about their mystical experiences during that trip. I spoke about it in their ceremony, reminding them of their shared experience. It was a clear reflection of the spiritual nature of their relationship.

Someone once told me he heard a priest describe a religious person as an individual who is looking for God, while a spiritual person is someone who has found God. While I think I understand what the priest was saying, I would put it differently, because many people are both spiritual and religious.

The Cultural

While religion and spirituality deal with theologies and cosmologies—how we view divine order—culture deals with people, their customs and lore.

These are the practices generated by a tribe, region, nation, race, or community bound together by common language or lifestyle. "The great religions are by their very nature transnational and multicultural," writes the psychologist Joel Crohn in his book *Mixed Matches*. "Culture is more particular."

Of course, culture and religion overlap, but they are distinguishable. For the purposes of an interfaith ceremony, it is often important to make that distinction, especially when a prayer or ritual may offend any of the families involved. Many religious rites have roots in cultural customs. Cultures that converted later to a particular religion, in other words, often adapted or merged certain rituals with local customs.

If yours will be a cultural intermarriage, you may want to incorporate practices from your heritage in your wedding. Indeed, doing so can be an important tool in creating an interfaith ceremony, for honoring cultural traditions can go a long way toward healing family issues. When the celebrant explains the meaning and symbolism of the selected rituals, the experience is enlightening for all those present. In a Jewish-Hindu ceremony, for example, one can make a correlation between the Jewish tradition of circling and the Hindu Seven Steps. The Kabbalists, the Jewish mystics, believed that circling helps the bride and groom enter into the seven spheres of the soul. In Hinduism, the bride and groom circle the sacred fire seven times while taking seven sacred vows. Also, in Hinduism there are seven levels of consciousness, or seven chakras. Celebrating the customs of both families brings a sense of belonging and familiarity.

The Personal

Bringing personal elements into your ceremony makes it come alive. It helps create a service that is reflective of who you are as people. This is a ceremony that will touch hearts, not only your own but also those of your families and friends. Think back to weddings you have attended: When were you most moved? Probably that feeling occurred when the bride and groom exchanged their vows, for that is a highly personal aspect of every wedding. Imagine having that feeling throughout your ceremony!

When a couple allows the personal to come into their ceremony, they give the gift of their spirits to all present. Everyone feels closer to the bride and groom, learns more about them and their relationship. All hearts open, and warmth resonates throughout the room.

Decide if you wish to incorporate personal elements in your ceremony, and to what extent. Some couples wish their wedding to be minimal and understated; others want it to be ceremonial and expressive. Your decision may stem from a cultural point of view. Through answering the questionnaire and through discussion with your partner, you will strike the perfect balance. It may take a bit of effort, but as most couples would agree: This is one of the most important days of your life! Among life's many profound events, the marriage rite is the most gloriously celebrated.

■ ■ ■

The path of the human being is not simple. Myriad elements shape one's life and beliefs. Some people need religion, some need spirituality to varying degrees, and some need neither. Interfaith recognizes and understands that reality. It is a dialogue that is evolving along with our global village. It is a bridge among the religions.

At a wedding ceremony, an interfaith celebrant (or officiant or minister) may bring the balance and healing often required; he or she helps build the bridge. We are all human beings with our individual biases, but an interfaith celebrant must be neutral. Since interfaith is not a religion, the celebrant has no vested interest in guiding the ceremony to a certain "religious" outcome. Her job is to listen without judgment, recognize what is needed, present possible solutions with sensitivity, and care for all parties involved. She should remain grounded in compassion and dedicated to serving needs. Then it is for the couple themselves, often with their families' approval, to choose the rituals and music, prayers and blessings for their ceremony.

> There is only one caste, the caste of humanity. There is only one religion, the religion of love. There is only one language, the language of the heart.
>
> —*Sathya Sai Baba*

Rebeccah and Paul, a Jewish-Episcopalian couple planning their wedding, wished to use the Jewish tradition of breaking a glass and the Christian tradition of lighting the unity candle. But they also wanted their processional music to be "Ave Maria." The bride liked the song and wanted her friend, a soloist, to sing it. Rebeccah told me this after saying that she had grown up in a conservative kosher home and attended Jewish schools. After further discussion, it came out that while she and her mother were no longer observant, her mother still had wanted a rabbi to co-officiate with an Episcopal priest instead of having me alone conduct the ceremony. (Rebeccah and Paul were paying for their own ceremony, so they felt freer to select the celebrant themselves.)

I did not know Rebeccah's mother at that point, but I was sure she would be upset about their choice of processional music. In fact, I distinctly remember saying, "Rebeccah, your mother is going to plotz!" (Yiddish for "fall over.") I told the couple to consider seriously the religious significance of "Ave Maria." If they really wanted that song, I suggested, we could begin with traditional Jewish music while the chuppah was carried in, and balance other components of both religions during the rest of the ceremony. I strongly suggested that they speak with Rebeccah's mother and prepare her. In the end, we had Jewish music *and* "Ave Maria," and Rebeccah's mother later wrote and thanked me for one of the most meaningful experiences of her life.

I often meet and work with parents as well as the bride and groom. It is all part of the process of learning about one another. Before we build the bridge, we need to clarify where everyone is coming from and what each one wishes. I also want to hear their fears and concerns. Only then is understanding possible. This process does take effort, but it's worth it—for at your wedding, you set the precedent for how you will conduct your lives together, and how your families and friends will relate to you. As Joel Crohn writes: "The act of getting married is a kind of dress rehearsal for a shared life. . . . Weddings symbolically condense and display how a couple intends to live their life in relationship to family, culture, friends, spirituality, and success. . . . [The wedding presents] an opportunity for the couple to start designing a blueprint and laying the foundation for the future cultural and religious framework of their new family."

You will find that the material in *Joining Hands and Hearts* will help you create the wedding you want, regardless of whether you choose an interfaith ceremony and celebrant or use interfaith aspects in a traditional ceremony with religious clergy from your own backgrounds. Your wedding will be enriched by whatever you choose. Remember that marriage is universal. Love, devotion, faithfulness, long life, health, happiness, children, and family—these are the concerns of every bride and groom, and they are among life's greatest gifts.

ANNA AND JOSH, A FORMER EVANGELICAL
CHRISTIAN–AGNOSTIC PROTESTANT JEWISH COUPLE

The love story of this young couple traces a long and often difficult path. Here, in Anna's words, is how their story unfolded:

The first time I saw Josh, in an acting class in Manhattan, I thought, Now there's a really intelligent, sensitive, Jewish guy. Since I was a Christian, very committed to my spiritual walk and to my conservative church, it didn't occur to me that he might be just the intelligent, sensitive guy I'd looked for all my life. The first time Josh saw me, he thought (as he confessed years later), "Great legs. There is a woman I could spend the rest of my life with." (I don't know the degree of correlation between his two thoughts.)

When Josh asked me out for the first time, I wanted to refuse. But he was so nice, and I couldn't think of a polite way to say, "I can't associate with you because you're not the same religion as me." So we went ice skating in Central Park.

Two more dates followed, and then Anna realized she had to break up with him.

I was in my mid-twenties, I wanted to get married someday, and I knew I'd never marry a non-Christian. So, even though Josh was pretty incredible in every other way, I told him I couldn't see him anymore because he was not a Christian. I missed Josh and prayed for him for years after we stopped seeing each other.

During those years apart, Anna went through a time of questioning. When she attended services in her church, she sometimes cried for no apparent reason. She finally stopped going, bowing out of all her church commitments.

I was afraid of the loving but judgmental God I'd been taught, and I finally decided that couldn't possibly be who the real God was. I longed for the Spirit of God but refused the many rules of the church, the literal interpretation of Scripture, the confession and intercessory prayer I'd always used. I went off that God cold turkey. I was free-falling.

Strangely enough, Josh began volunteering at the after-school center for teenagers where Anna worked. They started seeing each other again.

I was never afraid with him. I was never more myself. He told me he felt the same way. We delighted in each other. He listened to my spiritual struggles, and held me when I cried because I couldn't figure out who God was. Josh had some experience with Buddhist meditation, and I was beginning to explore meditation, although I kept insisting I didn't get it and couldn't do it. Sometimes we meditated together. Sometimes we annoyed other pedestrians by stopping on busy street corners to kiss.

I was happy. After a while, I knew deep down that I had found the one. Josh said that from the beginning when he held me in his arms a little voice inside would say, "This is my wife, this is my wife," but he would completely ignore it. Now he says he should have known the little voice was smarter than he was.

One thing disturbed Anna: What would her parents think about Josh? Anna and her mother and father were so close, and she didn't want to make them unhappy. They learned about the presence of Josh in her life; they knew he was not a Christian. Eventually, they all had lunch at a Chinese restaurant.

It is difficult to say which of the four of us was the most nervous, but everything went beautifully. What was there not to like about Josh, this incredible man who loved me so much? What was there not to like about my parents, this wonderful couple who gave me their all?

Two and a half years later, Josh asked me to marry him. By then, he had spent enough time with my parents to let them see who he really was, beyond the category they had always been trained to place him in: non-Christian. But I knew their misgivings about their own daughter marrying out of the faith, raising their grandchildren differently than they had always assumed, because my mother and I had touched on the topic. To their great credit, my parents were able to be purely joyful with me.

On a beautiful August day, filled with lovely flowers, gorgeous dresses, friends, family, joy, and an openness and acceptance that only love can create, Anna and Josh were married. Anna wrote:

We would marry in the Friends Meeting House I had finally found in my quest for communion with the Divine Spirit. Sunday services there are silent. The silence is deep and filled with light. The first time I walked into the Friends Meeting House I felt the presence of God wash over me. It was the only place I had been able to meet with God for several years. Josh sometimes went with me and meditated, too.

Anna and Josh had asked me to talk about what they called "our long and miraculous journey, the one that finally led us to each other." At their wedding I said, "Together against great odds, through love and perseverance and always, always with God's help and intervention, you stayed on course. You forged ahead to fulfill your destiny together. It is my belief that when a love of this magnitude occurs, it resonates throughout the universe, bringing us all closer to God's peace."

Anna's final thoughts:

The service was real and intimate and celebratory and emotional. When at the end Susanna said, "I present to you Mr. and Mrs. _____," the guests burst into spontaneous applause, and as they clapped for several long moments, we simply stood holding hands, grinning, looking out at our loved ones, basking in the elation of the entire room, Jews and Christians and not-really-sure-whats. It is a minute, pure and true and victorious, that I will remember as long as I live.

Chapter Two

Tell Me All About It!

A Questionnaire for Couples

TWO days after my ordination, I was asked to officiate at my first wedding ceremony. I was so nervous! The bride and groom, however, seemed delighted to be my very first couple and nuptial service. He was an American Jewish man, and she was an East German Christian woman raised on the teachings of Rudolf Steiner. Before meeting the couple for the first time, I asked myself, "How can I speak to these two faces, on this momentous day of their lives, without knowing them at all?"

I decided that I needed to get to know them better.

In their kitchen, over steaming cups of tea, we began talking. I asked them many questions. When and how did they fall in love? What did they want and not want for their wedding ceremony? Did they believe in God? We discussed their relationship, their backgrounds, their beliefs, their cultural and family issues.

I listened carefully.

That they loved each other was undeniable. I noticed a sweet gentleness between them, in the words they used with each other and in their caresses. I was attuning to their magic. I distinctly remember their ambiguous responses when speaking of God. When they spoke of nature, however, their faces became serene and illuminated. Ah, I thought to myself, *there* lies the quality of the transcendent for them. It is in nature! I took mental and written notes.

We connected—I to them and they to me.

At their ceremony I used metaphors of nature when speaking of love and marriage. We incorporated a Native American blessing. From the looks on their faces, I knew it all touched home. You see, I was speaking their language. They wrote their own vows, to everyone's delight. We honored the bride's mother, who had passed away. I quoted Einstein for the sake of the groom's father, who was a scientist. We spoke of their family and friends in Germany who were unable to attend. We combined desired elements from both their traditions with balance and sensitivity.

Afterward many commented that it was the most beautiful ceremony they had ever seen. What joy! What tears! I had taken a risk in creating something unique, and it had turned out beautifully.

Since that time I have developed a written questionnaire that I ask couples to complete. I am going to ask you to complete the same questionnaire. Most of my couples absolutely love the assignment. Here are the words of Rachel: "We loved the questionnaire! Sometimes when you are planning a wedding you get caught up in the stress involved and forget the real reasons for the joyous day. The questionnaire helped to bring us back."

The questionnaire gives you an opportunity to articulate your feelings and thoughts regarding your ceremony. As you write about how you love each other, you're creating a precious document. These are powerful words! They penetrate the exteriors of the day—the invitations, the table settings, the gown, the flowers—to the essence of why you are having this glorious celebration. Twenty years from now, when your hair is tinged with gray, you and your beloved will be able to pull out these pages, perhaps snuggled together on a favorite couch, and recapture how you felt as you began to plan for the moment you would formally join hands and hearts. It can bring you back again and again. You may even decide one day to pass it along to your children.

I ask that you and your fiancé or fiancée answer these questions separately. You will have different as well as common needs or wishes. Each side of the family may have particular requests. After you have gathered your thoughts and feelings individually, you can come together to share and discuss them. You then have the tools to build a bridge.

When you write your testimony for the section of the questionnaire called "Matters of the Heart: About Your Relationship," you may want to keep it a surprise from your partner. Perhaps you'd like some of these personal comments included in your ceremony. Imagine how you would feel hearing each other's words of love read by your celebrant without having seen them beforehand!

Occasionally there has been a reluctant participant. I remember Kurt, who procrastinated answering his questionnaire until just two weeks before the wedding. He returned his responses to me with the following note: "Dear Susanna, I must admit I was dragging my feet on this. Now having done it, I really see the value of it." After their honeymoon, he and his bride sent me a gourmet food basket with a lovely note. It seems he was especially moved!

Of course, you need not answer the questionnaire if you do not wish to, or if it makes you uncomfortable in any way. You can create a beautiful ceremony tailored to your needs and desires by choosing and combining elements from our later menu of selections. The choice is yours.

As a celebrant, I see my role as a facilitator or, perhaps a bit more fancifully, a weaver, a third party who helps to interlace diverse and sometimes seemingly divergent elements to form a rich tapestry. In answering the questions that follow, you will get down on paper some of the particulars that must be kept in mind, enabling you to give your own celebrant information that he or she should know, especially if you envision a personal ceremony that reflects your relationship and your beliefs. But more than that, couples seem to discover, the questionnaire is a way of getting in touch with their souls, of uncovering and disclosing more about who they are and what they want.

So I hope you will think of the questionnaire as a means of defining the unique magic of your relationship and discovering how you might share that magic with all who will attend your wedding. I encourage you, as I do the engaged couples who come to me, to put all your cards on the table. Don't hold back! Be completely honest. Be true to yourselves. Most important, speak from your heart. Remember that this is not a test or a college term paper. I tell my couples to imagine they are simply writing in a journal—and not to worry about punctuation or grammar! Answering the questionnaire is a process to be enjoyed.

You may wish to settle down with your laptop or a fresh pad of yellow paper, a cup of coffee or a glass of wine, and write at length, in your own words and at your own speed. Some find that short, to-the-point answers provide them with all the framework they need. Many couples write more extensively. One bride-to-be ended up with a fifty-two-page single-spaced essay.

The questionnaire is divided into parts. Like your ceremony, it is a spiraling circle that first encompasses everyone who will attend your wedding, then addresses your immediate families, and finally focuses on you and your relationship.

Logistics

Logistics include your names; wedding date, time, and location; contact information; family members; and so on. These basic facts and figures are likely to be discussed when you contact the celebrant you choose to conduct your ceremony, but it is wise to think them through at this early stage. Write them down and have them ready to present.

Envisioning Your Ceremony

This is a broad-strokes sketch of the wedding you see in your mind. At this stage, perhaps you have only general ideas—in the words of one bride, "a lovely vision, without a lot of details." Perhaps you are aware of one or two rituals you would like to include, such as breaking the glass in the Jewish tradition and the Christian unity candle, but not much else. Or maybe you have a particular reading in mind. However, you may be a couple with very definite ideas. In that case, here is your opportunity to organize them.

When you have completed this part, I make one request: Be open to possibility! You may very well change your mind as you look through the later sections of this book and see all the delectable options available to you. I remember one couple who thought they didn't want any readings or rituals apart from the exchange of rings. Then, after being shown our menu of possibilities, they chose a highly personalized ceremony richly laden with readings and cultural flourishes. Another example: Some couples are absolutely certain they want to write their own vows. After reading sample vows I provide for them (as I will for you), they prefer to adapt those words—editing, deleting, changing at will. So as you picture your ceremony in these various ways, think broadly. None of this is etched in stone!

Many couples want their ceremony to be touching, for themselves and for their family and friends. Aside from that, feelings vary. One of the questions I ask you to think about is the tone you'd like to set. Some tell me they envision a formal wedding, ceremonial and traditional. Others hope for a more intimate, warm feeling. One Catholic groom requested: "Spiritual, yes. Religious, no. Sacred, yes. Pomp and circumstance, no." His bride also asked for the ceremony to be "romantic and life affirming."

Another bride wrote: "We see our ceremony as being a reflection of our lifestyle. It should be solemn, reflecting the seriousness of our commitment, but not narcoleptic." In his questionnaire, her groom agreed, adding, "And not too long!"

Sometimes a bride or groom requests that laughter be present to reflect their joint sense of humor. As one bride put it, "Jake and I laugh a lot together. It is one thing that is so special about us. Is it possible to have laughter alongside the tears—as I have no doubt that we will both cry?" My answer: "Absolutely."

From one concerned groom-to-be I heard, "I'm a financial analyst, not really an emotional guy. My friends are not emotional people. I really see a plain, basically civil ceremony." His fiancée had different thoughts. She wanted something a little more spiritual, a little more emotional. The combined result was a humanist ceremony with heart. Touching but "not sappy," as he put it.

You will be asked to consider what you wish for family and friends to take away from the experience of your wedding. One bride answered that she wanted guests to feel not like observers but like integral parts of the ceremony. The groom had two requests: "I ask that everyone should cherish the evening and bask in each other's audience. And I want the fine gentlemen within this upstanding group of men to act as chivalrous and attentive towards their significant others as if it were their first date." I read this at the ceremony verbatim. It scored points with the ladies!

Your Backgrounds and Families

In this portion of the questionnaire I ask you to think about your backgrounds and how you were raised. Write about your families and what they mean to you. Here is an opportunity to voice your love and gratitude for them, and these are words your celebrant may include in a part of the ceremony.

Through his response, we hear Toi's admiration for his parents: "My parents are the embodiment of quiet strength, resilience, courage, selflessness, and a sheer determination to survive. Despite the fact that they both worked when I was a child, I was lucky to have home-cooked meals every night no matter how late they came home, and I was never denied an opportunity to succeed. For years, I never understood how I could ever repay them, but I realize now that it's not a matter of repayment but rather living my life in a way that they would be proud of and doing for my future children what they did for me. I just hope that, each day, I can comport myself with the dignity and grace that characterizes their lives."

Annette's parents divorced when she was young, and Annette was raised by her mother, to whom she paid tribute: "My mom has given me unconditional love. I admire her for the way she changed her life. With two young children, she went back to college and got her degree and hopes to retire in a few years from the New York Police Department. Money was tight, but we always managed to get by. Her life is and always will be for her children."

John expressed his feelings quite succinctly: "I want to tell my parents that they are in every way responsible for who I am, that they did an incredible job and I am grateful. I couldn't have asked for better parents."

> Two distincts,
> division none.
> — *William Shakespeare*

Often couples find their parents' marriages are inspirations. Catherine wrote, "My parents have been married for forty-five years. I'd like that to be mentioned somewhere. They stand as an example of what marriage should be. From both of them I got a great capacity for love and friendship and loyalty."

You will also be asked to describe your religious or cultural background. In this way, your celebrant can become familiar with how you were raised.

Catherine wrote, "I was raised Presbyterian, but it was mainly a social thing for me, with choir and handbells and kids my age. My parents used to come watch me sing and play on Easter and Christmas Eve. I come from Suburbia with a capital *S,* the kind of place where we rode our bikes to the pool and Little League, and climbed trees and played in the park."

Elliot wrote, "I was brought up Jewish. From about fourth or fifth grade through high school I attended religious school. As a family, we weren't particularly religious but went to temple for the major holidays—Rosh Hashanah and Yom Kippur. I did have a Bar Mitzvah and thought I didn't really like Hebrew school. I think I liked singing the prayers though."

From Sharifa: "I am a Muslim by birth. I don't consider myself a practicing Muslim. Having said that, I do consider Islam to be part of my heritage and culture."

From Tanner: "Since college, I have looked outside to various sources of spirituality. I don't believe that any one religion has all the answers. I find myself very much drawn to Native American spirituality and Buddhist thought."

From Kiki: "My parents grew up in Japan and are Shinto. I am not very religious but feel strongly tied to my culture. It is my hope that I will pass on a strong sense of Japanese culture to my children."

This section of the questionnaire also deals with any sensitive matters that need to be considered. Most couples tend to be keenly aware of situations that might present problems, and these may be of a religious nature (such as her parents really want a rabbi to officiate, but his parents are going to have a hard time accepting that idea). There are often family realities that might complicate the proceedings to come. These questions will help you begin to identify the sensitive issues.

When there are interfaith or intercultural differences, or when divorce and stepparents are part of the picture, these issues need to be discussed and navigated before the ceremony. At one wedding the father of the bride refused to sit in the front row beside his ex-wife. He indicated he'd walk his daughter down the aisle but then would join his current wife in the back. The bride was extremely unhappy at first. After we talked it over, she decided it was best not to make her father do anything that would be uncomfortable to him.

The sister of one bride, upset that the wedding would not be performed by a rabbi, was very vocal about her objections during the weeks leading up to the ceremony. I suggested asking this sister to do a reading regarding the chuppah. She then became an enthusiastic participant!

One interracial, interfaith, intercultural couple specifically wanted their families to better understand the beauty in their relationship through the ceremony. So we quoted the words of Dr. Martin Luther King, Jr., and I pointed out to the congregation that the bride and groom's marriage reflected King's great dream and vision.

Don't shy away from the difficult matters! You are setting the foundation for how you will deal with different issues throughout your marriage. With enough love and understanding, you can navigate an amicable solution for all. I have seen it happen successfully over and over again!

Perhaps you'll want to remember someone who is no longer with you. A Chinese-American bride wrote dearly about her affection for her grandmother, who had died recently at age ninety. Amelia missed her grandmother very much and wanted to honor her. Since both Amelia's parents worked, her A-ma had been her primary caregiver. From the questionnaire, I was able to lace her words into her ceremony: "My A-ma lived with us. We knew her beautiful smile, her laughter, her curiosity and common sense, her endurance and unconditional love. She was our devoted baby-sitter, an amazing cook, and knew how to do anything around the house. She never complained and was always so patient with us. She was an integral part of our lives."

Matters of the Heart: About Your Relationship

This is my favorite part of the questionnaire. The questions in this section are all about you and your beloved—what your future bride or groom means to you, what you love about this individual, how he or she has changed your life.

I hear the most romantic stories! Many describe their emotional "Will you marry me?" moment. Here is one: John and Robin met when both were members of a choral society, Robin as a singer and John as assistant conductor. He "always had a bit of a crush on Robin," John wrote, "but didn't act on it for fifteen years." They became good friends, however, and enjoyed "some real heart-to-heart conversations over the years," Robin said. Toward the end of that time, John separated from his wife, and one day a long-standing member of their chorus took Robin aside after a rehearsal and remarked, "The maestro is free." She just smiled and replied, "I know." Matters moved quickly after that.

> The best and most beautiful things in the world cannot be seen or even touched. They must be felt with the heart.
>
> —*Helen Keller*

John wrote, "I felt the need to propose in a unique, memorable, and romantic way." So one afternoon he e-mailed Robin that he needed thirty minutes of her time, met her at her office (she is a merchandising executive in the fashion industry), put his finger to his lips, indicating she was to say nothing, and led her to Carnegie Hall, a short distance away. "Having rehearsed and performed in Carnegie Hall many times over the past twenty years," John explained, "I knew the right person to ask if I could 'borrow' the main stage for the occasion."

Taking the service elevator to the stage level, John led Robin center stage, took her hands, looked deep into her eyes, and sang the chorus from "Our Love Is Here to Stay." He wrote, "With tears in my eyes I then got down on one knee and said, 'As a newly single person, I have the privilege to ask for your hand in marriage.'" With tears in *her* eyes, Robin answered yes—"at which point we heard applause from the dress circle!" As it happened, a tour of the hall was taking place at the time. They'd had an audience all along, echoing their musical history together.

When couples share their thoughts and feelings on the questionnaire, I ask permission to quote their tributes to each other at the ceremony, and that is when they hear their partners' words for the first time. This is the stuff that makes for stardust! Often, when I return home from a ceremony, my husband tells me that I am sprinkled with stardust. I actually glow from the power of these couples' love. You'll read some moving testimonies in our couples' ceremonies at the end of the book; here are a few examples.

Maestro John wrote about his Robin, "What qualities do I most admire in her? A—she is Accepting. B—she is Beautiful. C—she is Caring. D—she is Delightful. E—she is Ebullient." And he continued right on to the end: "X—she Xceeds my expectations. Y—she is Young-at-heart. Z—she is Zesty."

Toi wrote of his bride, "I admire Amelia's kindness and tremendous heart. Her beauty and positive energy always makes me feel wonderful, and she always lifts my spirits when I am down. Loving Amelia is easy. She has a quiet, reliable strength. Just the simple act of holding hands brings me unsurpassed joy, and falling asleep with her in my arms provides unparalleled contentment. She is beautiful in the morning (of course, I don't have my contacts in!), and I love watching her sleep. There is an aura she exudes that is always inviting and comforting."

Or consider Shawn and Karen's words about each other. Karen wrote, "From our first date, he had me smiling and laughing all night. I remember leaving him that first night with all his thoughts that he shared with me, and thinking, I want more of that! I feel we complement each other. He loves to talk, and I like to listen. He is messy, I am neat. I love to cook, and he loves to eat."

And Shawn wrote, "I realized from the beginning that she was the one. She is a very easy girl to love. I admire her strength and solid family upbringing. We are a good fit. The Bible speaks about things from God being 'first peaceable and easily entreated.' With Karen, things are first peaceable and easily entreated."

Jimmy wrote about his Carmen, "I love Carmen in totality, from her sparkling eyes to her strong character. When we are apart I feel at a loss. When we are together I feel whole. I love the way she takes the hurt with a soft touch. Every time the phone rings I hope that it is her. I feel deeply loved and appreciated when I see her next to me, her look of calmness, the energy that she releases when I hug her."

Katayone wrote of her Andrew, "He is the reason I get up in the morning, and knowing I'll see him again in the morning lets me sleep at night. He knows me so well, understands what I need (usually before I do). He is an endless source of support. He also makes me laugh, even at times when laughing does not seem possible. Not to mention that he is incredibly handsome!"

Catherine summarized her love for Elliot in nine words: "I am truly marrying the man of my dreams!"

Can you feel the stardust?

About Yourself

In this section, you will write something about what you enjoy doing, what inspires you, who you admire, what plans you have for the future. As you look at some of the questions, you may be thinking: Why? What's this for? In fact, I have used the answers to every single one of these in ceremonies, whether it was one groom's passion for golf or another's motto to live by. In this part, I also ask several questions that prompt soul-searching and elicit powerful feelings. Consider some of these diverse responses from people with spiritual beliefs ranging from the religious to the humanist:

Wrote a Mormon groom: "I see God as a caring and loving being who understands and empathizes with our predicaments, a true spiritual father in heaven. One belief in the Mormon Church is the idea that God was once as we are now and has 'evolved' to his present position, and as literal sons and daughters of God, all of us contain elements that are sacred and we all have the potential to become as he is now. What this means to me is there exists a true connection between God and ourselves: a parent and child connection. I find this reassuring."

A Jewish bride: "I feel very tied to the cultural and historical aspects of Judaism. I support the state of Israel. I feel that Judaism, at least the way I 'practice' it, is one of the more ecumenical and welcoming religions. I believe in God as a higher power and creator of all things. I almost feel that God is like the little wandering spots you sometimes see when you open your eyes. They are always there somehow in the fluid of your eyes. They are familiar, always with you, and you wonder what they are and what they are there for. I guess I sense that God is somehow in me or at least always with me in my surroundings. I feel most connected to God when I'm singing, especially in those rare times when I just feel like a musical instrument because everything is connecting."

A groom: "I was raised an Episcopalian, but I rejected dogma and adherence to a particular faith by age seventeen. I believe in creative spirit, but I do not believe in a Creator. I believe in the power of prayer, but I do not believe there is anyone to whom prayer can be addressed. I believe in the interdependence of all things visible and invisible, animate and inanimate. I believe that simply because I can't see the leprechauns on the lawn doesn't mean they don't exist."

From Neeha, a Hindu bride: "My family taught me to respect all religions and cultures. Everything is Brahman, including me and you. It is this tremendous sanctity and reverence of all life for which I am deeply grateful. I try to see God in everyone and everything."

From Carmen, a humanist: "I come from a pretty large Latin family. I believe that the idea of God is self-created on many levels, and that we create the image of God in accordance with what we think we need in a god. A patriarchy would obviously need a powerful, all-knowing, disciplinary, male god. I, as a woman seeking strength within myself, and solidarity within women, name my god a Goddess. I need, in my life, to invoke the sacred female and to lay within her for strength and solace."

From Shawn, a Born-Again Christian: "I believe strongly in the Bible and the Word. I do not think it is important what denomination I call myself as long as it is rooted strongly in God's Word, that is, the God of Abraham. I believe that the Holy Spirit lives inside me and anyone else who asks Him into their heart. I am inspired when I see God moving in people's lives. I like to see testimonies in action. I like to see miracles."

> The greatest thing about love is that when it's there, you know it.
>
> —*Bill Cosby*

Ted and Alison had had a baby before getting married. Alison wrote, "As I get older, I sense a certain connectedness with all things in the universe that I never felt when I was younger. And it got stronger since my becoming pregnant and giving birth. A sense that we are all part of the same struggle—a deeper sensitivity to others, the environment, and the world in general. I believe there's something going on out there—that's God for me. I felt most connected to that force when I was delivering Christopher. My sense was that I was holding on to a life force that was pulling me at an exorbitant speed through a tunnel. I believed in it and so I felt delivered. I cried and thanked God when I came home."

Or perhaps the words of Catherine and Gemma sum up how many see and feel God. From Catherine: "I see God in the baby goslings that are here for such a short time in the spring and in the sun glinting off a buttercup." From Gemma: "It's all about what is in your heart. That's where God is."

For me as the celebrant, the answers to the questionnaire help paint a portrait. That portrait helps me know to whom I am speaking and how I can address their hearts. To do that, I must speak their language. I seek two things: How can I best inspire this couple? What is it about them that inspires me? Then, attuned to their magic, I am able to reflect that essence back to them and to all those present.

Your answers will help your celebrant better understand you and speak to you in a way that resonates with your soul.

The Questionnaire

Logistics (to provide your celebrant)

- List your full names as they will appear on your wedding certificate. (It is a good idea to go over pronunciations with your celebrant.)
- List the names by which you wish to be addressed at the ceremony, if they are different from your given names.
- If known, give the date and time of your ceremony, and the address and phone number of the location.
- List your postal and e-mail addresses and your phone numbers. If you will be staying with friends or relatives on the day of the wedding, list the addresses and numbers where you can be reached.
- List the names of all close family members who will attend.
- How many people are expected to attend?
- If you will have a rehearsal, do you want your celebrant to be present?
- At what time do you wish your celebrant to arrive for the ceremony? Take into consideration the signing of papers (i.e., the ketubah, the marriage license). Also, your celebrant may have to change into robes and set up items needed for the ceremony.

Envisioning Your Ceremony

- Whom would you wish to conduct your ceremony? Will it be a member of one or both of your faiths, an interfaith minister, or a judge or civil officiant?
- If you don't yet have a site selected, where would you like your service to take place?
- How long do you wish the ceremony to last? (Ceremonies can range from fifteen minutes to well over an hour, with the average about half an hour.)
- What tone would you like for the ceremony? Intimate, ceremonial, minimal, sacred, warm, solemn, lighthearted?
- Do you want a spiritual, religious, humanist, or personal service (or combination thereof)?
- Are there any rituals or traditions you know you want to include?
- Are there any readings, prayers, or blessings you know you want to include?
- What do you definitely want and definitely not want for your ceremony?
- What would you like to convey to everyone in attendance?
- Do you wish to include, honor, or mention any family members or friends? If so, who?
- Do you want to mention anyone who has died?

- Will you write your own vows?
- Do you have a bridal party? How do you picture your procession?

Your Background and Families
- What are your religious, cultural, and family backgrounds? How were you raised?
- Are you close to your families? Please elaborate.
- Are there any sensitive issues between the two of you with regard to the ceremony?
- Are there any sensitive issues involving your families with regard to the ceremony?
- What did your parents and grandparents contribute to you as a person?
- For second marriages with children: How do you love them? Elaborate.

Matters of the Heart: About Your Relationship
- How did you meet and fall in love with your partner?
- How long have you known each other?
- When did you realize he or she was your partner for life?
- What is special or unique about your relationship with your partner?
- What qualities do you most admire in her or him?
- Would you like to share any touching, funny, or revealing stories about the two of you?
- When do you or did you feel closest to your partner?
- How and why do you love him or her? (Don't hold back!)
- How does he or she make you feel loved?
- What has your fiancée or fiancé given to you as a person? How has she or he made you better?

About Yourself
- How would you describe yourself?
- What do you do for a living?
- What do you hold sacred?
- What inspires you?
- What are your priorities in life?
- What are your goals for the two of you as a couple?
- Do you hope to have children?
- How do you view marriage generally and your upcoming marriage in particular?
- Do you believe in God? If you do, how do you perceive or feel God?

- Was there a time or experience when you felt most connected to God? Describe it.
- Where is your sacred spot, a place you feel most connected, most at peace, or most inspired?
- What do you enjoy doing? What do you consider just plain fun?
- What is your favorite art form, movie, piece of literature, poem, song, painting, sculpture, or dance?
- Who is your favorite artist or performer, your favorite sport or athlete?
- What is the motto you live by or would like to live by?
- Is there a person in history you admire greatly? Why?

Optional (and highly recommended!): Write for each other a life pledge. Include a promise and a vision for your future life together. Tell your partner just how he or she has affected your life. Express your gratitude. Seal this letter in an envelope and exchange it with your beloved on your wedding night. Save it for an eternity!

When You're Done

You may want to give your questionnaire to your celebrant, perhaps with an outline of the basic structure you'd like for your wedding. Tell your celebrant that he or she will get to know you a little better from your written comments and may want to weave some of them into parts of the service. You may decide to write portions or the entire ceremony on your own. You may also wish to have someone close to you say a few words based on your questionnaire responses.

Not every celebrant will go to the trouble of developing a personal address based on your questionnaire. You will most likely have to pay for this extra service. Most couples find it well worth it. Often, however, a clergy member or judge is perfectly happy to read a personal testimony if the couple has written it out. When a couple does not wish to answer the questionnaire, I ask both bride and groom to simply write me a short paragraph about their feelings for each other. I instruct them not to show one another what they have written. Then, at the appropriate time in the ceremony I pull out their notes and read them aloud. Your celebrant might do the same for you.

What could be more moving than your own words of love?

ANNETTE AND ROBERT,
A GREEK ORTHODOX–LUTHERAN COUPLE

She had prayed to God, Annette said, to bring her someone who would love her just for herself, just for the way she was. Someone she could laugh with and live with, a soul mate. For his part, Robert, who had been bruised in an unhappy first marriage, wasn't sure if he was ready to trust his judgment again when it came to women.

Enter the Internet. Deciding she wanted to change her life and "put myself out there" to meet someone, Annette discovered a personals website. "After checking it out," she wrote in her questionnaire, "I thought, Hey, why not take a chance? My family thought I was crazy!" After one disappointing contact, she decided to give it another try: "And then Robert e-mailed into my life!" The e-mails were great. Each felt hopeful that a relationship was under way. But even after talking on the phone, they were nervous about coming face-to-face. Annette wrote, "I was afraid to meet him for fear that he or I would be disappointed."

They did meet, for a pleasant dinner and a long walk at the South Street Seaport in Manhattan. "By the end of our first date," said Annette, "I knew everything was going to be just fine. Deep inside I knew he was the man I had been searching for my whole life." Still, she doubted herself, she said, "because I couldn't believe that it was this easy." Robert hadn't been eager to rush into marriage. He knew from the e-mails that they would be friends, he said, but during that "romantic stroll I fell in love with her."

Robert told the following story about how they became engaged: "At 5:30 A.M. on Thanksgiving, I started fumbling around for the ring. Eventually I found it. I got on my knees and said, 'Will you marry me?' Then after what seemed like quite a while, she said 'Yes.'"

Annette explained her version: "Robert was fumbling around for something. It was still dark out, and I was half asleep. He was at the edge of the bed on both knees holding my hand, asking me if I would marry him. I thought he was kidding until I felt something in my hand, and then I woke up. Then I asked him to turn on the light *so I could see the ring!*" (At their wedding, I related these details of the proposal, and added, "In case anyone wants to know, the diamond is a beautiful antique yellow diamond that belonged to Robert's grandmother and that he had reset in platinum. The man has taste!")

Annette was Greek Orthodox; Robert had been raised Lutheran. Their service, in a beautiful stone country club overlooking mountains with trees at their peak fall foliage, was spiritual and God-oriented; their families took part. What was most memorable about their ceremony, however, was this: It was to be a masquerade ball! All guests were asked to wear costumes, and on the grand day in walked minstrels with big pointy hats, damsels in distress, knights in armor. One elderly woman was a flapper, all in silver from head to toe, feathers in her hair, jewelry dripping.

Annette had ordered a Renaissance-style gown, but when it arrived, she was disappointed. So was her mother, who insisted, "You are not wearing that dress!" And so two weeks before the wedding, her mother—an angel, and, Annette said, someone who "has always been my best friend"—sewed her a new dress. Walking down the aisle, Annette was a vision in white, carrying flowers and holding a Venetian mask over her face. Robert was arrayed in a purple satin outfit with black tights, black shoes with huge buckles, and a Napoleonic hat with a luxurious feather. (Said Annette later, "Everyone remarked on what great legs he had, and that he must be in love if I got him to wear tights!") Annette's beloved boss (he gave one of the readings) was a knight with a mesh "helmet" and a fake goatee.

As the ceremony was about to begin and I stood before this remarkable assemblage of people, I was momentarily speechless! All in their masks and extraordinary outfits sat looking at me, very serious and solemn—and the picture could not have been funnier. Finally I asked, "Is anybody ever going to forget this wedding or what?"

There was much laughter as Annette and Robert joined in marriage, and many tears as well. Both bride and groom had written about their families with love and appreciation, and I shared their words of gratitude, including these from Robert:

I am grateful to my parents for being my friends. For knowing when to step in and help and knowing when to back off. For loving me but not smothering me. For giving me enough support for confidence but not so much that I lost strength. For letting me make enough mistakes to learn but not enough for disaster.

Their words of love for each other were equally moving. Annette had written,

It has always been so easy to love Robert. I love cooking for him and taking care of him. He makes me feel loved by the look in his eyes and the way he touches me. But most of all he tells me. He can be half asleep and still he will say, "I love you, honey." I felt so proud the first time Robert told me how I have changed his life.

In the questionnaire letter I suggest, to be exchanged and opened only after the wedding, Robert wrote, "To Annette, on our honeymoon." Here is some of what he told her:

I know I found my true love in you. Everything about our relationship just seems to have fallen into place. The reason is because we are each being ourselves and that is whom the other one loves. We are so comfortable with each other, we have no need to hide anything.

I wanted to create a literary masterpiece for you. I had to settle for what I am capable of—a nice pile of "mush."

Chapter Three

Practicalities

The Nuts and Bolts of Any Wedding

The evening before Bill and Cynthia's wedding at a suburban New York hotel, her priest informed the couple that he would be unable to co-officiate with Bill's rabbi because the hotel was unconsecrated ground. The next twenty-four hours were a nightmare—a hastily arranged early morning ceremony with neither rabbi nor priest and few witnesses at a nondenominational chapel, and the reception that night back at the hotel, featuring the shaken bride and groom and their confused guests.

Bill and Cynthia have gone on to years of happy marriage, but they still find it hard to laugh about their wedding day. The moral of the story: It's important to work out details! This chapter is about the details, or the nuts and bolts of any wedding.

The Setting: Where Will Your Wedding Take Place?

Perhaps you have already decided where your wedding will be held. Or maybe you have no particular ideas in mind. Like many couples, you may be checking out personal referrals, bridal magazines, local papers, websites, and the yellow pages for the perfect site. Your options are many!

Wedding ceremonies, of course, can take place in religious settings, such as churches, chapels, temples, or mosques. They can be performed in nonreligious settings, such as banquet halls and ballrooms, restaurants, hotels, and mansions, private homes or backyards or libraries; under elaborate outdoor tents and pavilions, in forests, on sandy beaches, on penthouse rooftops, at vineyards, on yachts, at quaint country inns, in city parks or botanical gardens, and at historical sites and buildings. I have led ceremonies in just about every one of these venues.

A Hindu–Russian Orthodox couple chose a pine grove near their home as the site of their wedding. The actual name of the grove was Cathedral Pines, so I was able to open the ceremony by welcoming the guests to God's cathedral, God's sacred temple. Later they all walked to the couple's tented backyard for the reception. In the presence of their guests, the bride and groom planted an apple tree as a lasting metaphor for their marriage.

For their wedding, a Chinese-American bride and her American, Catholic groom gathered about fifty family members and friends in a spectacular town house in Upper Manhattan, an Italian Renaissance–style palazzo built in the early twentieth century and a designated landmark. The ceremony was held on the first floor before a marble fireplace. For the reception following, the bride changed into a red silk gown—red signifying good luck in Chinese culture—and met her guests in the upstairs library, an immense Baroque-style room with twenty-five-foot-high ceilings and a coat of arms said to have been painted by Raphael, parts of a fifteenth-century palace. Tables and chairs were draped in pumpkin-colored shantung; flowers and fruit in crimson, eggplant, and peach were on every surface; golden candelabra holding four-foot-tall red candles lit the tables. Embellishments of gold were everywhere—on ribbons, place settings, and goblets. As we roamed our castle followed by serenading minstrels, everyone felt we were taking part in a grand Renaissance feast!

Because many religions impose restrictions on the use of their facilities, and family concerns may be strong, interfaith couples often find it most comfortable to select nonreligious or neutral settings. As you consider the options, think about the atmosphere you wish to create. A ceremony in a grand ballroom has quite a different mood from one at the seashore. A daytime wedding framed by an ocean vista with a lapping surf feels very different from an intimate, candlelit evening ceremony in a small chapel accompanied by classical music, or one at a country inn with the sun setting over the mountains as the backdrop.

For some couples, though, it's very important that their wedding take place in a traditional religious setting. Churches, chapels, temples, and mosques can range from the very simple to the ornate. Catholic, Episcopalian, and Eastern Orthodox churches, and Hindu temples typically display many religious icons, while university chapels, Unitarian Universalist churches, some Protestant churches, Zen temples, synagogues, and mosques are often minimal in visual symbolism. Quaker churches (also referred to as Friends meeting houses) are simple and unadorned. Your taste, and considerations of what will make your families feel most comfortable, will dictate.

In Chapter 8, I will describe particular conflicts or considerations that you may need to take into account; for example, divorced Catholics who have not obtained annulments cannot marry in a Catholic church.

Many interfaith couples find the question of religious or nonreligious setting a nonissue. They tell me, "We consider ourselves spiritual but not religious." But in some couples one may be more religious than the other or feel a stronger pull toward a particular faith. It can be difficult for the man or the woman who was raised as a Christian, for example, to accept the idea of not being married in a church. Many a Christian girl has grown up with an image of walking down the church aisle on her wedding day to organ music—adult though she is and no longer "religious," it's still hard to give up that vision. Suddenly she finds herself pushing for a church wedding while her groom is resisting. A Jewish groom, by contrast, may feel tremendous discomfort in a church setting. For him there may be thoughts of a history of pogroms, the Holocaust, and terrible persecution from the Christian community.

> Nothing is impossible to a willing heart.
>
> —*Heywood*

Each partner in an interfaith, intercultural union must try to put himself or herself in the other person's shoes, so to speak. We may never be able to understand what it feels like to have family or ancestors who are Holocaust survivors, but we can strive to imagine it. We may never fully comprehend the devastating impact of slavery on the African-American psyche, but we can try. Empathy is a powerful tool.

My feeling: If either one of you will be deeply uncomfortable in a church, temple, mosque, or other setting, or if one family will be, it is better to seek another option. Again, a university chapel may be an appropriate compromise, because these are usually nondenominational and open to people of all faiths. (And you don't have to be a student; you can rent the chapel.)

The Celebrant: Who Will Marry You?

For the interfaith couple, choosing—or finding—a celebrant to perform the wedding can pose difficulties. In fact, this might be your greatest obstacle or dilemma. As I've noted, many couples have come to me because an interfaith ceremony conducted by clergy from one of their religions would not be possible.

The person who performs your ceremony *does* matter. Your celebrant should be someone you can work with and someone who will conduct the type of ceremony you want. You can present elements you have selected as you tailor your wedding, but he or she is the one to implement them. Even a simple or basically civil script can be transformed into something memorable when conveyed with heart by a devoted and personable celebrant. My suggestion: Interview! There are many caring celebrants from every background. When interfaith or intercultural issues are prominent, you especially need to feel comfortable with your celebrant; it is essential that you trust this individual.

Perhaps most important, you must find a celebrant who is *willing* to marry you. That may be easier said than done. Some religions do not permit intermarriages. Some clergy will not perform intermarriage ceremonies at all, or will not conduct such services outside their own places of worship. Others may require that you join their congregation, or will perform the marriage only if you vow to raise your children in that faith.

Here are various options available to you:

- **You may elect to have a religious ceremony that is officiated by clergy from one of your religions.** If one of you does not feel any particular religious affinity while the other does, having a celebrant from one of your religions can be a suitable option. Remember, however, to be sensitive to your families' feelings and to be certain the celebrant of your choice will be willing to marry you. For example, Catholic priests cannot perform weddings on unconsecrated ground without a special dispensation. Imams will perform interfaith ceremonies for Muslim men marrying Christians or Jews but cannot do so for Muslim women.
- **You may decide to have a religious ceremony co-officiated by clergy from your two faiths.** Many interfaith couples find co-officiants to be the perfect alternative. They honor and acknowledge both their backgrounds, and everyone—often, in particular, the parents and grandparents—is happy. Again, however, this option is not always available. Conservative rabbis, Eastern Orthodox priests, and ministers of fundamentalist Christian sects will not co-officiate at an interfaith wedding. Some Reformed and Reconstructionist rabbis, and many Catholic priests and Protestant ministers, will perform a co-officiated wedding ceremony depending on the faiths involved. For example, Catholic priests and almost all rabbis will not officiate at a union in which one of the parties is Hindu.

- **You may have a religious ceremony officiated by clergy of a religion outside your individual religions.** Having a celebrant from a different religion may be an attractive option if neither of you is actively religious but one or both feel drawn to the teachings of a third religion. One couple, for example (she was "a lapsed Presbyterian," he considered himself an atheist), wrote their own ceremony and had it conducted by a clergy member of a Buddhist temple. During their engagement a Jewish and African-American Baptist couple investigated and then decided to join the Baha'i community, a religion that accepts people of all faiths and cultures. Later they had a Baha'i wedding, which allowed them to include aspects from both their backgrounds.

- **You may have two religious ceremonies, each performed by clergy of your separate faiths.** One couple felt it was important, both for them and for their families, that they be married in a synagogue by a rabbi and in a Catholic church by a priest. That decision required that they state their intention to raise any children, in the first case, in the Jewish faith and, in the second, in the Catholic faith. They are raising their children in both traditions. Please note: Depending on your traditions, this option may be problematic if one or both of your religions forbid it.

- **You may choose an interfaith minister or a Unitarian-Universalist minister for a spiritual ceremony including references to God but based on no particular religion.** An interfaith minister may also represent one side of the family if their clergy will not. For example, as an alternative to a Greek Orthodox priest, I have officiated with a rabbi.

- **You may choose an interfaith or a Unitarian-Universalist minister, or a licensed representative of Ethical Culture or of the American Humanist Association, for a humanist ceremony.**

- **You don't need a celebrant for a Quaker wedding, available in some areas.** You must obtain a Quaker wedding license and have witnesses present to sign it. Then you can create and essentially conduct your own ceremony.

- **You may have a civil ceremony officiated by a judge or other court-appointed official.** Many of these individuals will be happy to perform a ceremony written by the couple.

- **In at least one state (Massachusetts), a friend or relative can be licensed for a day to perform a wedding.** To find out if this is an option where you will be married, call your county clerk.

- **You may have two ceremonies, one universal and one more religious, to satisfy the feelings of both families.** One couple—the groom was Islamic, the bride a nonpracticing Christian—were married first by an imam in an

Islamic ceremony. I later led an interfaith service that focused on cultural aspects of the families.

The key to success in choosing who will marry you is to do some investigating. Research and interview. Pastors of many Protestant sects in particular have autonomy in deciding any number of matters relating to a wedding ceremony. If you haven't found the one who'll marry you, keep looking!

I have had couples tell me, "We really want a priest, but we've talked to four of them and they were dismissive, even sort of curt." And I reply, "Call up the fifth and the sixth priests, and see what they have to say." One woman phoned me after speaking to eleven rabbis, all of whom declined her request to marry her and her fiancé. She sought me out through a personal reference, she admitted, as a compromise. "You should not have to compromise," I said, "if you really want a rabbi." And I gave her the names of three Reformed rabbis who I knew would conduct an interfaith ceremony.

It takes a bit of effort. But if you're working so hard at every other aspect of your grand day, why not put some of that energy into finding the right celebrant? Some celebrants charge a fee for an interview, but the fee is generally deductible if you choose to work with them.

Working With Your Celebrant

Once you have selected your celebrant, arrange to meet to talk over how and why your marriage will take place. Bring your ideas. Read through the rest of this book, look through the standard wedding format, scan the wonderful options described in Part II, jot down the readings or rituals that appeal to you, and discuss it all with your celebrant. Here are some suggestions:

Bring a Copy of Your Written Responses to Your Questionnaire (Retain the Original)

One of the most important roles your celebrant will have is the address to you and to your guests—the more personal, less pro forma part of the ceremony. From the questionnaire, your minister, priest, rabbi, imam, cleric, or judge can better understand the backgrounds and needs of the individuals who are about to participate in this important rite. Ideally, your celebrant will be prepared to devote some time, thought, and creativity to the mission. A celebrant can make a wedding ceremony come alive by sharing some insights or news about the couple. That might be a funny story about their first date, a romantic story about how he proposed (or how she asked him), or a moving story about their affection for their parents or siblings. If your celebrant does not have the time to review your questionnaire, simply circle the sections you'd like him or her to read aloud. Most celebrants would be happy to include brief personal testimonies.

People remember stories! Stories bring the event right home. Listen to anyone who's a good speaker and you will hear that person tell stories. One couple, attending the wedding of a friend, asked for my card and contacted me—four years later—when they were planning their own wedding. "We're calling you because that was the most beautiful ceremony we've ever seen," they said. What did they like about it? I asked. Was it the readings? The vows? The procession? They admitted they didn't recall any of those details, but "we just remember that wedding was all about the couple. And you told that great story about how they met! We loved that!"

Discuss Any Sensitive Issues

A couple who had decided they would not have children and who had told their parents so (to the parents' dismay) wanted to avoid a delicate moment by making sure that no readings or other parts of the ceremony included references to future generations.

A bride who was detecting resentment and bad feelings among her sisters over which of them was "more involved" wanted to include each sister in a portion of the service.

This is the time to see what might be done to ensure not only that the mechanics of the day go off without a hitch but that no one inadvertently feels hurt, saddened, excluded, or offended.

When you talk to your celebrant, ask him about these sensitive matters. If a family member is very ill or has recently died, for example, you might ask, "How do you suggest we handle this in the ceremony so that people feel comforted and not further wounded?" If there's bad blood between a biological parent and a stepparent, talk to your celebrant about how each might feel suitably acknowledged.

Teach Your Celebrant

It's wonderful when a celebrant makes the effort to pick up foreign words— "hello," "welcome," "peace," "thank you," or other, commonly used terms— or to learn a small ritual of greeting. Doing something like this is in essence saying, "I acknowledge and respect your culture. I am reaching out." Teach your celebrant some simple expressions if they would be meaningful to your family members. Most celebrants, once asked, would love to incorporate them.

For example, if the bride or groom is Muslim, the couple can ask their interfaith or Unitarian minister to incorporate the greeting "Salaam A'leikum" in her opening words. She might also be taught the meaning and pronunciation of "Al-humdulilah," which means "praise be to God," or "Shukran," which means "thank you." A bride or groom of Portuguese origin could teach the celebrant an appropriate Portuguese opening greeting. Writing it down phonetically helps! If either of you is Japanese, you may explain to your celebrant that it is customary to bow as a greeting. Indeed, bowing is a sign of respect and honor, and Japanese participants will bow in return.

Decide How Your Celebrant
Will Be Referred to at the Ceremony

When you're describing your forthcoming wedding to family members, certain titles may be discomforting. For example, technically I am Reverend Macomb, but the term *reverend* sometimes bothers people. In that case, I tell the couple to refer to me as the celebrant, or simply to call me Susanna.

Wedding guests sometimes expect the celebrant to be an elderly person with a reassuring gravitas and reading glasses. Before one ceremony I introduced myself to the bride's father and we talked for a while. Suddenly he asked, "How old are you?" I was, I think, thirty-seven at the time. His reply: "Thank goodness! I thought you were in your twenties." I've heard similar comments a

> Love conquers all.
> 　—*Virgil*

number of times (now that I'm forty-three and do use reading glasses, however, not as often as I used to!). It's interesting, though, that such questions are always raised before the wedding, never after. During the ceremony, outer appearances melt away; we are speaking soul to soul and joined by the sublimity of universal spirit.

If you plan to have an interfaith minister perform your ceremony, she must be sensitive about the clothing she wears. Usually, for example, I have on a basic white robe that I can layer with different prayer stoles or shawls according to the situation, all without religious or other symbolism. But if one family is Buddhist, for example, an ocher or gray robe or conservative civil clothes (though not black) would be more appropriate than anything white, because white signifies death.

My point is, consider some ways you might help your family and guests feel most at ease with your celebrant. In interfaith, intercultural, interracial situations where there are serious issues, I often meet with the parents before the wedding. If it's possible, a face-to-face meeting helps, so that any sense of "other" is dissipated.

Discuss Sensitivities of Language

Language may need to be adapted. Here are some examples: In most inter-faith ceremonies, God is referred to as God (you will note that all the prayers in this book are adapted to praise God in this universal way). The mention of Jesus, Allah, Ganesh, Adonai, or Brahman can be extremely sensitive in interfaith company. This may be an important matter for the couple and their families to discuss. I have conducted ceremonies in which we men-tioned Adonai and Ganesh, or Allah and Jesus, but that is rare. My general rule is to join in common worship by invoking one God, recognizing that he or she is called by many names but in essence is one.

Many brides and grooms, of all religious back-grounds, like the short reading (you will find the complete text in Part II) that begins "From every human being there rises a light that goes straight to heaven." This saying was actually written cen-turies ago by a rabbi, and I have used it often—even at non-Jewish weddings. If the couple have specified they'd like a humanist ceremony, no references to God, I'll change the opening slightly and say, "From every human being there rises a light that goes straight to the heavens." Clearly, "the heavens" has a less religious sound than "Heaven."

> Under floods that
> are deepest . . .
> Over the rocks that
> are steepest,
> Love will find a way.
>
> —*Anonymous (adapted)*

In Christian ceremonies, perhaps the most popular Bible reading is 1 Corinthians 13, the passage that includes the familiar words "Love is patient; love is kind; love is not envious or boastful or arrogant or rude," and so on. In a Jewish-Christian ceremony, I am careful not to say "our next reading is from the New Testament" but will refer to First Corinthians, chap-ter 13. I'm often asked to say the "Our Father" when one of the couple has a Catholic background. Changing "Our Father who art in heaven" to "O God who art in heaven" makes the prayer more universal and acceptable to those from other religious traditions.

Words are important to people, and words can always be adapted—not only in the interest of making them religiously inoffensive but to modernize them. In explaining an Iranian ritual, for example, instead of saying, "to pro-tect the couple from evil spirits," I will say, "to protect the couple from all harm." I will adapt a passage that reads "the moral man" to "the moral man and woman." The biblical words "he who fears the Lord" I have read as "he who loves the Lord" or "she who worships the Lord." I announce that the words have been adapted—and often guests thank me.

These are small matters, but they reflect a sensitivity to the assembled company. If you have selected a prayer or reading in which a minor change in language might avoid discomfort, this is something to talk over with your celebrant.

The License

Obtain your wedding license before your ceremony. This is an especially important concern for the couple whose wedding is being performed in an unfamiliar place and by someone other than local clergy. Each state has its own laws—who can perform your ceremony, necessary witnesses, whether blood tests are required, how long the license is valid, and so on. Your local county clerk or state marriage bureau should provide you with all the information you need.

In New York State, for example, each member of the couple must provide two valid forms of identification and prior divorce papers, if applicable. No blood tests are required. The ceremony must take place at least twenty-four hours after and within sixty days of obtaining the license. Two witnesses are required. The bride and groom, the witnesses, and the celebrant all sign the wedding license. It is then the celebrant's obligation to mail the certificate within five days of performing the ceremony to the city clerk, who sends an official copy to the couple's home.

The Rehearsal

Do plan for a rehearsal; it eases everyone's nerves. Any questions the bridal party or parents may have can be addressed. If you are marrying in a facility that's accustomed to holding weddings, the staff can usually arrange the rehearsal. And if your celebrant can't be present, with a little effort you can easily guide this practice run on your own. The main purpose is to walk through the procession—its pace and spacing—making sure everyone knows where she or he will stand or sit. I will tell you the most common mistake people make at the rehearsal: They walk too fast! It's because they're nervous. Slowly does it. I tell brides and grooms that this is the walk of a lifetime, so savor it! Then practice the recession—how you will all leave. Once or twice is usually sufficient.

The Microphone

If you are having more than fifty guests at an indoor ceremony or will be married outdoors, it's wise for your celebrant to use a microphone, preferably a lapel mike clipped to the neckline of his robe or to his collar. He can then speak in a normal tone of voice and move about freely. Although most celebrants are able to project their voices quite well, I've found that talking in a normal voice creates a greater feeling of intimacy, especially with the bride and groom. At moments during the ceremony, I speak to them rather quietly, as if only to them, but the lapel microphone picks up the sound and the guests can hear both me and the bride and groom. If a lapel mike is unavailable, a standing microphone will do.

The Music

Music is key in creating the mood you want for yourselves and your guests. Generally you'll choose music for the procession and other music for the recession. Most couples select a classical passage for the grand entry of the bridal party, often changing to a different one to announce the bride.

But you are by no means limited to classical, and many couples pick music they feel is reflective of who they are, whether it's jazz or opera or modern. One of my brides arrived to the aria "Un Bel Di" from Puccini's *Madame Butterfly*, sung by a soprano from Juilliard. She chose this piece because she loved the song and it moved her soul. Another bride, desiring a more lighthearted entrance, walked down the aisle with a live jazz band playing and a vocalist singing Nina Simone's song "My Baby Just Cares for Me." Many couples choose music reflective of their cultural heritage, such as African drumming or Indian sitar. In interfaith services, one needs to be sensitive to religious music. For example, High Church Christian music might be offensive to the Jewish or Muslim family, while a cantor singing in Hebrew might be offensive to the non-Jewish family. Again, there are always exceptions!

The Sacred Space

Remember that you can create a sacred space in any setting—be it a hotel ballroom, a restaurant, a private home, or a mountaintop. The love, devotion, and commitment you bring to your wedding provide the sanctity of the event. And you can enhance the sense of the sacred by using elements from both your traditions and any other tradition you wish to include, be they flowers, wine, oil, the Jewish chuppah, the Greek Orthodox wedding wreaths, the Hindu fire, rose petals, candles, or any number of options.

In Part II you'll see suggestions on how to arrange a sacred space. A simple table, draped with a cloth and holding the items you'll use during the ceremony, becomes an altar. We are visual creatures. Your guests will feel comfortable and moved at the sight of this focal point. Make it beautiful!

CHRISTINE AND DAVE, A CATHOLIC–MORMON COUPLE

"I want your card! I'm getting married and I want to call you" was the voice I heard coming from atop a ten-foot ladder. A woman with a camera on her shoulder was waving me over. This was my introduction to Christine, a professional photographer who was taking pictures at the wedding ceremony I had just finished. "You have to do my wedding!" she said. "Just listen to my story."

It was a tremendously moving story, of great tragedy and great love, of answered prayers and the coming together of a sweet family. Christine's father died when she was sixteen, a loss that caused her to drift away from her Catholic religion. Years later her sister, pregnant and terminally ill, died within one week of giving birth—leaving Christine custody of her daughter, the miracle that is Maggie Lucia. In so short a time, this giving woman suffered the loss of her sister, and received the simultaneous blessing and enormous responsibility of motherhood. She wrote:

> I've always felt that I found God on my own. I felt most connected to him when Maggie Lucia was born and my sister died. To see God take a life and give a life all in the same week was a miracle to me. My faith started to grow, and my conversations with God became more frequent. From within my soul I can feel his strength and love.

But Christine, in her mid-thirties, was unmarried and unattached.

One day friends suggested that she get to know a friend of theirs—Dave, who was completing a graduate degree. Christine lived in the East; Dave, raised in the Mormon faith, lived in the West, but from the moment they began e-mailing, each felt something important was happening. The e-mails escalated to phone calls. Three months later Christine flew out to meet Dave and go camping, and by the end of that brief holiday they knew they were meant to be. Soon it was agreed: When his studies were completed, he would move East and they would marry.

Together we began the process of creating their ceremony. Their question-naire responses spoke volumes. Here is some of what Christine wrote:

I can't tell you how Dave has changed my life. He's given me security, a feeling I have never really had before. He brings me happiness in the purest ways. Dave has a happy soul, calm and pleasant. Being with him reminds me of being on a big, comfy hammock on a breezy day with the wind blowing softly and the sun shining sweetly.

Here is some of what Dave wrote:

Our coming together felt like something ordained. Pieces clicked, and there was a focus to life that had been lacking. The love I have for Chris is deep and life-changing. It has given meaning to what was once a routine, transcending all, making me smile when I think of the future.

For our ceremony, I know Christine would like some biblical passages. I agree but would also like a little Eastern flavor. Although I'm not well versed in Buddhist thought, I'm interested in the idea of an individual gaining a greater awareness and identity through marriage.

It would be wonderful to slide a little Winnie-the-Pooh into the cere-mony for our daughter. I want her to know that her presence is celebrated. I have fallen in love with Maggie Lucia. She needs a mommy and a daddy, and we learn from her far more than we could ever teach. While marriage has sometimes seemed elusive to me, being a father is something I've always desired.

Christine's patience with both Maggie and myself amazes me. I watch the straws multiply on her back, but she never breaks. Sometimes I get scared of the idea of marriage, but the idea of Christine and Maggie Lucia with me forever overpowers everything and I am constantly amazed at the power of love. Being a father makes my heart ache with pride and happi-ness. Being a husband puts a very silly grin on my face. Being the son of my parents makes me proud.

Such wonderful words to incorporate in their service! Christine and her daughter arrived by horse-drawn carriage at the charming restaurant in the middle of New York's Central Park and walked in on a muslin runner that Maggie Lucia and her preschool classmates had painted. The ceremony included a biblical reading from Proverbs that ends with the line "He who finds a wife has found a very precious thing" and a bit of Buddhist philosophy, a marriage homily that begins, "Nothing happens without a cause." Christine and Dave wrote their own vows. Here is Dave's vow to his wife:

Yes, respect always
shall be yours to name your own.
Smiles too in your heart.
Yes, never changing
my love for you,
I shall not forget.
I adore you, Christine.
Hope and everlasting love,
two shoes on the stairs.

Maggie Lucia, a four-year-old angel in a pretty dress and ballet slippers, was very much a part of the proceedings. After they exchanged their own rings, Dave and Christine presented a ring to Maggie as a symbol of their love and commitment to her.

Life's miracles always leave me with a sense of awe. The possibilities are endless. Christine and Dave's wedding seemed to me a celebration of nothing less than a miracle.

Chapter Four

Family Matters

Working with Family and Friends Throughout the Wedding Process

> Our family is a circle of strength and love.
> With every birth and every union, the circle grows.
> Every joy shared adds more love.
> Every crisis faced together makes the circle grow stronger.
>
> —Anonymous

Planning a wedding is a complex business! There's always an incredible amount of work, with never-ending details to be ironed out. Throughout this process, emotions are heightened—the delightful ones, such as happiness, excitement, anticipation, and hope, and sometimes more difficult ones as well, like worry, nervousness, frustration, anger, stress. It's common for a couple to feel that what should be a joyous celebration of their love is turning into a scenario in which everyone tells them how things should be done! Sometimes the bride or the groom or both get caught in a cross fire of varying opinions and wishes, all coming from those dearest to them, their family and friends.

Your wedding is a public statement. Unless you've decided to elope, it's usually a family affair, with mothers and fathers, grandparents, and other relatives involved to some degree. If you will be paying for the ceremony and celebration yourself, you may feel relatively free to do as you please. If parents are footing the bill, however, they probably believe, reasonably enough, that they should have a say in the process, which may begin to infringe on your own vision of your wedding. *Whatever* the circumstances, family issues are sure to surface; if you are an interfaith, intercultural couple, they may be particularly emotional and fraught. Through some solid communication tools, you will be able to bridge any differences you may have. Moreover, it is my hope that, in reading this chapter, you will feel you are not alone. Many others, like yourselves, have gone through similar issues and come to satisfying resolutions.

This chapter is meant to help you interact with your family and friends in the most harmonious and magnanimous ways, to encourage love, support, understanding, and healing throughout the wedding process. You will find here—partly through the examples of other couples—some solid ideas on how to work through differences, honor family members on your most meaningful day, and truly share the joy of your love. The very issues that seem to divide you or to be causing problems and tears are what can draw you all closer! They can bring healing, and the circle will grow stronger—*if* you face them head on.

Before one wedding at which I was the celebrant, the bride and her mother argued over a particular part of the ceremony (the Catholic passing of the peace) that the mother wanted in and the couple wanted out. The argument got heated, the bride started to cry, and Mom, now feeling terrible, said, "Okay, okay, we love you, we'll do it your way, we don't care." But she *did* care. And the matter needed to be addressed in an appropriate manner or the unhappiness behind it would pop up again, somewhere else. When I presented the ritual to the bride in a universal manner—as creating a community of love and peace through a handshake or a hug and the words "peace" or "shalom," as opposed to a community in Christ—it became an acceptable compromise for both mother and daughter, and her Jewish fiancé's family.

That's the most important message I want to share in this chapter: Face your family differences and difficulties, and deal with them lovingly. Don't be afraid of the tears. Think of ways your ceremony can include and embrace, celebrate and heal. Work with your celebrant to come up with happy alternatives (a third party can be invaluable when discussions are under way). This is a time of great possibility, a time to set the tone for family gatherings and conversations over all the years that lie ahead.

> Darkness cannot drive out darkness; only light can do that. Hate cannot drive out hate; only love can do that.
>
> —*Rev. Dr. Martin Luther King, Jr.*

Weddings are about people, family, and life, with all its variables and scenarios; they don't take place in a vacuum. For one thing, couples are often in the midst of difficult job or career changes or a major geographic move during the preparations for the wedding. In my experience, in at least one out of every four weddings *something else* of great significance to the family has been happening recently—the death of a family member, for example, or some sickness or loss. Couples don't know what, if anything, to do about these circumstances that seem so out of keeping with a joyous occasion, so I have included here some thoughts about and examples of how to address death and illness within the family or circle of friends. Occasionally there is a family member who is so negative and destructive that he or she becomes toxic. Abuse of any kind is unacceptable. If you have a family member who is of this nature, do seek professional counseling.

Communication Is Key. Listen from the Heart

One of the first things I suggest to all couples, especially interfaith couples, is simply to ask their parents what is important to them about the ceremony to come. Find out if they have particular thoughts or wishes. Is there a reading, blessing, or ritual they would like to see included? Hear what they have to say; listen openly and respectfully, without taking offense or going on the defensive. Even if you don't agree with your parents' point of view, try to understand it. Remember that empathy is a powerful tool! If there is ambiguity, ask for clarity. Often when I work with couples and their families, I listen to what they are saying between the lines, the underlying issues that one or another is reluctant to speak out loud. In an atmosphere of respect and openness, these issues will usually surface. When you feel yourself contracting because of tensions, take a deep breath and expand. Become bigger.

When I meet with the families of an engaged couple, or maybe with one set of parents, I tell those mothers and fathers the same thing: Listen to what your children have to say. Try to understand things from their perspective. And remember, it's their wedding!

When you can maintain an atmosphere of respect and really listen to one another, the circle grows stronger. Transformation becomes possible. I have had the mother of a bride instruct me that she wanted a specific scripture from the New Testament to be read in the ceremony, but she would not say as much to her daughter. The father of a groom asked me if we planned to include the traditional seven Jewish blessings, but he hadn't questioned his son and future daughter-in-law for fear of interfering. Your celebrant may serve as a bridge—and even, at times, a family counselor—but communication begins at home. Fear does not make a bridge; only love can do that, and it takes courage to communicate honestly and lovingly.

Letting Go May Be Hard

Your marriage is a major rite of passage—for your parents! I often joke that the most nervous person at the wedding is the mother of the bride. Even if your family knows and loves your fiancé or fiancée, and couldn't be happier about your upcoming marriage, letting go can be hard. In some ways, they may have envisioned and prepared for this day all of your life. Then, with astonishment and perhaps some tears, they can hardly grasp it all. The transitions required for life's rites of passage are not always easy. I have heard mothers and fathers say:

"Where did the time go?"
"I'm thinking of the day she took her first steps, just as if it were last week."
"I remember the moment they handed my son to me in the hospital."
"He is my firstborn!"
"My baby is getting married!"

I am a parent myself. I watch tearfully as the mother of the groom dances with her son, anticipating the day I will dance with my own son at his wedding. Each time I see a bride dancing that special dance with her father, I remember my wedding, and dancing with my father. At these moments there is great joy, but also a bittersweet sadness for time that has passed. It takes a parent's courage and grace to let go, openly and freely, and to adjust to the fact that now your marriage and relationship must take first priority and your parents must come second. Sometimes, it's actually the children who find it difficult to make the transition. But remember, if you're not united as a couple, you are sending your parents mixed signals.

Ask for Your Parents' Support and Blessing

Deep down, we usually want our parents' approval of our choices and decisions. This is a need that began in the womb, and it lives on throughout our lives. I encourage couples simply to ask their parents outright for their blessing.

Children, even as young adults, expect their parents' unconditional love and acceptance; they often just assume it's there. But isn't it better to ask for their support and blessing? For an interfaith marriage, this love and support may seem elusive or challenged. Do tell your parents that you're happy in your choice, that you have found the man or woman you wish to build your life with, and that their support would mean so much to you and your beloved. Ask gently, "Can you give us that?"

When approached in that manner, most parents will not turn away in disapproval. You're making a powerful statement: "I love my partner, just the way he or she is." You're *not* saying, "I love my partner but, yes, it would be nicer if he or she wasn't _____ (fill in the blank: Catholic, Jewish, black, white, Asian, et cetera). You're showing your parents how your love has expanded, and asking them to expand too, to embrace this new person entering your family. Couples often tell me that they are already married in spirit, but remember, your parents may not be there yet! They don't love this person yet, but in time they can.

Sometimes simply asking can make all the difference. Occasionally, however, couples need to go further and, after stepping back, going to their hearts, expanding and opening to possibility, they become bigger and are able to meet a parent more than halfway.

Michael called me two days before his wedding. Michael and Julia, from Jewish and Greek Orthodox families respectively, had decided on a spiritual ceremony that would celebrate their traditions in a universal way. To accomplish this, they had thought it best to keep both Hebrew and Greek out of the service. Two days before the event, Michael's mom called the bride to ask if Uncle Sol could bestow a blessing over the wine in Hebrew, instead of the universal blessing in English, as had been agreed. When Julia replied that she would feel a bit uncomfortable with this idea, Michael's mother said "Okay" and hung up. Hearing about this, the groom, very upset, confronted his mother, an argument ensued, and the conversation ended with Mom declaring, "I guess you don't want me walking down the aisle either, so I won't!"

Michael's next phone call was to me. His mother had been "criticizing," "making power plays," and "causing trouble" throughout the planning process, and this was "the last straw." After talking a bit, however, Michael was able to acknowledge that his mother, a widow, was probably feeling very much alone and, because Michael was her only child, her emotions may have been in turmoil. I suggested that Michael take a deep breath and come from his heart, call his mother and say, "Mom, I really do want you to walk down the aisle with me. It would mean so much to me. Would you feel comfortable doing that?" Of course, Michael's mom did walk down the aisle, and proudly. She just needed to know that she was wanted. She needed her son to extend a hand and ask for her support.

Let Your Parents Find Their Own
Peace With Your Marriage

When you've done all you can to reach out to your parents, realize that they must ultimately find their own peace with your marriage.

A friend once gave me this wonderful saying: "When in doubt, do the loving thing." This is a good way to approach your parents. Be loving. Yet sometimes the loving thing is to set boundaries, to leave the ball in their court. Most parents do love their children deeply and truly want what is best for them and, most often, they find it in themselves to make peace with their doubts.

Murray, a devoted Jewish father, called me one day (it was around Christmastime) on the recommendation of a friend to tell me that his youngest child and only son was engaged. "Alan is getting married to a Methodist girl," he said, "so you have to do the wedding!" Upon discovering how religious Murray is, I asked why not have a rabbi and a Methodist clergyman? "No, no," he said, getting very emotional, "I am Conservative and we just don't do that!" The bride had agreed that their children would be raised in the Jewish faith, which pleased Murray, and yet: "They've got a Christmas tree up in their apartment!" The bride had explained her feelings; the tree for her was not a religious but a festive cultural symbol, and she enjoyed the gift giving and celebration that went along with it. The Christmas tree was important to her, and her groom-to-be had no objection to it. In the end, it was up to Murray to find his own inner acceptance. Loving his son deeply and not wanting to interfere in his happiness, he did. Murray is now a doting grandfather of two little girls.

Unfortunately, it is not always the case that parents put their child's best interests first.

When Carrie came to me, I knew something was very wrong. Most brides are happy planning their nuptials, but she was in deep pain. Adopted as an infant by fundamentalist Evangelical Christian parents, Carrie had fallen in love with Glen, a Jewish man, and her mother and father strongly expressed their disapproval. Carrie, very much in love, as well as financially and geographically independent, continued the romance and began to plan her wedding. Her parents would have nothing to do with it, and refused to meet with me.

Their reactions were agonizing for Carrie. She questioned whether her parents had ever truly loved her; she thought perhaps their feelings were due to the fact that she was adopted and not "of their blood." At first Carrie considered arranging a five-minute civil ceremony without a reception, to avoid the anguish of her family's absence, but the groom and his close-knit family couldn't imagine not having a wedding. In the end they settled on a simple, small, and intimate ceremony and reception. It took place two weeks before New Year's Eve, and I mentioned in my address that this was a time for new beginnings, a reason to rejoice; Carrie and Glen would create their own family now. During the ceremony a blue jay flew to the railing inches from where we were assembled, and we took it as a sign of hope. Later the bride told me that she would always cherish her memories of this small but meaningful wedding, and that despite the pain, there was great joy because she knew she had found the love of her life.

Perhaps one day her parents will come to accept the marriage; perhaps not. Carrie will have to go through a tremendous process of self-healing, but the rightness of her choice pulled her through.

Ultimately, it is *your* marriage, *your* wedding, and the beginning of *your* new life. In the end, we hope that Mom and Dad will find their own measure of inner peace. Do your best in working with your families; then it is up to them to work with you and with one another. When all else fails, go within. Contemplate. Meditate. If it is part of your belief system, pray. "Prayer from the heart," said Gandhi, "can achieve what nothing else can in the world." One needs to quiet oneself to hear the inner voice of wisdom and peace. Right action will then follow.

Let There Be No Uncomfortable Surprises

When I meet with parents, they often start asking me many questions:

"What is an interfaith minister?"
"What will you wear?"
"You won't mention Jesus Christ, will you?"
"Please, tell me we're not going to have an all-Jewish ceremony!"
"Are you familiar with our culture?"
"Have you read the Koran?"
"Do you speak any Greek?"
"Have you ever been to India?"
"Confidentially, who is having the greatest say in planning all this?" (During the preparations, it's not unusual for a parent to tell me, "I don't think my daughter really wants this in the ceremony, but her fiancé is pushing

her. He's taking advantage of her kindness." Or, "My son has a very easy-going nature. Is he giving in too much to her wishes?")

One groom's mother, a Muslim, questioned me about the ceremony, my work, and my beliefs. I knew what she was searching for: Is there any discomfort here? Are you religiously biased? Can you handle this for my family? Are you going to be there for us?

I welcome all these questions, listen, answer openly, and try to build a bridge. But I would guess that for every mother, father, or grandparent who asks me something, there are many more who do not—out of hesitancy, or a feeling that it is not appropriate to express their uncertainties. Yet loved ones often have questions too. Almost always, I believe, the more family members are "filled in," the better able they will be to relax, accept, and celebrate.

Do let your parents and loved ones know what to expect. Let there be no uncomfortable surprises. Explain the meaning of an interfaith ceremony and describe your celebrant, if it will be someone with whom they're not familiar.

Reassure Your Parents That Your Heritage Need Not Disappear

One bride, an American-born Chinese woman, fell in love with and married an all-American, Anglo-Saxon man. Although her parents had always welcomed her friends of all races and religions, suddenly they admitted to her that they had hoped she'd marry a Chinese man. It was unsettling to them that she wasn't, and surprising to her that they felt this way.

"My mother," wrote another bride, "is very skeptical of mixed marriages. She has heard many horror stories. She's afraid of the unknown. She needs to be convinced."

When a new family member enters the picture, relationship dynamics shift. A mother or father might blame the newcomer for dominating a child's views or beliefs. Sometimes the parents become deeply concerned about future grandchildren, about whether this next generation will learn anything about the traditions that have gone before. They may feel, truly, as if their heritage is about to be annihilated!

Try to be reassuring. Address your parents' concerns one at a time. Let them know that you will pass on knowledge of your family's traditions to your children, if this is your intention. If you are proud of your heritage, tell them so. If your spouse supports you in this, share that fact with them or even have him or her speak to them directly. Fear of "the other" is so often removed by talking, and by exploring ideas together.

Take comfort and courage *yourself* from the fact that your children-to-be may greatly benefit from the knowledge of two heritages, or three or four. Children are naturally attuned to spirit; it is we adults who have developed so many layers and filters over the years. Perhaps someday you and your children will begin a spiritual search together. They may be your inspiration! They may even teach you!

> E veryone should carefully observe which way his heart draws him, and then choose that way with all his strength.
>
> —*Martin Buber*

Yelena Khanga—journalist and author of the book *Soul to Soul*—has black, white, Russian, American, African, Jewish, Baptist, and Muslim roots. Her story describes the challenges and the great rewards of being raised as a child of a multiracial, multicultural, and multifaith heritage. "We need a language," she writes, "through which we can respect differences while embracing common humanity, a language to speak *dusha vi dusha,* soul to soul."

I have also been deeply impressed by the story of James McBride, whose Christian mother, daughter of an Orthodox rabbi, married a black man who founded a Baptist church. As a child, James would question his mother: "What color is God?" and she would answer: "God is like the color of water." McBride shares his story in the book *The Color of Water: A Black Man's Tribute to His White Mother.*

Your marriage—especially an interfaith, intercultural marriage—is an opportunity for all to learn, grow, and embrace a more expansive and compassionate view of life. A new member of the family has new gifts to bring to the table, gifts of the spirit. For example, Trenton, a quiet Mormon, married Tina, a lively Spanish Catholic. After their ceremony, Trenton told me that Tina had brought his family closer together by adding an emotional dimension to their lives. Charles, an Anglo-Saxon Protestant, the son of a military officer, spoke of his father as a man who would control every facet of his life if he would let him. Charles's new wife, an Indian Hindu woman, helped heal her husband's feelings of resentment toward his father, and now family gatherings are getting to be more fun.

Change is a part of living, and acceptance of change is what really brings peace. Indeed, the Buddhists say that the one constant in life is impermanence! But it may take time, and your reassurances, for your parents to reach that point. The mother and father of one Muslim Afghani groom became withdrawn upon hearing that his bride-to-be was an American Christian. Taking their silence to mean disapproval, the young man pointed out to them passages from the Koran which state that Islam is not exclusive, that Muslim men can indeed marry Christian women. He explained to them the Afghani rituals he and his bride intended to include in the ceremony. He did everything he could think of to ease his parents' tension—at the same time, he set a clear boundary and conveyed the strong conviction behind his choice. He told them, in fact, that his future bride was "the perfect woman for me!" Through these efforts, he was able to ease their tensions.

Again, I believe that empathetic appreciation of parents' concerns, and of the fact that they may need to wrestle for a while in their minds and hearts, is the loving approach—and far more likely to lead to acceptance than a bristly, this-is-what-I'm-doing-whether-you-like-it-or-not attitude. I remember this story told me by Rabbi Joseph Gelberman, founder of the New Seminary and All Faiths Seminary: The Orthodox parents of a young Jewish woman called him, deeply distressed over the fact that their daughter had fallen in love with and planned to marry an African-American Christian. Said the rabbi, "I understand completely how you feel. My parents would have sat shivah for such a thing!" Then he went on, "I have met him, he's a good man. I ask you this: Is it a sin to fall in love with someone of a different color complexion and faith? Go to the synagogue and pray. There you will find your answer."

I think of a quotation from Antoine de Saint Exupéry's *The Little Prince:* "It is only with the heart that one can see rightly; what is essential is invisible to the eye." Your family members may need time to think, or to pray, to learn to see your fiancé or fiancée with their hearts instead of their eyes.

Assure Your Parents That You've Chosen Your Partner Out of Love, Not Rebellion

Let your parents know they haven't done anything wrong in the way they raised you!

If it's taking a while for a mother or father to come around to welcoming a child's choice, if understanding and acceptance aren't easy, parents may be questioning whether they gave a child too much or too little structure. Did we not teach him enough about our own traditions? Were we lax in expressing our values and thoughts? Were we too strict? Is she getting back at us now for some failure on our part? I have heard parents express such concerns—often between the lines.

Be reassuring. Emphasize to your parents just how much you and your partner love each other. Write them a letter, if that seems easier. Leo Tolstoy wrote, "When you love someone, you love the whole person, just as he or she is, and not as you would like them to be." Your parents might need to hear this in so many words.

Listen to David's words to his parents: "When you get into your late thirties, you begin to doubt whether you will ever find someone. But Ella was worth the wait. At this point in my life, it matters most what is inside a person. I have never been happier in my life. I believe that when you get to know her you will see just how special she is."

Hear Vicki's words to her mother: "We really see our wedding as the joining of two families. Karl will take very good care of me, and not to worry— he loves you also." To her fiancé's family: "I am fully aware of how lucky I am to have found such a special person, and I will take very, very good care of him. You need not worry—I will never hurt him."

These are soothing words for any parents, especially for parents of children who are intermarrying!

It may become clear that, despite your efforts to build a bridge, your family will remain intractable in their opposition to your marriage. Understandably, such an attitude is deeply painful for you; you may benefit from professional counseling. You can hope for the best in the future. Given time—perhaps after the wedding—and faced with the inescapable choice of accepting what is or essentially losing their child, most parents will come around.

Do Not Assume You Know How Your Parents Will React

Sometimes the most conservative, orthodox religious parents will embrace the interfaith marriage, while the more liberal or reformed-thinking parents will object. Sometimes it is the couple themselves who are the worriers, who have "issues" on their parents' behalf.

A Chinese-born nonreligious man fell in love with a Chinese-born Catholic woman and nervously informed his parents that he planned to convert. Their reaction: "We trust you, we trust her, and we believe this will make you happy." African-American, Born-Again Christian parents happily welcomed their new Buddhist Vietnamese daughter-in-law. A close-knit Greek Orthodox family that had been displaced by war adored their Jewish son-in-law, raised in a Conservative kosher home.

The list goes on and on. When I meet these blended families, I think of these words from Willa Cather: "Where there is great love there are always miracles." How the older generation reacts is often as reflective of their personalities, character, and experiences as it is of their religious beliefs or backgrounds. Intermarriage truly is an education-in-progress for the entire family, one that cannot help but be enriching when carried on in an atmosphere of mutual respect.

Your family may find it easier and more natural to embrace your interfaith marriage than you might anticipate. Keep open the lines of communication, and listen well.

Having a Sense of Humor Helps

During a meeting involving one bride and groom and both sets of parents, things were getting a bit tense. The groom stood up and said, "That's it. Molly and I are getting married alone, naked on a beach in Bora Bora." Holding his fiancée's bangle bracelet up to his nose, he asked her, "What do you think about exchanging nose rings?" He delivered the lines with ease and a deadpan sense of humor, and everyone just laughed and laughed. The conversation became a great deal more relaxed after that.

At another meeting of a bride, her mother, and myself, Mom was constantly interjecting her opinion. Her daughter began imitating a scene from the first *Austin Powers* movie. In a good-natured and hilarious way, she would say "Shoosh" to her mother, combined with a ducklike gesture of the hand. Then she'd say, "That was a preemptive shoosh!" Her mother, who had obviously seen the movie, started laughing out loud. After that everyone—including me!—lightened up and began to take things a little less seriously.

Sometimes a little humor is a perfect tension breaker!

I believe it is also wonderful to allow for a touch of humor at the wedding itself. When you read the ceremonies I have conducted for couples, one thing missing on the page is the glints of humor that happen—usually unplanned, a sweet and spontaneous moment that pops up. Humor can seldom be written in; indeed, when a joke or lighthearted reference has been put down in writing, the listeners can almost always tell it's a remark the celebrant has made twenty times before. But I do believe there should be laughter at a wedding, which of course is not only a serious occasion but a joyous, ebullient life passage as well. Some weddings and some couples, however, lend themselves to the humorous moment more than others.

One man had written that his bride-to-be was "the best woman I've ever met in my life." In person, he added, "And I've met quite a few!" I included this amusing aside in my talk to the couple and their guests, while quickly appending, "Or so he boasts!" Another bride had elected to say the blessing over the wine in Hebrew, but when the time came she went blank. "She's a little nervous here, everybody," I called. "Can we help her out?" And after laughing a fair number of the guests were able to recite the prayer aloud and in unison. Humor can enrich the moment.

Encourage Your Parents to Reach Out to Your Spouse and His or Her Family

Perhaps you and your intended's families have come to know each other over time, through casual family get-togethers. Or maybe you've had just the one let's-all-meet-one-another dinner at a restaurant. Sometimes one set of parents won't end up meeting the other until the wedding. Almost always, however, the more opportunity families have to spend time together, the more comfortable all will be at the ceremony.

I think it is a loving and welcoming gesture if parents can reach out to "the other side" during the ceremony as well. Before Mabu and Jerry's wedding (she was Japanese, he a product of Jewish and Protestant parents), the groom's father asked me if he could say a few words. So before the closing blessing I said that Jerry's father would like to speak briefly, and I called him forward. I will never forget the surprised and delighted expression on the face of the mother of the bride (she was dressed in a most beautiful traditional kimono and head-dress) as Jerry's father began his speech in fluent Japanese. Later I learned that he had spent two months with a tutor, practicing for this moment! The gesture melted all our hearts; it was a form of outreach that at once embraced his son, his new daughter-in-law, and her family.

For the wedding of Jen, a Chinese atheist, and Edward, a Korean Presbyterian, Jen's parents flew in from Singapore. After Jen's father walked her down the aisle and approached her waiting groom, he shook the young man's hand and said in a strong, dignified voice for all to hear: "Welcome to our family."

If Your Parents Are Too Shy to Reach Out, Do It Yourself

Reaching out is so important. I tell the couples I work with, Do it! And they often ask, How can I? There are so many ways: Learn your prospective spouse's family customs. Show interest in their culture. Go to the mosque, or church, or temple. Prepare some dishes from their country's cuisine. Participate joyfully! At a Hindu-Christian wedding, the Christian bride had her hands decorated with henna, a ritual she delightfully adopted from her spouse's culture.

I've already mentioned how comforting and tension-relaxing it can be for the celebrant to say a few simple words—welcome, greeting, peace—in the languages that are spoken by the bride's and groom's families. This is a lovely gesture coming from the couple themselves as well. I conducted one ceremony that was translated for a handout in three languages: Arabic, English, and Spanish. At another reception the new bride surprised everyone by speaking briefly in her in-laws' native Russian. These are charming and touching gestures of welcome.

Lean On Your Friends for Support

More than one couple has said to me, "Our friends are our real family." Especially if parents and siblings are scattered and aren't much in touch, if a cool estrangement (or perhaps it's outright antagonism) has grown over the years, the bride and groom may feel most cherished by a loving circle of friends. During a time when emotions are running high, these individuals can be a welcome presence.

It's also the case that friends will often have something—maybe too much—to say. At one wedding of a couple with many friends, there were eighteen bridesmaids and groomsmen, and in the months leading up to the ceremony, a great deal of jockeying for position had been going on among this group. In her questionnaire the bride said, "It's tense when everyone is around. If maybe at the wedding you could mention how important friendships are and how petty differences should never come between friends, that might be really great and help to put things back together."

> He who is in love is wise and becoming wiser.
> —*Ralph Waldo Emerson*

In my address to the guests, I opened with some of the groom's own words. On his questionnaire he had written, "We would like to tell our family and friends that they each have a place in our hearts. Although the years pass, people go or have gone their separate ways, we all have a bond of love for each other that can never be broken." This offered an affirmative, nonconfrontational way to talk about how much this young bride and groom valued their friends, and perhaps lead everyone to reflect and to focus on what really matters once again.

If there's a message you would like to convey to your friends, explore with your celebrant ideas about how to get it across.

Consider Honoring Your Parents, Stepparents, or Other Close Family Members

In the next chapter, which outlines the basic format for an interfaith wedding, you will see a part of the ceremony called honoring of family members. Bringing your parents into the ceremony can have warm rippling effects. You give them the gift of your love and appreciation on this most special and significant day in all your lives. It's a way of saying, "You meant so much to me all these years. You still do. You are also part of my new life." The gift spreads to everyone else in the room, for each of us is a son or daughter, a parent or a grandparent.

There are many wonderful ways to include these most important people. Of course, having your mother and father walk you down the aisle honors them. But perhaps you will want to go further. You may decide to present flowers to your parents, offer a personal tribute, involve them in a ritual, include readings or prayers in their honor, or incorporate a meaningful family heirloom in the service.

Of course, this will be easiest if both sets of parents have been contentedly married to each other for a hundred years and present a picture of wedded bliss. Often these days, however, the older generation has been through divorce; Mom and Dad's relationship might range from perfectly amicable to downright hostile. To make sure everyone is comfortable, ask your parents and stepparents well ahead of time if they have any special thoughts or requests. I have officiated on two occasions in which the bride walked down the aisle with three fathers—biological father, first stepfather, and present stepfather. All had played significant roles in these young women's lives. The brides wanted them there.

Another bride faced this troublesome situation: Jamie called me in tears. Her mother had died several years earlier, and now Jamie realized that her stepmother assumed she would be walking down the aisle with Jamie and her father, as is the Jewish custom. Although Jamie was very fond of her stepmother, who had done much to help plan the ceremony, she was deeply upset about this scenario. Finally, gently, she told her stepmother how much she appreciated her offer, but that she preferred to walk down with only her father, because "I know my mother will be walking with me in spirit." The stepmom was clearly hurt but accepted her wish gracefully. The day before the wedding Jamie presented her stepmother with a plaque containing a personal inscription of gratitude, and at the ceremony we acknowledged her for her love and support. Jamie's stepmother was both visibly moved and a bit surprised. Whatever rift had been caused by the bride's decision to walk only with her father was healed.

Another bride wrote about her stepfather, "He's the glue that put the family back together. I could just cry when I think of all he has done for us. He put up with my teenage years, and that was not easy." We honored him during my address. We also asked him to come forward with the biological fathers, right before the vows, and bestow a silent blessing. All three fathers participated by placing their right hands on the hands of the bride and groom and joining me in a moment of silent prayer.

These are just a few of the transformations possible. A little care and effort can go a long way when it comes to family. Marc Chagall said, "If I create from the heart, nearly everything works; if from the head, almost nothing." It is the same with the art of relationships.

Think of Ways to Involve the Children

Ben, a sixty-five-year-old widower with six grandchildren, married Arlene, forty-three. For the procession, all six grandchildren walked out before the bride. What a joyful sight! At the end of the ceremony they blew bubbles on Grandpa and his new wife.

Another bride and groom had, between them, sixteen nieces and nephews, some of them very young. This couple did not want a large bridal party, so they chose to have just one attendant each. After they arrived at the altar, all those nieces and nephews came down the aisle holding hands, not in a formal row but walking naturally—accompanied by many *ooohs* and *aaaws* from the guests. Young children bring delight to a wedding event no matter what they do.

Especially if you or your partner have children from a previous marriage, including them in your ceremony in some way makes a powerful and tender statement—that they are and will remain an important part of your lives. This is the reassurance they long for. Children from previous marriages, even "cool" teenagers, so often have fears regarding the new marriage: "Will Mom or Dad still love me the same?" "Where does this leave me?" I remember one father telling me that he wanted his kids to know that in his new wife, their stepmother, they had an excellent friend, someone who'd always be on their side.

I encourage parents and stepparents to address their children's fears before the marriage, and to speak to their children honestly, lovingly, gently, and respectfully throughout the planning process. Then, at the wedding itself, acknowledge them, bless them, even celebrate them.

Carla was divorced and had three children. Her fiancé, Tommy, was also divorced but had no children. During the ceremony, before the bride and groom said their vows, I asked the three children to come forward and spoke quietly to them: "Billy, John, and Kate, your mom and Tommy want you to know just how important you all are and that you will always be in their lives. They love you very much and want your blessing. Will you join me in blessing their marriage?" I instructed them to place their right hands upon the hands of their mom and Tommy, and we all closed our eyes in silent prayer. Later each child sprinkled the bride and groom with rose petals.

At one wedding the groom's son and daughter—shy and uncomfortable adolescents—turned down their father's request that they participate and elected to remain sitting quietly next to their grandparents. I addressed them personally, briefly, along with the couple's parents, using their father's own words from the questionnaire. I told them that when I asked their dad what his priority in life was, he answered, "My kids." The happiest day of his life, he said, was the day he was reunited with his children (this was after a prolonged custody battle). As I spoke, I saw their faces soften. Later the boy came and questioned me about God and spirituality. Many doors open when we open our hearts.

Consider Acknowledging the Death of a Loved One

Perhaps a family member or a close friend has passed away recently, or many years ago. It's perfectly appropriate to acknowledge that individual at your wedding, and you may find it an immensely moving and loving moment for you and for your guests. Many people initially shy away from this idea. It strikes them as introducing a sad note, a downer, on a joyous day. The moment may be poignant but does not need to be in any way maudlin.

Barbara insisted she and her fiancé had no major differences or issues on which they needed to compromise, yet she seemed uncomfortable, even somewhat forlorn, as we talked. I asked if anything was upsetting her, and tears began to flow. Her mother, to whom she was extremely close, had died the previous year, and planning the wedding without Mom was emotionally overwhelming. I suggested that sometimes it's healing to acknowledge these feelings of loss, and that we could give her mother a place at her wedding. During the ceremony we spoke of her mother's presence in heart and spirit, and said she was sorely missed and would never be forgotten. Barbara also paid tribute to her Ireland-born mother by having bagpipes played during the procession and ending the ceremony with a traditional Irish wedding blessing.

One bride and groom had a separate table on which they lit five candles, one each for the family members who had passed on. During the ceremony some couples use articles belonging to those they loved and lost—a mother's Bible, the kiddush cup of a beloved grandmother, a tray holding the sacred objects in a Hindu service that had belonged to a much-loved aunt. You can ask your celebrant to say a few simple words expressing your affection for the individual who meant so much to you.

I have seen over and over how a bride's or groom's expression of love and thanks for a departed grandparent brings a moment of tenderness and joy to the parents. The grandmother of one groom had died several days before his wedding. He mentioned this to me in a phone conversation shortly before the ceremony, and I asked, "Do you think it would be nice if we said something about her? Was she a good grandmother?" Well, yes, he said, she had always been kind to him. At the beginning of the ceremony, I was able to mention his grandmother's passing and say, simply, "She was a kind bubbe." Afterward, the groom's mother thanked me.

From the experiences of one young couple whose ceremony I conducted, I felt again the spiritual interconnectedness of all the monumental passages of life. Sara and Jake had known each other since seventh grade, fallen in love during their college years, struggled through some relationship ups and downs, and were at last happily planning their wedding. Then one evening Sara called, in tears, and explained that Jake's mother, earlier diagnosed with cancer and expected to recover, had abruptly taken a turn for the worse and was near death. At their request, I joined Jake and Sara and family members who had flown in from all over the country at the bedside of this clearly much-loved, fifty-two-year-old woman. Leaving the subway station near the hospital, I felt suddenly surrounded by a presence pulling me in. It was, I knew, the soul of this woman, whom I had never met, pushing me to get a move on. (Later, as I was telling family members about my experience, they said, "Yep, that was Stephanie, all right. If she wanted you to do something, you did it!")

All spoke so highly of Stephanie—of her hospitality, her grace, her love for her son and for the young woman he would marry. We said prayers. We did a meditation to help Jake's mother and her emotionally and physically exhausted family members accept what was imminent, and to let her go. Before I left I felt compelled to speak to Jake, telling him that I believed his mother would soon let go, and that he might be surprised to feel, at that moment, great joy. She died ten minutes after I left. And, some days after that, Jake told me that at the moment of her death he had experienced her presence "all over. It was incredible! I had to keep myself from smiling!" Clearly this young man, an only child and devoted to his mother, felt a joyous communion with her soul at the point of her death. Spiritual communion is an ecstasy, a bliss.

In her questionnaire, Sara later wrote, "The time I felt most connected to God was during the passing of Jake's mom. Beginning with the two weeks leading up to her death, I began feeling so much love, not only for her but for Jake, his family, my family, our friends who helped us. I feel a much deeper sense of love for Jake now after the experience we've been through together."

It was Stephanie's wish that her son and his bride go ahead with the wedding, and they did, just a month after her death. Although all were burdened with a great sadness, we made certain the wedding didn't feel like a funeral; as one aunt said, "We already did that." Yet it felt absolutely right to talk about the woman who wasn't there. In my remarks to the couple and their guests, I spoke of how we honored her, we missed her presence, we knew how happy she'd been for this day, and I read the passage Sara had written, ending by saying, "Jake's mother left you with that great gift. Hold on to it. Keep it inside you and affecting your lives, always."

If a Family Member or Close Friend is Ill, Consider Acknowledging Them

Most people do not like to bring up the subject of illness at a wedding. Yet illness is a part of life. A marriage ceremony can actually be an uplifting experience for a family member who is ill. On several occasions when a parent of the bridal party was very sick, the bride or groom has told me how good the planning felt for the parent, saying that it was something to distract him or her in the most pleasant way and something to look forward to. A wedding represents hope.

Often a bride or groom whose parent suffers from a chronic illness is powerfully inspired by that mother's or father's spirit. In answer to the part of the questionnaire that says, "Is there a person in history you admire greatly?" one young woman named her mother—"my hero"—in part because of her strength and determination in living with multiple sclerosis for years. At the ceremony we told her mom just that. Particularly if people are ill, how wonderful to let them know they are loved, appreciated, and admired!

At a humanist ceremony that took place at the United Nations Chapel, I read the words that Carlos, a Spanish-American groom, had written about his dad. His father, suffering from an advanced neurological disorder, was present but not able to speak or to be entirely in control of his movements. Carlos had said on his questionnaire, "My dad. What a warrior! My dad worked so hard on those ships, sometimes eighteen-hour days. He is a rock. He got hurt seriously a few times on the job, but he didn't stop. I remember when I graduated college and I saw a big smile on his face. He was proud of what I accomplished, and I had just scratched the surface."

Both father and son were passionate about sports, especially soccer, and Carlos remembered one glorious game they had attended together, a quarter-final match for the World Cup. Their team won, and they danced in the parking lot: "He wasn't my dad that day, he became my buddy. A close buddy."

As he listened intently to this tribute, Carlos's father's uncontrolled gestures and facial expressions became still. Later he tried to thank me, but his illness prevented him from doing so. I took his hand and held it to my heart, closed my eyes, and bowed my head. We understood each other.

The dear friend and mentor of one bride and groom, a forty-year-old man suffering from AIDS, was clearly bound and determined to be present for their wedding, although it was physically difficult for him. He glowed—especially when the couple presented him during the ceremony with a small plaque that expressed the meaning of friendship. Another wedding took place on a yacht. Upon arriving I greeted the bride's sister, who had been battling cancer with determination and courage. I told her how happy the couple was that she could be there and asked her how she was doing. "Okay," she said, "except that I'm afraid all this wind will blow my wig off!" She also was presented with a gift at the ceremony, a piece of jewelry that had special meaning for the sister. It was a moment filled with tears of joy.

Embracing an ailing family member or friend in some small way need not mean calling attention to something sad; rather, it can widen the circle of love and thanksgiving. If you will be dealing with such a situation, make your celebrant aware of what's going on. He or she will need to be sensitive and extremely careful in editing the ceremony. I believe it's best to keep the language throughout grounded in the present. For example, I might hold the couple's hands and say, "Remember always to be in the moment. Remember to smell the roses. Remember to cherish each other." Stay away from phrases such as "grow old together" or "until death do you part." Even the words *eternal* and *immortal* might better be avoided; but if the ill person is of great faith, the idea of the eternal may provide comfort.

At the same time, remember that your wedding is a joyous occasion! Do not diminish the joy! Done with care and love, your ceremony can be uplifting for the family member or friend who is ill, giving comfort, joy, and healing by demonstrating your love and appreciation.

To have a loving, supportive family and friends is surely one of life's greatest treasures. It is a gift, one that not everyone is fortunate to have. Having people who love you at your wedding speaks much about them as caring human beings. And it also says much about you.

SVEN AND ELIZABETH,
AN EPISCOPALIAN–CATHOLIC COUPLE

Elizabeth is tall, beautiful, with a wholesome face and an open personality. Sven is a quiet, gentle man with a refined intellect. Theirs is a delightful love story.

Sven, who had been wounded by his divorce, kept rejecting his friend Hedi's promptings to call Elizabeth, her former co-worker. Hedi persisted for six months, convinced the two should meet. Exasperated by Sven's noncompliance, Hedi finally shouted, "Sven, you don't have to marry her!" At that moment, Sven says, he heard a voice in his head: "It clearly said, 'Oh yes, I do!' And I wondered, where did that come from?"

(It was at my meeting with Sven and Elizabeth that he revealed the message of that voice within. Elizabeth, staring at him with open mouth, said, "You never told me that!" He looked at her shyly, almost embarrassed, and said, "Well, it just seemed so silly at the time." After a moment I observed quietly, "And look where you are now.")

Elizabeth, by contrast, had been really working on herself. In their ceremony I referred to it as "the kind of courageous introspective work that transforms one's life." Elizabeth had changed. A pattern of emotionally destructive behavior had ceased. One spring day she had a quite remarkable experience. She was standing on a corner, putting a large bundle of pictures and résumés into a mailbox (Elizabeth is a professional actress). "It had just finished raining, and the sky was opening up," she wrote in her questionnaire. "I looked up, and over Central Park was the most beautiful rainbow! I couldn't believe it! When do you see a rainbow in Manhattan? I felt it was just for me." She took it as a sign that something good was about to happen to her. It did. A few months later, Elizabeth met Sven. Little did she know at the time that she was standing outside the church in which she and Sven would marry.

Many of us go in search of miracles. Some of us never quite believe in them. Yet they are all around us, happening to ordinary people every day.

Sven's words from his questionnaire:

I admire Elizabeth's contributions of sense and sensibility (borrowed from Jane Austen). Her sense manifests itself in her forthrightness, her "roll up your sleeves and get it done" approach to problems. Her sensibility becomes a compass for her forthright nature and helps her to locate herself in the middle of a task or while at rest. There is a sweetness about Elizabeth that seems to come somehow from candor and a sense of surprise.

Elizabeth's words:

Sven and I met on a blind date—my first and last. My soul realized he was the one almost immediately. My mind took about two months.

From day one we have been a constant comfort for each other. We are always there to catch each other if we fall. I admire his vast experience and knowledge. He remembers details of everything he reads. He is endlessly sweet and caring to me and his children. He would do anything for them. (Sven had a son and daughter from his previous marriage.) He is hardworking, creative, fun, funny, but most important . . . he cooks! And finally, he always puts the toilet seat down! What else could a girl want? But, seriously, I am marrying him because he is the only person in my life who has made me feel loved. It is as simple as that.

For their wedding in a Unitarian-Universalist church (Sven had been raised Episcopalian, Elizabeth, Catholic, but neither wanted a religious ceremony), Sven envisioned "a celebration of boundless potential." Wrote Elizabeth, "We see our ceremony as simple, pure, and elegant. We want it to be touching, short, intimate, and fun." Sven's two children would take part, "but their participation should allow them to feel at ease in front of many strangers," Sven requested.

Sven wrote their vows. He studiously went through a book I had recommended and wrote down all the words that appealed to him. Then, according to Elizabeth, in a flash of inspiration he wrote the following within minutes:

I, Sven, take you, Elizabeth,
to be my wife,
to love and to cherish,
to hold ever foremost in my thoughts,
my plans,
my dreams.
To support and defend with heart and soul,
with loyalty and faithfulness,
that we may together form
a common place for ourselves
where we will comfort, support, and nurture
each other and those we love,
so that we may be united
one with the other
even when apart.
Because in our love will we
preserve our intention
to return always to our common place,
the one single place
where we are when we are together.

Sven's elderly father lived with them. They affectionately called him Far Far, meaning Father's Father in Norwegian. Sven's father was still very much in love with his late wife, though many years had passed since her death. After the wedding ceremony I introduced myself to Far Far, who was frail in body but sound in mind and spirit. We spoke of his wife, and he said something I will never forget: "I do not know where she is, but there is one thing I do know. Wherever she is, I will find her." Beloved Far Far has since passed on. There is no doubt in my mind that he has found his wife.

A postscript: When I contacted Sven and Elizabeth to ask if they would grace this book with their story, Elizabeth shared with me another not-so-small miracle in her life. She'd been at home one afternoon, baking cookies, when her stepdaughter called loudly, "Come look, a rainbow!" This again was a glorious rainbow, stretching across the skies. And this time the entire family saw it. The following week Elizabeth learned that she was pregnant.

I must add that, though I have lived in New York City my entire life, I have yet to see a rainbow. Elizabeth assures me that she will call me the very next time she sees one.

Chapter Five

The Interfaith Ceremony

Its Components and Structure

If you lived in one of the world's remote places and were marrying someone from an unfriendly village, your wedding might feature wrestling matches, the exchange of insults, and other ancient ritualized hostilities. Interfaith weddings in the Western world are usually more peaceful! Your interfaith ceremony will draw out the spiritual essence from competing and sometimes discordant traditions in a harmonious way.

The ceremony should mirror your love. Like life, it should be a full experience. There can be poignant moments of reflection and silence, of reverence, of joy and elation. Laughter, tears, talk, praise, prayer, blessing, and ritual all have a place in the joining of hands and hearts. A wedding is a time to feel connected and elevated.

Before you begin to structure your ceremony with your partner or start negotiations with your families, you must know the possibilities available to you. This chapter presents them. The possibilities may seem a bit overwhelming, but it really is not difficult. The readings, prayers, and rituals we offer here speak to all hearts; they are universal and exclude no one. Remember the interfaith premise: Never instead of, always in addition to.

Many people attending their first interfaith ceremony are amazed at how deeply touched they are to hear words about love that are unfamiliar to them, celebrating tradition that is foreign to their own. One feels richer inside, somehow greater than before. There is a joy when we recognize—suddenly, unexpectedly—the similarities behind the clothing of our different faiths and cultures. When we celebrate the unity in our diversity, we become one with the world. We are one with God. This is the strength of interfaith. It takes courage. It calls upon our humanity.

A Word About Rituals

In the context of an interfaith wedding, rituals are any ceremonial acts that punctuate the service. They may be religious, cultural, or social; they include blessing and drinking of wine, the Christian unity candle, the Catholic passing of the peace, the Greek wreath exchange, the Japanese rice wine ceremony, the Hindu garland exchange, the Iranian sofreh. Regardless of their religious or cultural origins, most rituals are adaptable for an interfaith service. They can be explained and universalized so that it becomes meaningful and inclusive for both sides of the family.

Rituals are physical, symbolic manifestations of what is going on inside you spiritually. After all, the marriage ceremony is a transformative moment, and ritual can help define and convey that sense. Many rituals are inserted at specific times in a wedding ceremony. The Jewish tradition of breaking the glass, for example, takes place at the final moment. Celtic handfasting takes place just before the vows. Rituals such as drinking from a common goblet of wine are a bit more flexible. Later you will find guidance on where and how to place them in your ceremony.

Many couples have come to me saying they want a simple ceremony without ritual. Yet, as I mention practices that might be appropriate for them, often they become enthusiastic about the possibilities. When you celebrate ritual in a universal context, you may find yourselves surprisingly embracing of it. Ritual for ritual's sake can feel devoid of meaning. But ritual to which you feel connected will uplift and transform you.

Building Your Ceremony

My collaborator on this book has jokingly compared my structure for an interfaith service to working with an Erector set! To demonstrate how you can create the wedding ceremony that satisfies your needs, we present here a basic format on which you can layer the rituals, prayers, blessings, and readings of your choice. Interfaith is a sumptuous buffet of cultural and religious diversity. Select what you wish!

The basic interfaith ceremony consists of these elements:

Procession
Ritual (optional)
Opening words
Reading(s) (optional)
Honoring of family members (optional)
Celebrant's address
Prayer (optional)
Declaration of intent
Ritual(s) (optional)
Silent prayer (optional)
Vows
Blessing and exchange of rings
Pronouncement
Kiss
Closing blessing
Ritual (optional)
Recession

Procession

I often refer to the procession as "the Walk of a Lifetime." This is the moment you have been waiting for; the product of all your preparation begins to unfold. But, of course, it means more than that. Many brides—grooms too—have anticipated the wedding procession all their lives. It is the beginning of a major rite of passage for the couple, as well as for their parents, and one to which our society gives great attention. You now become part of something bigger than yourselves. Even if you have been living together for several years, or if this is not your first marriage, something uniquely powerful takes place when you publicly present your chosen partner in life before family and friends.

A procession can be a quiet, simple entrance by the bride and groom from a side door, or it can be a ceremonial parade down a center aisle with family members and friends of honor. One very old tradition made new (and becoming quite popular) is a variation on the ringing of bells. Churches have often rung their bells at the end of a wedding ceremony, announcing the bridal couple to the community; historically, the ringing of bells was a means of keeping evil spirits from interfering with the nuptial pair. In Buddhist weddings, one to three solemn bells are rung to begin and conclude the ceremony. In this modern variation the bride is announced to all in attendance by "bell ringers"—one, two, or even four young boys who process in before the bride ringing handheld bells. At the conclusion of the ceremony, the bell ringers may recess before the bride and groom. The children, as well as the guests, always seem to enjoy this chiming spectacle.

How you walk into your ceremony makes a statement about your relationship with each other and with your family and friends. To some extent the form of your procession will be dictated by the setting you have chosen. Traditional ceremonies also often include a preferred sequence.

In a Christian ceremony, grandparents are seated first, then the parents of the groom, followed by the mother of the bride; finally the bridal party enters. Often there is a change of music when the bride walks down the aisle with her father. The congregation usually stands for the bride's entrance. The bride walks to the left of her father. The groom, who is already up front, offers his arm to his bride and brings her before the celebrant.

> In marriage you are neither the husband nor the wife; you are the love between the two.
>
> —*Nisargadatta*

In a Jewish ceremony, the chuppah (the wedding canopy) is held up by four poles carried by male members or close friends of the groom. He follows, with his mother and father on either side. Sometimes the chuppah is an elaborate construction that is not carried but already in place; attendants simply follow the grandparents. Often the rabbi leads the procession. The bride walks down the aisle with her mother at her right side and her father at her left. She joins the groom with both sets of parents under the chuppah. The congregation usually remains seated throughout.

A Jewish-Christian procession can take place as follows: The Jewish groom, the groom's family, and his attendants may walk down in the Jewish tradition; the Christian bride, her family, and her attendants may walk down in the Christian tradition. Processional music can be classical or another neutral selection. It is important to avoid the use of music by the German composer Richard Wagner, because he was a known anti-Semite.

In a Hindu ceremony, the groom is first welcomed by the parents of the bride with several delightful rituals. He then takes his place within a ceremonial pavilion, and the bride is escorted by her family to assume her position beside him.

For a Jewish-Hindu wedding, the Jewish groom might walk down in a customary manner, with the chuppah serving as the pavilion. In Hindu fashion, the bride's parents could wait up front to greet the groom, his parents, the attendants, and finally their daughter, symbolically welcoming everyone into their family. Another option would be for the bride to walk down with her friends and family preceding her and her parents at her sides. For a Hindu-Sufi wedding I celebrated, the entire female contingent of the Afghani bride's extended family walked behind the bride and her father.

The point is that adaptation of all traditional procession rituals is possible in an interfaith ceremony.

Ritual (optional)

Between the procession and the opening words, it is possible to insert a ritual. This is the first of at least two opportunities during the ceremony to honor families. One ritual that couples from many backgrounds choose is honoring the mothers with the symbolic gift of a flower. The presenting of roses originated in the Catholic tradition, evolving from honoring the Blessed Mother to honoring one's own mother. It is a way to distinguish Mom when Dad has the honor of walking the bride down the aisle.

Two flowers, often yellow or blush pink roses, are left at the table or altar, ready for presentation. One Japanese Buddhist bride chose orchids. Another bride selected lilies because her mother's name was Lily.

I often suggest that the flowers have notes attached, rolled and tied with beautiful ribbons or fabric. In the note, you can convey to your mother what she means to you. What more wonderfully appropriate time, after all, to thank her for all she has done for you? Tell her the contributions she has made to you as a person and to your life. Though this tradition is usually designated for mothers, many couples have chosen to give both parents flowers, attaching notes to both mother and father.

If a parent has passed away, the flower can be placed in a vase at the altar, with or without a note. One bride found it healing to write a note to her mother, who had recently died. Remember, these decisions are yours. There is no right way or wrong way. You are the one who must feel comfortable.

Opening Words

I always begin a ceremony by welcoming the guests on behalf of the bride and groom and their families. No matter what the religious or cultural situa-

tion, a warm welcome and a friendly smile bridges boundaries and puts people at ease. "How wonderful it is to see the minister smiling!" is a comment
I've heard more than once.

At an intercultural wedding, I often say "Welcome!" in the languages of
the families present. This small gesture has great meaning. It demonstrates a
celebrant's willingness to reach out. There are smiles all around when "Bon-
jour!" or "Salaam A'leikum!" or "Nea how!" or "Shalom!" comes out of my
mouth.

The opening words (in Christianity they are often referred to as the convocation) are meant to invoke the sacred and to encourage all present to
open their hearts. This is the time to gather everyone in a circle of intent so
that all feel unified in support of the couple. Words of inspiration are offered
to uplift each person. Both in the opening words and in the address to the
couple, inspiration is key.

Since I work with so many traditions and family situations, the way I
open a ceremony varies. Opening words for a ritual-heavy wedding that fully
celebrates both sides of an intercultural marriage will be very different from
those for a simple humanist ceremony for a couple of the same culture. This
is one opening statement I have used:

**Welcome, everyone! Today we witness the joining of two lives, two fam-
ilies from two ancient and rich traditions. And God is smiling! In honor
and in celebration of their heritages, [bride and groom] have chosen rituals
from each of their backgrounds for their ceremony. This couple, as an
interfaith couple, embodies the meaning of respect, tolerance, and understanding. This ceremony will celebrate their oneness as well as their
uniqueness. They will learn from each other and grow. Together they will
expand to something greater than themselves. Theirs is a love that knows
no boundaries. They stand as a beacon of light inspiring all of us to love.
They give us hope.**

The opening words can be personalized in countless ways. For the wedding of a couple whose families had been strongly opposed to their relationship, I opened by reading excerpts from supportive letters written to me at
my request by close friends of the bride and groom. The couple knew that I
had asked their friends to write about them; the friends did not know that
their letters would be read. After the ceremony I gave the bride and groom all
the letters their friends had written.

After reading the excerpts, I added, "It is said that when the one man loves
the one woman and the one woman loves the one man, the very angels desert
heaven and sit in that house and sing for joy." This was a very fitting reading
for this couple, but its source, the Kama Sutra, was not appropriate to name

for their Jewish and Catholic families. I personalized the quotation by immediately adding,

**The angels are here. Just look around you. You are this couple's angels.
For you have come here with joy, with love in your hearts. You are the ones
who have stood by their sides through the years, the tears, the joys and sorrows. Your very presence adds meaning and sanctity to this occasion.**

After the service the couple's parents told them that they now understood
their relationship. We had built a bridge through interfaith.

Reading vignettes personalizes any ceremony. Eddie and Lili were both
Chinese-born, American-raised, of Buddhist and Christian backgrounds, to
which their attachment was more cultural than religious. When I asked
members of their large families and many close friends to send me their
impressions of Eddie and Lili, I received dozens of replies. I read several
excerpts and followed with the Chinese legend that a couple is bound at
birth by an invisible thread that becomes shorter and shorter until they meet,
fall in love, and marry. The effect was so personal that a number of the guests
believed I was one of the couple's close friends.

Interfaith couples often ask me to begin by acknowledging and explaining
what they are about to do, or by telling something about how they met and
fell in love, using sentiments expressed in the questionnaire. Omi, a divorced
Muslim-American with two children, and Rose, the American daughter of
Hispanic Catholics, had written beautifully about each other: "He is the
kindest, most supportive, and loving man I have ever been with. He is a
wonderful father, and that is important to me. I can't imagine my life without him." "I love her intelligence and spirituality. I love the way she is with
my children. She is the most giving woman I have ever met. We've known
each other for four years, but forever in our souls." Rose and Omi heard their
words about each other for the first time when I read them at the opening of
their wedding.

Another effective way to open your wedding is by honoring your heritage
with a traditional story. People love and remember stories! There are wonderful tales and legends about love in every faith and culture.

If your ceremony is taking place in a natural setting that has specific
meaning to you, you may want to begin by calling attention to it. I opened
the ceremony of a couple who were married on their favorite mountain with
these words:

**This is Mohonk, named long ago by Native Americans. Translated, it
means "lake in the sky." These mountains are very old and were considered
sacred by the Native Americans. Many, many others have found this to be
a mystical place. Many come here for peace and healing. No one more so**

than Bill and Emily. You see, this is where it all started for them. They began their courtship in these mountains. It is here they fell in love. And it is from the sky above us that Bill falls thousands of feet skydiving with his buddies.

Bill's hobby was competition skydiving. The wedding invitations were sealed in wax paper with clouds on it!

I opened another ceremony, on a beach with a magnificent sun setting behind us, by saying, "Behold God's handiwork! Listen to the sound of the ocean, the sound of God." Then I explained to everyone that the couple, a Catholic and a Protestant, had chosen to be married by the ocean because it was sacred to them; it was there that they felt most at peace and inspired.

Often a less personal statement is appropriate. Here is a portion of the opening words I might use:

Welcome everyone!

There are moments in our lives that are ruled not so much by time but by the heart. This is such a moment for [bride] and [groom]. These two people have fallen in love—so deeply, so completely—that today they make a bond, a sacred covenant whereby their hearts, their bodies, and their souls shall be united as one in marriage for the rest of their days.

Today, before all of you, their most cherished family and friends, they will say the most powerful, most loving words two people can say to each other. They will take their wedding vows. And it is our honor and privilege to stand witness. For this blessed act, my friends, is magnificent and so tender to behold.

I am going to ask all of you now to go to your hearts and open them as wide as you can and raise your spirits high, as we come with our full presence to honor [bride] and [groom] as they join together as husband and wife in the holy state of matrimony.

These examples may give you some ideas for the words that will open your ceremony. With your celebrant's support, you can develop a statement that in many ways will set the tone for your service, which may be formal and serious or highly personal, affectionate, and amusing. You will find other suggestions in Chapter 7 and throughout Part III.

Reading(s) (optional)

After the opening words is a good time to insert one or two readings, and these may be offered by the celebrant or by a family member or friend. You might even begin your service with a brief reading instead of opening words; this option works well for couples who want a humanist ceremony, "a civil ceremony with heart." In either case, readings convey to everyone in attendance how you feel about love and marriage. They offer insight into who you are and how you think as a couple.

If you choose only one reading, it should be agreeable to both of you. Two readings can reflect different but not mutually exclusive perspectives. Many couples, for example, select one passage from a religious text to reflect their beliefs (or to please observant family members) and one literary or poetic reading to express their personal, romantic relationship.

There are appropriate and quite beautiful selections from any number of sources. A Greek Orthodox–Jewish couple chose Marge Piercy's chuppah reading and a poem by Homer. A Portuguese Catholic–American Protestant couple paired a biblical reading and a selection from Elizabeth Barrett Browning's *Sonnets from the Portuguese*. A Muslim bride and Protestant groom chose verse from Rumi and Walt Whitman. An African-American interfaith couple chose a Maya Angelou poem. A Lebanese Catholic and American Protestant couple selected a poem from the Lebanese poet Kahlil Gibran. A German-born couple, a Catholic and a Lutheran, chose a Rainer Maria Rilke poem. Whether you are same-faith or interfaith, the possibilities are endless.

In Part II and Part III you will find many of these and other selections. How do you know when a reading is suited to you? It moves you. It feels right. You experience that sense of "Aha!"

Wedding readings are jewels. Let them speak to you. When I was suggesting possible readings to one bride, she said excitedly that she felt like a kid in an ice cream store! She and her fiancé were tasting all the flavors and deciding which ones they liked best. Enjoy the process of finding the passages that best reflect you. As you look through the suggestions in Part II, you are scanning thousands of years of humanity's most exquisite expressions. These words reflect the world's perspectives on love; they represent the heart, mind, body, and soul of our spiritual relationship to marriage and love.

Honoring of Family Members (optional)

You may have decided to honor your parents by including them in the procession, or by presenting flowers to them after it. Later in the ceremony, they can be asked to participate in a ritual like the Celtic handfasting or to bless the union with the celebrant during a silent prayer. Now is an opportunity to honor them in a broader manner. The section of the questionnaire regarding your families is intended to suggest ways your celebrant can speak directly to family members.

Some couples want their ceremony to focus completely on them, with no mention of their parents or other relatives, because of estranged relationships or for other reasons. I have officiated at interfaith and interracial weddings where, despite efforts to include them, one or both sides of a family have refused to attend. I have worked with couples whose parents have been happily married for half a century, and with couples who have so many parents and stepparents it's hard to keep track! Some couples are intimate with their families, some are friendly but distant, some don't speak. There is always a way to honor family, or *not* to acknowledge them but in a way that does not dishonor.

If you wish, arrange with your celebrant to speak directly to family members during the ceremony, possibly including some of your own words about them from your questionnaire responses. Or you may prefer a less personal address, including a general quotation or two in their honor. Here is one I have often used:

This is the portion of the ceremony we dedicate to family, for as Alice Walker states, "To acknowledge our ancestors means we are aware that we did not make ourselves, that the line stretches all the way back, perhaps to God. The grace with which we embrace life, in spite of the pain, the sorrows, is always a measure of what has gone before."

"What we do for ourselves dies with us, but what we do for others and the world remains and is immortal." [from Albert Pine]

[Bride's] and [groom's] parents, you have given your children immortal gifts. The light of this marriage would not, could not be possible without you. At a wedding we see firsthand how this sublime torch, this lineage of love, gets passed along from generation to generation and, in a very real sense, we become immortal.

Emerson defined success this way: It is to leave the world a better place, by virtue of a redeemed social condition, a patch of garden, or by way of a child. We congratulate you on your success! You have brought forth life. You have brought forth love. It is most appropriate on this, your children's wedding day, that we thank you. We bless you.

We dedicate this quotation, from Linda Hogan, a contemporary Native American writer, to all [bride's] and [groom's] extended families: "Walking, I am listening to a deeper way. Suddenly, all my ancestors are behind me. Be Still. They Say. Watch and Listen. You are the result of the love of thousands."

This is also a suitable place to acknowledge loved ones who cannot be at your wedding because of sickness or old age, or family members who have died. As mentioned in the previous chapter, a wedding can sometimes be a bittersweet time for families, especially those who have recently lost a loved one. All your feelings about the loss will be rushing through your mind on this day, and many couples and their families find it healing to acknowledge briefly the individual they are missing. Here is how I referred to the death of a groom's mother:

We acknowledge that her spirit resides among us today. Shawn says that he can feel her effervescent smile, smiling down on him today. She remains and will always remain in Shawn's and his father's hearts. Lilies were her favorite flowers. They are here today, dedicated to her.

A vase of lilies had been placed on the table that served as an altar; comments honoring the surviving parents followed.

Here is how I referred to the death of a bride's brother in a car accident several years earlier:

Rose misses Victor very much and says she knows he surely would not have missed this event. He so often wondered who she would marry, and is probably quite surprised that Eddie is not a musician, artist, or poet. Victor remains in and will never leave the hearts of the family.

This point in the ceremony is also a wonderful time to speak directly to children. To the two young children of a remarrying groom, I said,

McKayla and Zoe, your dad calls you his incredible, amazing girls. He says he loves your happy dancing feet. He looks forward to coming home because of how you jump into his arms. He says that you have taught him so many things—to love, to play, and to dance. [Bride] and your dad want you to know how very much they love you, and how important you are and always will be in their lives.

Celebrant's Address

Now your celebrant speaks to you directly about love and marriage.

When I start to work on my address for a couple, I am thinking about how I can best inspire these two individuals, and what about them inspires me. I recall our meetings and conversations, and I read and reread the questionnaire responses. I look for expressions that moved me, especially expressions of love that I might quote. Each pair has their particular magic. I seek out what that magic is so I can convey it back to them and their guests. Do ask your celebrant to reflect deeply on your written and spoken words to her.

If you wish her address to be personal, give her permission to use your questionnaire responses.

It is my hope that the following examples will not only guide you in determining how you wish to be addressed but also help celebrants in conducting interfaith ceremonies that touch the heart and inspire unity.

Here is an address I offered for an interdenominational couple who did not wish a highly personalized statement. These words are a good sample of an address that can work for all couples:

[Bride] and [groom], in just a few moments something magical occurs. A transformation takes place. You will transform into family, a nuclear family for all to see. Now this is quite profound, because family means that you literally become part of each other. You carry each other deep inside, wherever you may go. No matter what life may bring, whether it is the wonderful sound of laughter or the anguish of tears, whether life brings abundance or hardship, sickness or health, now you walk this walk called life hand in hand, committed as husband and wife, eternally.

This is quite something! It is the beauty and power of marriage, and it is difficult. It is upon the strength of the foundation of this nuclear family that you shall build the temple of the rest of your life. Its beauty, its significance, is completely up to you. You are the architects of your marriage. Let it be magnificent to behold! Let all who come into your home benefit from the warmth of its radiance. Let it stand as a beacon of light inspiring others to love.

[Bride] and [groom], let your arms be a safe haven, a refuge for each of you to come home to every day. Drink from each other's inner well, and feel renewed, refreshed, each and every day. Enjoy each other. Laugh much. Enjoy the process, the dance of life. Cherish your time together, for life is a gift. Be slow to anger and quick to forgive. Use kind and gentle words. Yes, even in the bad times—especially then, for the storms of life will inevitably come. It is then you are called upon to hold each other even closer.

When times get tough, when things get very frightening, think of the sky at the ocean's shore. Storms at sea are frightening, and yet, when is the sky at its most beautiful? It is usually right after a difficult storm, for that is when the sky is clearest and so full of hope. That is when the rainbows appear.

(Taking the couple's hands) [Bride] and [groom], put your relationship on the altar of your lives and dedicate yourselves to it. Remember, as long as you have this, you have everything. Beauty and youth fade away, money comes and goes, but your love is irreplaceable. Love is eternal.

Here is a portion of a very personal address I used in the ceremony of an American Protestant and Portuguese Catholic couple:

Susan and Antonio, you both mentioned that you felt the hand of God in Fatima, that something mystical happened. That was no accident or coincidence. Because something much greater than yourselves, wiser than yourselves has brought you together. That is why you balance each other so well. Antonio, you worry and Susan calms you down. And, Antonio, you will keep her laughing. Laughter is a wonderful tool in life!

Susan, let your arms be a safe haven, a refuge for Antonio to come home to every day. Let him drink from the well of your inner beauty and feel renewed every day. And, Antonio, this woman has chosen to bestow all her love on you, over all others. This is an honor. A sacred trust. Let her know that to you she is the most beautiful woman on this earth.

If you find that your celebrant will not or cannot take the time to craft a personal address to you, you can write your own for him to read, or give your questionnaire responses to someone significant in your lives who will write and deliver the address. Be sure to select someone who is comfortable with public speaking and will address you and your guests clearly, sincerely, and with emotion. Select someone who will feel honored to be asked to play this important role in your ceremony.

Prayer (optional)

Prayer has several meanings. It is communication with the divine through word or thought. It can be conveyed with music or with ritual. Prayer can be a request for something particular, or for blessing; it may express gratitude or good wishes, or simply be a way of saying, "Hello, God, I'm here." Prayer may be formal, casual, traditional, or invented. The writer Anne Lamott says her two favorite prayers are: "Help me God, help me God, help me God," and "Thank you God, thank you God, thank you God." The offering of a simple prayer is a wonderful way for an officiant to open or close her address. In a profound sense, she is asking for the deepest and greatest good for the couple's marriage.

Prayer is universal. People of every faith and culture pray, and when you look through the various selections from different religions and cultures in Part II, I think you will be amazed at their similarities. Among the religious prayers, remove the terms Father, Adonai, Ganesh, Allah, and refer to God universally as God and, you will see, there'll be nothing to argue over! You may choose to have your celebrant read a prayer of religious or cultural origin, or a broadly spiritual prayer (containing no religious language), or a secular prayer.

Prayers contain heartfelt energies that elicit goodness. Prayers filled with hope and love emit and amplify light.

Many couples like this spiritual, nondenominational prayer, which I have adapted from Marianne Williamson's book *Illuminata* (divine references can be eliminated for a humanist ceremony):

[Dear God],

Please [We] bless this couple.

Please make [Let] their relationship be a great and holy adventure.

May their joining be a sacred place. May they find rest here, a haven for their souls.

Bring them together, heart and mind, body and soul.

Guide their way into light. Guide their way into wisdom. Help them grow.

May this marriage now receive your [our] blessing [and carry your great power]. We thank you [give thanks] for the gift of their precious love. Amen.

Declaration of Intent

The official portion of the ceremony encompasses the declaration of intent, the vows, the exchange of rings, and finally the pronouncement.

With the declaration of intent (sometimes called the declaration of consent), you are officially declaring before all your guests your intention to wed. When I begin this portion, I change my voice slightly from the earlier, more spiritual and informal portions of the ceremony. Now I am speaking in my "official" capacity. Here is a declaration of intent I often use:

The covenant of marriage is one that can be entered into only by persons who are both legally and spiritually free to offer themselves to each other. Therefore, in the presence of God and in the presence of all the witnesses here, I will ask [bride] and [groom] to state their intention. [Bride] and [groom], have you come here freely and without reservation to give yourselves to each other in the holy state of matrimony?

The couple answer yes.

Since it is your intention to join in marriage, kindly join hands, and with your hands your hearts.

Ritual(s) (optional)

If you choose, this is a lovely time to include a ritual. One that I have often used in interfaith ceremonies is handfasting, also called handwrapping or binding. Its origins are in Celtic, Eastern Orthodox, Hindu, and many cultural traditions, in which the bride's and groom's hands were bound by a ribbon symbolizing their indissoluble love. Many couples, regardless of their backgrounds, are charmed by this ritual when I explain it to them.

In ceremonies that I co-officiate, I often ask the other clergy member if, instead of a wrapping, I may place a portion of one of his or her garments— for example, a rabbi's tallith—on the hands of the couple. Most clergy are happy to consent, and the ritual takes on a powerful unifying significance.

Handfasting is one of many rituals (described in Part II) that may be used at this point in the ceremony.

Silent Prayer (optional)

As the ceremony moves toward its essential moment—the exchange of vows—I usually hold the couple's hands first in silent prayer. I speak quietly to the couple to calm them and help them focus. In a voice that can be heard only by us, I ask them to be truly present and to feel the words they are about to speak. Often, their eyes are closed. In some ceremonies, couples have asked their parents or children from a former marriage to come forward and join in the blessing.

I am particularly deliberate at this moment because, to me, the vows are everything. They are the culmination, the reason for the entire ceremony. As you develop your service, consider whether this is a point at which you might benefit from a few calming words from your celebrant and a moment of silent prayer. It may help if you try to imagine that you are the only two people in the room!

Vows

The vows are the essence of the wedding rite. Everyone comes to witness the bride and groom intently gazing into each other's eyes while pledging themselves to each other.

Technically and officially, the celebrant is a witness. In signing your marriage license, she in effect states that before her this couple have declared their solemn vow. When other witnesses are required to sign the license, they are stating the same. For this reason, the wedding ceremony is also called the solemnization act or act of solemnization by civil authorities: The wedding is solemnized through the act of taking vows in the presence of a state-appointed officiant and witnesses.

Some brides and grooms elect to write their own vows. Others choose from a selection that may be presented to them by their celebrant. Traditional religious ceremonies may not offer the couple a choice; many Protestant denominations, for example, require specific vows. In a traditional Jewish ceremony, in which the exchange of rings is the most significant rite, the ceremonial vows are very brief. Muslim vows are also brief, while Hindu vows—the essential seven steps—are more extensive.

You may read your vows or recite them from memory. Usually, however, the vows are repeated by a couple, following the lead of the celebrant, for two reasons. First, you are nervous! Your celebrant knows as much and will supply you with only a few words at a time. But second, without having to look down at a piece of paper or worry about what comes next, you are free to gaze openly into your beloved's eyes while holding her or his hands. Following the celebrant's lead also avoids the sense that the vows are something of a performance staged by the couple.

> The bride comes from the heart of dawn,
> And the bridegroom from the sunset.
> There is a wedding in the valley.
> A day too vast for recording.
>
> —*Kahlil Gibran*

One groom had written his own vows as a surprise for his bride, giving them much thought and spending the week before the wedding trying to memorize them. Then he thought he would read them. Immediately before the ceremony started, he asked me if I could read them for him to repeat because he was too nervous. I said of course—and that turned out to be a good thing, because when the moment arrived, his hands were shaking so much that he couldn't possibly have read them! Instead, he was able to repeat his words with great poignancy as he heard them spoken slowly and calmly by me.

For another wedding, two songwriters had written their vows together in the form of verse and recited them by memory while holding each other's hands. English was not the bride's first language, and she hesitated at some of the words; the groom was there to help her remember. They spoke in soft, patient, melodic tones, and the moment was tremendously touching.

Do what feels comfortable. Whole books are dedicated solely to wedding vows. In Part II, you'll find a selection of vows. Remember that you can adapt and edit at will to arrive at the expression perfect for you and your partner.

Blessing and Exchange of Rings

In almost all contemporary wedding ceremonies, rings are exchanged. The wedding band is a lasting symbol, and this custom, European in origin, is now common throughout the world. You will, of course, choose rings that reflect your personalities and that are comfortable. But you should feel more than comfortable with your wedding bands—you should love them! You will wear them all of your lives!

Before the exchange of rings, it is customary for the celebrant to bless them and speak a bit about their symbolism. Typically, I ask for the rings from the best man (or best man and best woman, or the pillow bearer) and say,

These rings are powerful symbols. The circle symbolizes the wholeness of your love, unbroken and everlasting. The precious metal represents the sincerity of your commitment. It is strong, enduring, and does not tarnish. As you wear them, may you be reminded of your eternal love for and devotion to each other. [By the grace of God,] these rings are hereby blessed. For a humanist ceremony, I delete the reference to God.

Most interfaith couples choose universal words like these for their ring exchange. In a more traditional ceremony, the rings are blessed according to the religion. In Jewish tradition, the ring exchange is most significant, while in Christian tradition the vows are most important. In co-officiated ceremonies, therefore, the rabbi will preside over the rings and the minister over the vows. In the Jewish tradition, the couple exchange simple gold wedding bands during the ceremony; afterward they may wear more ornamented rings if they wish.

Though it is customary, not every couple chooses to exchange rings. Katlyn and Glynn, an American architect and an English scholar of Chinese history who had met and fallen in love in Hong Kong, placed white gold Chinese wedding knots hung from ribbons around each other's necks at this point in the ceremony. Glynn disliked jewelry and didn't want to wear a ring that would hold no meaning for him. Katlyn, however, did want to wear a wedding band, so in a private library after the ceremony I did a blessing over a ring, which Glynn then placed on her finger with a brief vow. In the presence of a few witnesses, we signed their license.

Pronouncement

After the exchange of vows, the couple turn from each other and face the celebrant for the pronouncement. This is a deciding moment. Your celebrant declares to all present that you are now officially husband and wife.

The words can vary. Clergy may declare the couple married by the tenets of their particular faith. A civil officiant may pronounce: "By the power vested in me by the state of . . ." Many interfaith couples prefer a more universal statement, such as this one, which I frequently use:

By the love that has brought you here today, by the vows you have exchanged, and by the integrity of your commitment, in the presence of the witnesses here, [and in the presence of God,] it is my pleasure and my honor to pronounce you husband and wife.

For a humanist ceremony, I delete the reference to God. You will find several variations on the pronouncement in Part II.

Kiss

Now the celebrant tells the couple they may kiss—not by way of giving permission, of course; these two individuals are usually so caught up in their emotions that they simply don't know what to do next! At one Catholic wedding I attended, the priest made no mention of the kiss after his pronouncement. After a brief, awkward moment, the groom timidly asked, "May I kiss the bride?" Amused, the priest replied, "Well, if you don't, I will!"

I kid couples to practice the kiss in the days and weeks before their wedding. I tell them that if they don't do it right the first time, try, try again! Though it is obviously not necessary to solemnize your marriage, I consider the kiss mandatory.

After the kiss, the guests usually break out in spontaneous applause or cheering. Often I'll join in by clapping my hands, because guests are sometimes unsure if applause is appropriate until they receive this indication from the celebrant.

Closing Blessing

At these final moments, when the bride and groom stand together before family and friends (and especially if an interfaith couple has faced some familial opposition to their marriage), the celebrant has a perfect opportunity to send a message of support for the couple. I often precede the closing blessing with these words:

Will everyone now please go within and fill yourselves with all your good intentions, your hopes, prayers, and good wishes for [bride] and [groom] for the many years to come? Let us send them forth with many points of light.

The closing blessing follows, and you will find an array to choose from in Part II—my favorites from various religious, spiritual, and humanist sources. Many couples, of all backgrounds and beliefs, have chosen the Apache wedding song or prayer that begins, "Now you will feel no rain, for each of you will be shelter for the other." (It's usually listed as a reading in wedding books, but it works ideally as a closing blessing.)

Shawn wrote in his questionnaire, "I am Irish, Irish, Irish on all sides." His father, then in his seventies, still spoke with a lovely Irish brogue. For Shawn and Marla's wedding, we used a traditional Irish wedding blessing that an Irish cousin provided and his brother read. It began, "May the road rise up to meet you. May the wind be always at your back." (You will find the full text in Part II.)

Julie wrote in her questionnaire how much she loves angels, how she believed that her car was once lifted in the air to avoid a crash. She referred to that incident as "the heavenly work of an angel." As a closing blessing for her wedding, I invoked four archangels to walk with the couple through their life together (a rabbi taught me this invocation):

To your right is the angel Gabriel, who will be there to give you faith and encouragement. To your left is Michael, who will protect you. Behind walks Raphael, who shall be there to heal you. In front of you walks Uriel, whose name means "the light of God." This angel shall light your path, as you walk hand in hand on your journey as husband and wife.

Ritual (optional)

You may wish to add a final ritual at this point. At African-American weddings, for example, many couples choose to jump the broom at the end of the ceremony. In Jewish weddings, the breaking of the glass has become synonymous with the ending of the ceremony and the beginning of the banquet, regardless of the degree of religion in the ceremony. This cultural ritual has evolved to hold various meanings, as we'll explain in Chapter 8. In an interfaith ceremony, the celebrant can state that the bride and groom wish to signify the breaking of barriers between people of different faiths, cultures, or races.

Other cultural rituals—the sprinkling of rose petals traditional in a Hindu ceremony, for example—when universalized for an interfaith wedding are quite lovely, for their symbolism of love and acceptance, beauty and strength, speaks to all hearts.

Recession

The ceremony is over. Recessional music begins. The bride and groom walk arm in arm down the aisle at a cheerful pace. What I would most like to suggest to you about the recession is this: Coordinate beforehand with the musicians the precise moment the music should begin. I have been at ceremonies in which the music started immediately after the kiss or at a quiet moment before the end of the closing blessing.

For the recessional music, your choice is wide open. Tastes range from traditional wedding music through contemporary songs to something particularly relevant to the couple's personalities or cultures. Franklin and Sharon, an interfaith, interracial couple, began their ceremony with her cantor singing in Hebrew and ended it with Bob Marley. Anjali, a Hindu bride, chose the music of Ravi Shankar. Erika and Steven, a Christian interdenominational couple, chose "Ave Maria" for the processional and classical guitar music played by a friend for the recessional.

> One half of me is yours, the other half yours—
> Mine own, I should say; but if mine, then yours,
> And so all yours.
>
> —*Shakespeare*, The Merchant of Venice

The recessional historically has been followed by the throwing of rice as the bride and groom leave the wedding site, an originally pagan tradition symbolizing fertility and abundance or sustenance. Most places of worship and other establishments no longer allow this tradition because it is harmful to birds who eat the uncooked rice. Some venues suggest birdseed instead, although I agree with many brides who find this option less than appealing.

Rose petals are a lovely alternative. Confetti and streamers, also visually appealing, are often discouraged by cleanup-minded venues (though couples can arrange ahead of time to pay these costs). Blowing bubbles is an increasingly popular alternative. The couple walk out surrounded by floating pearlescent spheres, each one symbolizing a good wish. Bubbles often add a dramatic effect to photos, too!

After the ceremony, all your family and friends will want to embrace and congratulate you. You may choose to have the traditional receiving line or escape for a few private moments as husband and wife. (The idea of private time for the couple before the festivities is actually rooted in a Jewish custom, the yichud, which means "union" in Hebrew.) Some couples move with their bridal party to a private room, where they have a toast to the bride and groom before joining the other guests. Of course, this is also typically a time for taking photographs with the bridal party and family members. However you spend your first few moments of married life, remember that the next several hours are the time for feasting and dancing and celebration!

■ ■ ■

With this broad outline before you, and with a few preliminary suggestions on how the pieces fit together, you have now a foundation on which to create your ceremony. An interfaith wedding is universal; it is a rite that speaks to and from the heart and soul. You can craft a ceremony that lingers in everyone's memories long after the last dance, and the following chapters—Part II—provide you with all the options you need to do so.

GINGER AND STEVIE, A JEWISH–CATHOLIC COUPLE

Their friends, said Ginger and Stevie, are like family. "Ginger and I," Stevie wrote, "are the Gibraltar of our group of friends. People always say, 'I love your house, it looks lived in but not messy, comfortable, I could fall asleep here so easily. Good food, good music, good people, good conversation.'" So, early in our preparations for their ceremony, they had e-mailed their friends saying, "The minister wants to get to know us. Would you send Susanna your thoughts about us as a couple?"

From the lively batch of responses I received, I chose several to include in my opening words. "They have created a home, a place of celebration, a temple," wrote one of these friends, "where feelings and ideas are bountiful, dancing with yourself is encouraged, and you are moved to sing."

From another: "Their relationship is like a game of Tetris. They fit. I think they've both taught each other what love truly is, and I wish them a lifetime of it."

In their questionnaires, the couple themselves provided me with eloquent expressions of their love, many of which I used in my address. Wrote Ginger:

Trust is a big, tough issue for me, and I trust Stevie more than any man in the world. I guess most of all, Stevie tried so hard to listen and achieve my desires when I told him what I needed and wanted out of my life and my marriage. There were so many times I thought we were too different to survive, and so many times I tried to push him away. I think the fact that he didn't walk away made me finally realize, here was a man who was in it for the long haul.

There are so many things I love about him—his eyes, his smile, the way he gets little beads of sweat on his nose that I have to fondly wipe off. His romantic, sensitive, and poetic nature. His integrity, which is so much greater than most people's. He spends a lot of time now thinking about how we will raise our kids. I find this incredibly touching.

From Stevie, I read:

I see our wedding as an incredible culmination of six years of chasing Ginger. I see it as Ginger saying to me what I've said to her, that we are soul mates, that she will be my Muse, as I will be hers. I see our ceremony as an extension of the journey we have been taking, a bridge to commitment, one that Ginger has finally trusted enough in me to give to me.

What is special and unique about my relationship with her? I would have to say what comes directly to mind—everything. The fact that I knew from the minute I first saw her that she would be my partner for life, that there could be no other woman in my life. To feel that as fact, with every shining blood cell in my body immediately; only to have the feeling overtake the fiber of my soul, grabbing me at the end of each day with her, telling me I finally did something right. Something true.

What qualities do I most admire in my partner? Her incredible brilliance, intellectually, charismatically, and especially spiritually. When I say spiritually, I mean it—she is truly a woman who runs with the wolves.

In a beautiful, castlelike historic mansion in the country, in the autumn with leaves turning golden and red, Ginger and Stevie were married. For the procession, she walked down a grand staircase with her dad, then was escorted by her stepfather the rest of the way to the front of the fireplace, where we performed the ceremony. The couple had elected to have a ceremony with primarily Jewish elements—the chuppah, some Old Testament readings, the seven blessings, the blessing over the wine, the breaking of the glass. We included also the Christian unity candle and a beautiful Christian prayer. Stevie had chosen some vows that, he said, "are what it's all about with Ginger and me. I feel they speak to the heart of what we see as marriage." But he had adapted them a bit, he said, "and worked in the word Beloved, which is something I always use when referring only to Ginger or the New York Mets." Here was his last line:

I call you my Beloved. I give you my devotion.

Part II

THE MANUAL

*Turning Religious, Cultural, and
Universal Rituals, Prayers, Vows,
and Blessings into Interfaith Celebrations*

Chapter Six

A Menu of General Wedding Rituals and Traditions

Some very popular and much-loved practices cross many religious and cultural borders. In this chapter, we present several traditions that are commonly observed in many modern weddings—their origins and symbolic meanings, and some suggestions on how you might incorporate them in your ceremony.

Veiling and Unveiling of the Bride

When working with a couple, I suggest that the bride carefully consider her preferences regarding veiling. Will she have the veil covering her face? If so, who will unveil her? Would she prefer not to wear a veil at all? Various meanings have been attached to the veiling, from a sign that the bride is protected from evil spirits to a symbol of purity and virginity. In contemporary terms, I prefer to think of the unveiling as a rite of passage into matrimony—or simply as the public presentation of the bride.

Whoever escorts the bride down the aisle may unveil her before kissing her farewell. In a Christian or Western-style ceremony, this is usually her father (or, for various reasons, a brother or uncle). He shakes the hand of the groom, who then extends his arm to his bride. If the bride's escort is her father, I sometimes ask if he has any parting words.

If the bride is processing with both parents, the mother usually does the unveiling. And mothers typically know more about veils than fathers! Mom embraces her daughter, who then embraces her parents and bids them farewell. This is the signal for the groom to take his place beside the bride. In a lovely gesture, the groom may embrace his future in-laws; tender words are exchanged, a tear or two may fall. This is a moment of symbolic farewell. Then the groom gallantly offers his arm to his bride and brings her forward before the altar.

Another option: The bride remains veiled, until the nuptial kiss, at which time the groom lifts her veil and kisses her for the first time as his wife. Romantics favor this option!

Exchanging of Rings

Do you know why the ring is worn on the left hand? It is because this is the hand closest to the heart. Also, the placement of the ring on the third finger, as in Western tradition, comes from the Greeks, who believed that the third finger was connected directly to the heart by "the vein of love." And it was in Rome that rings came to be made of gold, symbolizing unending love and commitment.

Sharing of a Cup of Wine

As you will see in Chapters 8 and 9, and in the ceremonies described in Part III, sharing wine between the bride and groom is a popular practice in many cultures and religions, so the wine ceremony can be adapted to celebrate two heritages or two religions at an interfaith wedding. These variations can be made to suit your spiritual, cultural, and personal needs. Have your celebrant include a bit of verse that has special meaning to you. Use a cup that represents your heritage. If you are Ethiopian, you may wish to drink honey wine from your native land. If you do decide on a personal variation, make mention of it. Here are some examples, from services I have conducted, on which you might model your wine ceremony:

> For love is heaven,
> and heaven is love.
>
> —*Sir Walter Scott, "The Lay of the Last Minstrel"*

Celebrant: This goblet of wine represents the cup of life. Within it is port, which symbolizes the sweetness of life. If this port is any indication, our couple's life will be very, very sweet! The port is also a tribute to the groom's Portuguese heritage. [Bride] and [groom], we now ask you to drink from the cup of mirth and abundance.

Celebrant: The bride and groom will drink a cup of wine. This is especially appropriate as the groom sells spirits for a living! [He was the European sales manager for a liquor company.] In ancient Greece, wine was considered the nectar of the gods. [Bride] and [groom], we pray that your life be as sweet as the sweetest nectar.

Breaking of Bread

The breaking and sharing of bread, which is often wrapped in a white cloth and kept on the altar or table, is another common tradition. The celebrant might say something like this:

Celebrant: The breaking and sharing of bread among family and friends is an ancient tradition. It symbolizes that we are all nourished and sustained by the very same love that brought our bride and groom together.

[The celebrant then breaks the bread and offers it to the bride and groom. If the bread is being shared with the bridal party or all those in attendance, the celebrant adds:]

Celebrant: Today, they share this love with you.

[The celebrant gives a piece of bread to each of those participating, and partakes herself as well.

For one Greek Orthodox–Jewish ceremony, the mother of the bride had baked an enormous, circular, braided, quite beautiful challah bread, which was later shared with all the guests at the reception. The ritual felt familiar to the Jewish side of the family, as challah is the bread shared on Shabbat, the Jewish sabbath. We made special mention of it:]

Celebrant: This bread has special significance because it was made by the loving hands of the mother of our bride. It will later be shared with all of you at the reception as a symbol of the bride's and groom's sharing their love with us on this blessed day.

[At one Catholic-Jewish wedding, the challah was broken for the bride and groom and the bridal party. The bridal attendants then passed around small, precut pieces arranged in baskets to the entire congregation.]

Handfasting, or Binding of the Hands

The binding of the hands ritual is universal; it has numerous meanings and can take many forms. Handfasting existed in the Pagan Celtic period, when the hands were bound with a ribbon or cord. In some Buddhist ceremonies, the couple's hands are bound with the Buddhist rosary, the mala. In a Catholic service, the priest will sometimes wrap the hands with his prayer stole. In the Hindu wedding ceremony, the hands are bound with a special thread. In an African-American union, the celebrant may wrap the couple's hands in kente cloth and explain something of its significance to the guests (you will find further details in the African-American section of Chapter 9).

One multicultural, same-sex couple asked that their hands be bound with a cord made of seven different-colored-ribbons—the colors of the rainbow, a symbol of both gay pride and their cultural diversity. As I raised the ribbons high so all could see, I said, "[Name] and [name] have asked that this braided cord made of the seven colors of the rainbow stand as a symbol of our celebration of diversity, unity, and hope."

I have done many variations on this theme, which can be simple or elaborate, ecumenical, humanist, or cultural in tone. Typically, the handbinding fits most comfortably after the couple's declaration of intent and before they take their vows. Here are some suggestions:

The Basic Handfasting

If the celebrant is using her prayer stole, she may first take the stole in her hands.

Celebrant: This prayer stole indicates that something within yourselves yet infinitely greater than yourselves has joined you together. [Or, This prayer stole indicates that God has joined you together.] As your hands are bound, so are your hearts, minds, bodies, and souls.

[The celebrant wraps their hands, closes her eyes in a few moments of silent prayer, then unwraps their hands. The ritual may end there, or the celebrant may say the following words, adapted from a Celtic handfasting. Supporting the couple's joined hands with her right hand from below:]

Celebrant: As you hold the hands of your beloved, listen to what I am about to say. Above you are the stars, below you is the earth, as time does pass, remember: Like the earth should your love be firm, grounded in your humanity. Like a star should your love be constant, imbued with the light of God [or, imbued with light]. Let the powers of the mind and of the intellect guide you in your marriage. Let the strength of your wills bind you together. Let the power of love and desire make you happy, and the strength of your dedication make you inseparable.

Anointing and Wrapping of the Hands

The anointing of the hands with oil is a ritual I have developed. Anointing marks a rite of passage into the new and sacred life of marriage, considered by many an ordained life. Usually, I combine the anointing with the wrapping or binding of the hands.

Celebrant: Since it is your intention to join in marriage, kindly extend your hands, palms facing upward.

[The celebrant places her hands, palm to palm and one at a time, upon the hands of the bride and groom.]

Celebrant: Your hands represent giving and receiving. I now anoint them into your new life. May your giving and receiving never end.

[She blesses the oil and then may anoint the hands with a single touch or with the sign of infinity (a sideways figure eight). In a Christian marriage, she may use the sign of the cross. She then asks the couple to join hands and wraps their hands loosely together in her prayer stole or the designated piece of cloth.]

Including Family Members

If the mothers are being honored at another ritual during the service, such as in the lighting of the unity candle, you may wish to involve the fathers at this point by asking for their blessing on the union. Alternatively, all parents—perhaps stepparents as well—may come forward. In one large Latino family, all eleven of the couple's brothers and sisters came up one by one to bless the marriage. I encouraged each to say a few personal words to the couple; there were moments of tears, of laughter, and of reverence. It was deeply meaningful for this bride and groom.

Celebrant: Will the fathers of the bride and groom please come forward? Your children ask your blessing upon their marriage. Do you bless this union? [They respond, Yes.] Then will you each place your right hand upon the hands of your children and join me in a silent prayer.

For it was not into my ear you whispered, but into my heart. It was not my lips you kissed, but my soul.

—*Judy Garland*

[The celebrant places one hand on top of the fathers' hands and one hand below the couple's hands, in a cradling or cupping gesture. There follows a silent prayer (thirty seconds or so), or the celebrant may say a brief prayer. She then thanks the fathers and asks them to be seated.]

Holding Hands in a Moment of Silence

If you do not like the idea of your hands being bound, your celebrant may simply hold your hands in a reverent moment. After the declaration of intent, the celebrant asks, "Since it is your intention to join in marriage, will you now join hands and with your hands your hearts?" These words are from Shakespeare. Then she holds your enjoined hands with both of hers—gently, reverently, with closed eyes, for a moment of silent prayer and blessing. This is a wonderful and reverent prelude to the vows. It focuses and prepares the couple to say the powerful words to follow.

Candle Lighting Ceremony

In this much-loved ritual, three candles are placed on the altar or table, two side candles representing the individual spirits of the bride and groom, and a center candle that signifies the light of their relationship. Usually this ritual follows the vows. If the mothers are not lighting the side candles, the celebrant lights those candles at the beginning of the ceremony. Otherwise the couple may light their own individual candles first with a match; then each lifts his or her lighted candle and together they light the center candle. You may wish your celebrant to use one of the following statements:

Celebrant: [Bride] and [groom], you have committed yourselves through solemn vows. Your life is now one. May your love be an indestructible force. May it shine as a beacon example. Together please now light the candle symbolizing your sacred union.

"From every being there rises a light that reaches straight to the heavens, and when two people who are destined to be together find each other, their streams of light flow together, and a single brighter light goes forth from their united being." [From the *Baal Shem Tov*]

Celebrant: We will now ask the bride and groom to light a candle symbolic of their relationship and their individual selves.

[Bride] and [groom], these two candles represent the light of your individual spirits. The center candle represents the light of your relationship. In allowing the flames of the two smaller candles to remain lit, you accept each other's individuality as a means to fulfilling your oneness. May your love so endure that its flame remains a guiding light unto you. [Adapted from Weddings Galore Website, c. 1995–2001, Leslie P. Fowler]

Celebrant: [Bride] and [groom], you have entered into a union that is most sacred, requiring of those who enter it a complete and unreserved giving of self. It will bind you together in a relationship so close, and so intimate, that it will profoundly affect your whole future. [The celebrant lights the two side candles.]

For over three thousand years, human beings have used candles as a source of light. They are also symbols of warmth, of hope, and of life itself. Would you now each, from your own candle, light a third as a symbol of your new relationship? [From the American Humanist Association]

Celebrant: Receive this holy fire. Make your lives like this fire. A holy life that is seen. A life of God that is seen. A life that has no end. A life that darkness does not overcome. May this light of God in you grow. Light a fire that is worthy of your heads. Light a fire that is worthy of your children. Light a fire that is worthy of your fathers. Light a fire that is worthy of your mothers. Light a fire that is worthy of God. [This passage, adapted from a Masai prayer, from *African-American Wedding Readings,* edited by Tamara Nikuradse, is particularly appropriate if the bride or groom is African-American.]

Celebrant:
Beloved, bring beauty into my lonely life
Just as you once did in my house.
Sweep away the dust of hours,
Fill the empty lamps,
And mend all this, my neglect.
Then open the door of the shrine,
Light one candle, and in silence we'll be joined
Before our God.
[Adapted from the Indian poet and saint Rabindranath Tagore; this poem would be a beautiful addition at this point to a Christian-Hindu ceremony.]

Releasing of Butterflies

The butterfly release is visually magical and a popular ritual these days. At the conclusion of the ceremony, after the closing blessing is recited, perhaps

I shall light a candle of understanding in thine heart, which shall not be put out.

—*Apocrypha 11
Esdras 14; 25*

twenty, fifty, or a hundred monarch butterflies are released to flutter over the heads of the couple and their guests. Typically this is done at an outdoor ceremony, though some couples have their bridesmaids release the butterflies during the recession. However, the practice is politically and ecologically controversial.

An ecologically conscious couple might adapt the ritual in the following manner: Capture two wild butterflies that will remain in small, aerated boxes until the conclusion of the ceremony. The bride and groom then each release one butterfly while their celebrant recounts a Native American legend. (It should be noted, however, that the butterfly release is not a Native American tradition.) Here are two versions (adapted from a butterfly website):

Celebrant: A Native American legend says that if you have a secret wish, capture a butterfly and whisper that wish to it. Since butterflies cannot speak, your wish is secure in her safekeeping. Release the butterfly and she will carry your wish to the Great Spirit [you may wish to substitute God], who alone discerns the secrets locked within a butterfly. By setting the butterfly free, you are helping restore the balance of nature, and therefore your wish will be granted. Please, [bride] and [groom], share now in this ritual by making your silent wish and releasing your butterfly.

Celebrant: Native American legend states that if you capture a butterfly and whisper a wish to it, she will carry that wish to the heavens and it will be granted. Would you all please make your silent wishes now for [bride] and [groom] for their life together, as we release two butterflies?

Releasing of Doves

I have seen this ritual take place with just two doves and with as many as fifty. Inevitably, there is a symphony of *oooos* and *ahhhhs* from the guests. Often the doves fly away, in one massive, fluttering swoop. Again, this practice is ecologically and politically controversial.

The dove release comes at the very end of the ceremony, or after the closing blessing. The celebrant may end her blessing with one of the following passages:

Celebrant: The dove has long been a sign of peace and hope. It is seen as a symbol, an omen of good. In conclusion of our ceremony, [bride] and [groom] will now release the doves, and with them go all our hopes and good wishes for this couple's new life to come.

Go in peace to love and serve the Lord [an Episcopal blessing].

Ma' Salaama [a Muslim blessing].

Om Shanti, Shanti, Shanti Om [a Hindu blessing].

Shalom [a Jewish blessing].

Go now with love in your hearts and peace in your souls [universal].

Celebrant: White doves have long been a spiritual symbol of hope and peace. Our bride and groom will now release two doves. As the doves are released, we ask all of you to fill yourselves with a hope, a prayer, a good wish for [bride] and [groom] for the many years to come. Their love is our great hope for peace.

Chapter Seven

Universal Passages for Almost Any Wedding

Romantic Selections from Literature, Philosophy, and History

The following selections correspond to the main elements of an interfaith wedding ceremony. They are universal, by which I mean they speak to all hearts. You will find our selections filled with the language of love and humanity. Couples I have worked with have chosen many, if not all, of these passages for their ceremonies, and I know that they have found them moving and uplifting. Many books devoted to wedding readings or vows are available, but here is a good place to start.

Look through the menu and choose any passages you like. Additional possibilities are included in Chapter 5, and I also suggest you read through the sections corresponding to your religious backgrounds in Chapter 8; many other prayers and elements are listed there. Gather your ideas, see what touches you, then copy out your choices as you draw up a draft of your ceremony to bring to your celebrant. Enjoy walking through verse that spans the globe!

Opening Words

Your celebrant will have her own way of opening the ceremony, welcoming your family and guests, and beginning the proceedings. In Chapter 5, I suggested several openings: highly personal or more formal. Decide what tone you would like to strike, and talk it over with your celebrant. Here are several more selections, to give you ideas:

Selection 1

What greater thing is there for two human souls than to feel that they are joined together to strengthen each other in all labor, to minister to each other in all sorrow, to share with each other in all gladness, and to be one with each other in the silent, unspeakable memories? [George Eliot]

Today two people, two lovers, two best friends have come before us to join in the sacred covenant of marriage. And our hearts respond with joy and reverence to the significance of it all.

Selection 2

The poet John Milton once wrote: "Hail wedded love, mysterious law, true source of all humanity!" My dear people, it begins here. [Bride] and [groom] will join together on bended knee. Two hearts will beat as one. Two souls will comfort and support each other for the rest of their lives. Children, gifts from the divine, will come from this union. Not only is marriage the source of all humanity but it represents the best of humanity—for it is rooted in love and ordained by a force much greater than our common understanding. It is by the grace of this divine mystery that we now come together.

> There is no more lovely, friendly, and charming relationship, communion, or company than a good marriage.
> —*Martin Luther*

Selection 3

It is said that "there is no surprise more magical than the surprise of being loved: It is God's finger on man's shoulder." [Charles Morgan] [Bride] and [groom] have been joined together by the mystical, magical, eternal presence that is love. God is love. Our bride and groom have gathered all of you, their beloved families and friends, to bear witness to this sacred union. Today they will join their hands and hearts for the rest of their days and, if God wills, beyond the walls of life.

Readings

A reading may be introduced shortly after the opening words, toward the end of the service, or at any other point that feels appropriate or that will help the ceremony flow harmoniously. You may choose a passage from scripture, a poem you love, a bit of prose that has special meaning to you and your relationship. The selections here offer a cornucopia of possibilities.

Selection 1 (Kahlil Gibran's much-loved verse "On Marriage," from The Prophet)

> You were born to be together, and together you shall be forevermore.
> You shall be together when the wings of death scatter your days.
> Ay, you shall be together even in your silent memory.
> But let there be spaces in your togetherness,
> and let the winds of the heavens dance between you.
> Love one another, but make not a bondage of love.
> Let it rather be a moving sea between the shores of your souls.
> Fill each other's cup, but drink not from one cup.
> Give one another of your bread, but eat not of the same loaf.
> Sing and dance together and be joyous, but let each of you be alone,
> Even as the strings of a lute are alone, though they quiver with the same music.
> Give your hearts, but not into each other's keeping,
> For only the hand of life can contain your hearts.
> And stand together, yet not too near together,
> For the pillars of the temple stand apart,
> And the oak tree and the cypress grow not in each other's shadow.

Selection 2 ("The Art of a Good Marriage II," by Wilferd Arlan Peterson)

Across the years I'll walk with you, in deep green forest, on shores of sand, and when our time on earth is through, in heaven too, you will have my hand.

Happiness in marriage is not something that just happens. A good marriage must be created. In the art of marriage, the little things are the big things:

It is never being too old to hold hands. It is remembering to say, I love you, once each day. It is never going to sleep angry. It is forming a circle of love that gathers in the whole family.

It is at no time taking for granted. The courtship should not end with the honeymoon, but continue through all the years. It is doing things for each other, not in the attitude of duty or sacrifice, but in the spirit of joy. It is the speaking of words of appreciation and demonstrating gratitude in thoughtful ways. It is not looking for perfection in each other.

It is cultivating flexibility, patience, understanding, and a sense of humor. It is having the capacity to forgive and forget. It is finding room for the things of the spirit. It is a common search for the good and the beautiful. It is not marrying the right partner, it is being the right partner.

[Many couples choose to end there, although the reading concludes with this line:] It is discovering what marriage can be at its best, as expressed in the words Mark Twain used in a tribute to his wife: "Wherever she was, there was Eden."

Selection 3 (by Roy Croft)

I love you,
Not only for what you are
But for what I am
When I am with you.

I love you,
Not only for what
You have made of yourself
But for what
You are making of me.

I love you,
For the part of me
That you bring out;
I love you,
For putting your hand
Into my . . . heart
And passing over
All the foolish, weak things
That you can't help
Dimly seeing there,
And for drawing out
Into the light
All the beautiful belongings
That no one else had looked
Quite far enough to find.

I love you because you
Are helping me to make
Of the lumber of my life
Not a tavern
But a temple;
Out of works
Of my every day

Not a reproach
But a song.

Selection 4 ("The Greatest Gift," by Katharine Whiteside Taylor; adapted)

All things I would give my love,
All things tender, caring, serving, true.
I would enwrap her in my loving arms
And shield her from all stress and pain.
I would enchant him with the vision bright
Of those rare gifts that are his deepest self.
And I would carry her on wings of joy
To all the heights the soul of man can know.

Selection 5 (by James R. Scher)

Whenever two people begin
To write
Their lives' poem
On a single leaf
Of hammered paper,
The angels sing,
And the ends of the universe,
Bright with stars,
Move somehow closer.
So
Their joy together
Eternally
Becomes
God's smile.

Selection 6 (by Rainer Maria Rilke)

For one human being to love another human being: that is perhaps the most difficult task that has been entrusted to us, the ultimate task, the final test and proof, the work for which all other work is merely preparation. Loving does not at first mean merging, surrendering, and uniting with another person. It is a high inducement for the individual to ripen, to become something in himself, to become world in himself for the sake of another person; it is a great, demanding claim on him, something that chooses him and calls him to vast distance. . . .

Once the realization is accepted that even between the closest people infinite distances exist, a marvelous living side-by-side can grow up for them, if they succeed in loving the expanse between them, which gives them the possibility of seeing each other as a whole and before an immense sky.

Selection 7 (from Gift from the Sea, by Anne Morrow Lindbergh; a wonderful reading for musicians, dancers, and lovers of music!)

A good relationship has a pattern like a dance and is built on some of the same rules. The partners do not need to hold on tightly, because they move confidently in the same pattern, intricate but gay and swift and free, like a country dance of Mozart's. To touch heavily would be to arrest the pattern and freeze the movement, to check the endlessly changing beauty of its unfolding. There is no place here for the possessive clutch, the clinging arm, the heavy hand; only the barest touch in passing. Now arm in arm, now face to face, now back to back—it does not matter which. Because they know they are partners moving to the same rhythm, creating a pattern together, and being invisibly nourished by it.

Selection 8 (by Walt Whitman)

I do not offer the old smooth prizes,
But offer rough new prizes.
These are the days that must happen to you:
You shall not heap up what is called riches,
You shall scatter with lavish hand all that you earn or achieve.
However sweet the laid-up stores,
However convenient the dwellings,
You shall not remain there.
However sheltered the port,
And however calm the waters,
You shall not anchor there.
However welcome the hospitality that welcomes you
You are permitted to receive it but a little while.
Afoot and lighthearted, take to the open road,
Healthy, free, the world before you,
The long brown path before you, leading wherever you choose.
Say only to one another:
Camerado, I give you my hand!
I give you my love, more precious than money,
I give you myself before preaching or law:
Will you give me yourself?

Will you come travel with me?
Shall we stick together as long as we shall live?

Selection 9 (Sonnet 116, by William Shakespeare)

Let me not to the marriage of true minds
Admit impediments. Love is not love
Which alters when it alteration finds
Or bends with the remover to remove.
O, no, it is an ever fixed mark
That looks on tempests and is never shaken,
It is the star to every wandering bark,
Whose worth's unknown, although his height be taken.
Love's not time's fool, though rosy lips and cheeks
Within his bending sickle's compass come,
Love alters not with his brief hours and weeks,
But bears it out even to the edge of doom;
If this be error, and upon me proved,
I never writ, nor no man ever loved.

Selection 10 (Sonnet 43, by Elizabeth Barrett Browning)

How do I love thee? Let me count the ways.
I love thee to the depth and breadth and height
My soul can reach, when feeling out of sight
For the ends of Being and ideal Grace.
I love thee to the level of everyday's
Most quiet need, by sun and candle light.
I love thee freely, as men strive for Right;
I love thee purely, as they turn from Praise.
I love thee with the passion put to use
In my old griefs, and with my childhood's faith.
I love thee with a love I seemed to lose
With my lost saints, I love thee with the breath,
Smiles, tears, of all my life! and if God choose,
I shall but love thee better after death.

Selection 11 (by Jalal al-Din Rumi)

Apart from Love, everything passes away. The way to heaven is in your heart.
Open and lift the wings of Love! When Love's wings are strong, you need no
ladder.

Though the world be thorns, a lover's heart is a bower of roses.

Though heaven's wheel be mired down, lovers' lives go forward.

Invite love into each dark corner. The lover is bright as a hundred thousand candles!

Even if a lover seems to be alone, the secret Beloved is nearby.

The time-span of union is eternity. The life is a jar, and in it, union is the pure wine. If we aren't together, of what use is the jar? The moment I heard my first love story I began seeking you, not realizing the search was useless. Lovers don't finally meet somewhere; they are in one another's souls all along.

Selection 12 (author unknown)

What is a Friend? I'll tell you.

It is a person with whom you dare to be yourself.

Your soul can go naked with him.

He seems to ask you to put on nothing, only to be what you really are.

When you are with her, you do not have to be on your guard.

You can say what you think, as long as it is genuinely you.

She understands those contradictions in your nature that cause others to misjudge you.

With her you breathe freely. You can avow your little vanities and envies and absurdities and in opening them up to her, they are dissolved on the white ocean of loyalty.

He understands. You can weep with him, laugh with him, pray with him: Through and underneath it all he sees, knows and loves you.

Selection 13 (From a letter by Vincent van Gogh to his brother, Theo; a wonderful reading for artists!)

I want to paint men and women with something of the eternal which the halo used to symbolize. . . . To express the love of two lovers by a wedding of two complementary colors, their mingling and opposition, the mysterious vibration of kindred tones. To express the thought of a brow by the radiance of a light tone against a somber background. To express hope by some star, the eagerness of a soul by a sunset radiance.

Selection 14 ("somewhere i have never traveled," by E. E. Cummings)

somewhere i have never travelled, gladly beyond
any experience, your eyes have their silence:
in your most frail gesture are things which enclose me,
or which i cannot touch because they are too near

your slightest look easily will unclose me
though i have closed myself as fingers,
you open always petal by petal myself as Spring opens
(touching skillfully,mysteriously)her first rose

or if your wish be to close me,i and
my life will shut very beautifully,suddenly,
as when the heart of this flower imagines
the snow carefully everywhere descending;

nothing which we are to perceive in this world equals
the power of your intense fragility:whose texture
compels me with the color of its countries,
rendering death and forever with each breathing

(i do not know what it is about you that closes
and opens;only something in me understands
the voice of your eyes is deeper than all roses)
nobody,not even the rain,has such small hands

Selection 15 (From The Little Prince by Antoine de Saint Exupéry)

In Antoine de Saint Exupéry's classic story, the Little Prince came upon a flower that he believed to be unique—only to discover a field of roses just like his own. He was disappointed, until his encounter with the fox, who taught him an important lesson. Afterward, the Little Prince went back once more to look at the garden of roses, now with new eyes. Here is a passage from *The Little Prince:*

"You are not at all like my rose," he said. "As yet you are nothing. No one has tamed you, and you have tamed no one. You are like my fox when I first knew him. He was only a fox like a hundred thousand other foxes. But I have made him my friend, and now he is unique in all the world. . . .

"You are beautiful, but you are empty," he went on. "One could not die for you. To be sure, an ordinary passerby would think that my rose looked just like you—the rose that belongs to me. But in herself alone she is more important than all the hundreds of you other roses; because it is she that I have watered . . . because it is she that I have sheltered . . . because it is she that I have listened to, when she grumbled, or boasted, or even sometimes when she said nothing. Because she is *my* rose."

And he went back to meet the fox.

"Goodbye," he said.

"Goodbye," said the fox. "And now here is my secret, a very simple secret: It is only with the heart that one can see rightly; what is essential is invisible to the eye. . . . It is the time you have devoted to your rose that makes your rose so important. . . . You become responsible, forever, for what you have tamed. You are responsible for your rose."

Selection 16 (from an unknown author of ancient Egypt)

I breathe the sweet breath which comes forth from Thy mouth. I behold Thy beauty every day. It is my desire that I may hear Thy sweet voice, even on the north wind, that my limbs may be rejuvenated with life through love of Thee. Give me Thy hands, holding Thy spirit, that I may receive it and may live by it. Call Thou upon my name unto eternity, and it shall never fail.

Selection 17 (From "Fidelity," by D. H. Lawrence; please note that couples usually change the word orgasms to read chaos)

> And man and woman are like the earth, that brings forth flowers
>   in summer, and love, but underneath is rock.
> Older than flowers, older than ferns, older than foraminiferae,
>   older than plasm altogether is the soul of a man underneath.
>
> And when, throughout all the wild orgasms of love
>   slowly a gem forms, in the ancient, once-more-molten rocks
>   of two human hearts, two ancient rocks, a man's heart and a woman's,
>   that is the crystal of peace, the slow hard jewel of trust,
>   the sapphire of fidelity.
> The gem of mutual peace emerging from the wild chaos of love.

Selection 18 (adapted from Iphigeneia at Aulis, by Euripides; this is a wonderful reading for a Greek interfaith ceremony)

Let me know love within reason, and desire within marriage, and feel your presence. . . .
> The natures of humans are various, and human ways of acting are different, but everyone knows what is right, and teaching inclines them at last to virtue.
> Humility is wisdom, making us see the right way as something beautiful.
> And from this beauty honor is born and life earns immortal fame.
> It is a great thing, the pursuit of virtue: at home, it is a stillness in their love;
in the world, multiplied ten thousand times among citizens, it makes a city great.

Selection 19 (from "Wedding Song," by Naomi Long Madgett)

I cannot swear with any certainty
That I will always feel as I do now,
Loving you with the same fierce ecstasy,
Needing the same your lips upon my brow.
Nor can I promise stars forever bright
Or vow green leaves will never turn to gold.
I cannot see beyond this present night
To say what promises the dawn may behold.
And yet I know my heart must follow you
High up to hilltops, low through vales of tears,
Through golden days and days of somber hue.
And love will only deepen with the years
Becoming sun and shadow, wind and rain,
Wine that grows mellow, bread that will sustain.

Selection 20 (Sonnet 17, Pablo Neruda)

I do not love you as if you were salt-rose, or topaz,
or the arrow of carnations the fire shoots off.
I love you as certain dark things are to be loved,
in secret, between the shadow and the soul.

I love you as the plant that never blooms
but carries in itself the light of hidden flowers;
thanks to your love a certain solid fragrance,
risen from the earth, lives darkly in my body.

I love you without knowing how, or when, or from where.
I love you straightforwardly, without complexities or pride;
so I love you because I know no other way

than this: where I do not exist, nor you,
so close that your hand on my chest is my hand,
so close that your eyes close as I fall asleep.

Selection 21 ("Variations on the Word Sleep," by Margaret Atwood)

I would like to watch you sleeping,
which may not happen.
I would like to watch you,
sleeping. I would like to sleep
with you, to enter
your sleep as its smooth dark wave
    slides over my head.

and walk with you through that lucent
wavering forest of bluegreen leaves
with its watery sun & three moons
towards the cave where you must descend,
towards your worst fear

I would like to give you the silver
branch, the small white flower, the one
word that will protect you
from the grief at the center
of your dream, from the grief
at the center. I would like to follow
you up the long stairway
again & become
the boat that would row you back
carefully, a flame
in two cupped hands
to where your body lies
beside me, and you enter
it as easily as breathing in

I would like to be the air
that inhabits you for a moment
only. I would like to be that unnoticed
& that necessary.

Honoring of Family Members

In Chapters 4 and 5, you read some examples of how family members—those present and those who have passed away—may be mentioned, celebrated, and honored during the wedding ceremony. Here are other possibilities:

Selection 1 (a poem on family)

> Our family is a circle of strength and love.
> With every birth and every union the circle grows.
> Every joy shared adds more love,
> Every crisis faced together
> Makes the circle grow stronger.

Selection 2 (an address to the parents)

[Parents' names], many years ago, though it may feel like only yesterday, two perfect children were born into this world. When you first gazed at them, you marveled at their perfection and you felt truly blessed. In your children you saw infinite potential and you placed great hope.

With you they uttered their first words. With you they took their first steps. You rejoiced in their victories, you cried at their sorrows. You guided them, nurtured them, educated them, loved them to the best of your ability. You gave them all you had to give, so they would grow up strong and independent, capable of great love, capable of what they are doing here today. Without you, this marriage would not, could not be possible.

Now, today, all the love and caring you gave to [bride] and [groom], they will give to each other. And it does not end here. For in turn, they will pass it along to their children. And we see firsthand how this sublime torch, this lineage of love, gets passed along from generation to generation, and in a very real sense we become immortal.

[Parents' names], we thank you. We honor you.

> My greatest good fortune in a life of brilliant experiences has been to find you, and to lead my life with you.
>
> —*Winston Churchill, in a letter to his wife*

Prayers and Blessings

Prayers and blessings may be recited at various points in the service. Several of the following selections sound most appropriate as the closing blessing.

Selection 1 (adapted from Illuminata
by Marianne Williamson;
this prayer is extremely popular with my couples)

Dear God,

Please bless this couple. Please make their relationship a great and holy adventure. May their joining be a sacred space. May they find rest here, a haven for their souls.

Bring them together heart, mind, body and soul. Guide their way into light. Guide their way into wisdom. Help them grow.

May this bond be a channel of healing for themselves, their families and the world at large. May this marriage now receive your blessing and carry your power. We thank you for the gift of their love.

Amen.

Selection 2 (by Susanna Macomb)

[Bride] and [groom],

We pray that the chariot of your marriage takes you to heights you never dreamed.

We pray that together you will know many moments of sublime peace.

We pray that you will have fine healthy children whom you will love, and they you in return.

We pray that you will live to know your children's children.

We pray that you will walk in God's grace with your feet firmly planted on this earth and your arms reaching up towards the heavens.

Selection 3 (an Irish blessing, good for a closing blessing)

May the road rise to meet you.

May the wind be always at your back.

May the sun shine warm upon your face, the rains fall soft upon your fields.

May the light of friendship guide your paths together.

May the laughter of children grace the halls of your home.

May the joy of living for one another trip a smile from your lips, a twinkle from your eyes.

And, when eternity beckons, at the end of a life heaped high with love,

May the good Lord embrace you with the arms that have nurtured you the whole length of your joy-filled days.

May the gracious God hold you both in the palm of his hand.

And today, may the spirit of love find a dwelling place in your hearts.

Selection 4 (an Apache wedding prayer or blessing; many couples choose this as a closing blessing)

Now you will feel no rain,
For each of you will be shelter for the other.
Now you will feel no cold,
For each of you will be warmth for the other.
Now there is no more loneliness.
Now you are two persons, but there is only one life before you.
Go now to your dwelling, to enter into the days of your life together.
And may your days be good and long upon the earth.

Selection 5 ("This Marriage," by Rumi, translated by Kabir Helminski)

May these vows and this marriage be blessed.
May it be sweet milk, this marriage, like wine and halvah.
May this marriage offer fruit and shade like the date palm.
May this marriage be full of laughter, every day a day in paradise.
May this marriage be a sign of compassion, a seal of happiness here and hereafter.
May this marriage have a fair face and a good name, an omen as welcome as the moon in a clear blue sky.
I am out of words to describe how spirit mingles in this marriage.

Selection 6 (by Susanna Macomb)

[Bride] and [groom],
May you grow glorious in each other's arms.
May laughter and warmth reign supreme in your home.
May you have fine healthy children whom you will cherish, and they you in return.
May you live long.
May you live well.
We wish you this until the dying of the light.

Selection 7 (an adapted Celtic blessing; this works beautifully with the Christian passing of the sign of peace)

Peace between neighbors.
Peace between kindred.
Peace between lovers.
Peace between person and person.
Peace between wife and husband.
Peace between parents and children.
The peace of God above all peace.

Selection 8 (a very short Irish blessing)

Length of life and sunny days, and may your souls not go homewards until your own child falls in love.

Selection 9 ("The Blessings of Unknowing," by Wendy Egyoku Nakao)

On this day, two lives join as one. Who can know from where this union comes? Who can know how far into eternity this will go? These are the blessings of Unknowing.

On this day, two hearts beat as one. Who can know how many other hearts this joins? Who can know how far this love will flow? These are the blessings of Unknowing.

On this day, two eyes shine as one. Who can know how many are the gifts of joy? Who can know how far this light will glow? These are the blessings of Unknowing.

On this day, two hands meet as one. Who can know how many other beings this holds? Who can know how far this touch will grow? These are the blessings of Unknowing.

On this day, one is no longer one. Two are no longer two. Who can know how far these blessings go? Who can know? Who can know!

Let us rejoice in the blessings of Unknowing.

Selection 10

May your love cast out small fears.
May your hope endure.
May your faith in each other
and in this radiant universe
grow and flourish. Amen.

Vows

The words of your vows are like music that will resonate throughout your married life. Here, I have included vows for all sorts of couples: those who wish the traditional, a variation of the traditional, the simple and elegant, the deeply touching, the unconventional, the romantic, and the short and sweet. You will also find vows appropriate for second marriages and marriages with children.

Selection 1 (simple and elegant)

I, _____, take you, _____, to be my beloved wife/husband, to have and to hold you, to honor you, to treasure you, to be at your side in sorrow and in joy, to laugh with you in the good times, to comfort and solace you in the bad, and to love and cherish you always.

I promise you this from my heart, with my soul, for all the days of my life, eternal.

Selection 2 (adapted from Weddings from the Heart by Daphne Rose Kingma)

I, _____, take you, _____, to be my beloved wife/husband, to have you and hold you, to honor you, to treasure you, to be at your side in sorrow and in joy, to grow with you and to be transformed, to love and cherish you always.

I promise you this from my heart, with my soul, for all the days of my life, and, if God wills, beyond the walls of life, beyond the bounds of time.

Selection 3 (the most traditional)

I, _____, take you, _____, to be my lawful wedded wife/husband, to have and to hold, from this day forward, for better, for worse, for richer, for poorer, in sickness and in health, to love and to cherish, until death do us part. This is my solemn vow.

Selection 4

I, _____, take you, _____, to be my husband/wife, and these things I promise you:

I will be faithful to you and honest with you. I will respect, trust, help, and care for you. I will share my life with you. I will try with you to better understand ourselves, the world, and God, through the best and the worst of what is to come, as long as we live.

Selection 5 (standard civil ceremony vows)

_____, I take you to be my lawfully wedded husband/wife. Before these witnesses I vow to love you and care for you as long as we both shall live. I take you, with all your faults and your strengths, as I offer myself to you with my faults and my strengths. I will help you when you need help, and will turn to you when I need help. I choose you as the person with whom I will spend my life.

Selection 6 (a Quaker vow)

In the presence of God and these our family and friends, I take thee to be my husband/wife, promising with Divine assistance to be a loving and faithful husband/wife as long as we both shall live.

Selection 7

I, _____, take you to be my husband/wife, to laugh with you in joy, to grieve with you in sorrow, to grow with you in love, serving humankind in peace and hope, as long as we both shall live.

Selection 8 (a variation of the traditional)

(Many of my couples choose vows such as these to be asked by the celebrant *after* they have stated more personal vows.)

Celebrant: Do you, _____, take this man/woman, _____, to be your lawful wedded husband/wife, to have and to hold him/her, to love and to cherish him/her, to be true to him/her, through times of sorrow as well as joy? Do you promise this heart, mind, body, and soul? Do you commit before God to honor this vow all the days of your life?
Bride/Groom: I do.

Celebrant: Will you have this woman/man to be your wedded wife/husband, to live together in the holy estate of matrimony? Will you love her/him, comfort her/him, honor and keep her/him, in sickness and in health, for as long as you both shall live?
Groom/Bride: I will.

Celebrant: Do you, _____, take this man/woman to be your lawful wedded husband/wife? Do you promise to be patient, kind, giving, understanding and loving in the face of life's unexpected twists and turns, in the face of strife and hardship, as well as in the gleeful resolve you find in each other? Do you promise this heart, body and soul? Do you commit to one another before God to honor this vow all the days of your life? [Written by Dana Bradley Junior for his beloved Marla]

Bride/Groom: I do.

Selection 9 (very brief vows!)

I _____, take you _____, to be my wedded wife/husband. With deepest joy I receive you into my life that together we may be one.

Selection 10 (even briefer vows!)

_____, I take you this day and for all days as my husband/wife.

Selection 11 (vows for the very romantic man and woman; adapted from Wedding Vows by Michael Macfarlane)

I do swear and promise, as I take this lady/man by the hand, that I shall love and cherish her/him, that I will be faithful to her/him and to no other for all the days of my life. I have for the first time found what I can truly love—I have found you. You are my sympathy, my better self, my good angel. I am bound to you. I think you good, gifted, and lovely. A fervent, solemn passion is conceived in my heart; it leans to you, draws you to my center and spring of life, and wraps my existence about you. This pure and powerful flame fuses you and me as one.

Selection 12 (vows for couples who have seen much of life, and for marriages involving children; from Complete Book of Wedding Vows by Diane Warner)

_____, as we become one on this, our wedding day, we become part of each other. Your feelings become my feelings, your sorrows become my sorrows, your joys become my joys, your worries become my worries. I promise to be a true and faithful husband/wife, always there to comfort you and rejoice with you and endure all the complexities of life that we will face together [as a family] in the years to come. My love for you is pure and unshakable and I hereby commit myself to you from this day forth and forevermore.

Selection 13 (a Celtic vow)

We will keep faith until the sky falls upon us and until the seas arise and overwhelm us.

Blessing of Rings

The celebrant may simply say, "These rings are hereby blessed." Or you may prefer a more extended blessing, such as these. In Chapter 5 and in our sample ceremonies in Part III you will find additional selections.

Selection 1

A circle symbolizes wholeness, a state in which nothing is missing and everything is possible. Let these rings therefore represent wholeness. Let them remind you of the coming around of an eternal cycle: from sickness to health, from want to plenty, from despair to joy, from failure to possibility, from loneliness to love. Let these rings also be a sign of substance, as is the precious metal from which they are made. It is strong and does not tarnish. I give you the words of the I Ching: When two people are at one in their innermost hearts, they shatter the strength of iron or even of bronze.

Selection 2

These rings are symbols of your inner spiritual bond. They have no beginning and no end. They will endure forever. So may it be with your love.

Selection 3

These rings represent circles of love and circles of life. We wish for you love never ending, and may your life together be as strong and radiant as the precious metal from which these rings are made.

Ring Vows

After you have spoken personal vows and your celebrant has blessed the rings, you will exchange rings as you speak a ring vow.

Selection 1 (very simple)

With this ring, I thee wed.

Selection 2

I give you this ring, and with it, all that I have and all that I am.

Selection 3

_____, with a free and unconstrained soul, I give you all I am and all I am to become. Take this ring, and with it my promise, patience, and love, for the rest of my life.

Selection 4

(The following vows, from *Illuminata* by Marianne Williamson, are so compelling that I would estimate about two out of every five of my couples have chosen to use them in the complete or in an edited form. A good sequence would be: first, the bride and groom exchange rings; second, each, in turn, speaks these deeply touching vows; finally, the celebrant asks one of the questions listed earlier, to which the bride and groom respond with the immortal "I do." Get out your hankies!)

With this ring, I give you my promise that from this day forward you shall not
*   walk alone.*
May my heart be your shelter and my arms be your home.
May God bless you always.
May we walk together through all things.
May you feel deeply loved, for indeed you are.
May you always see your innocence in my eyes.
With this ring, I give you my heart. I have no greater gift to give.
I promise I shall do my best.
I shall always try.
I feel so honored to call you my husband/wife.
I feel so blessed to call you mine.
May we feel this joy forever.
I thank God.
I thank you.
Amen.

Selection 5 (adapted from a Hindu marriage poem or mantra)

You have become mine forever. Yes, we have become partners. I have become
*   yours.*
Hereafter, I cannot live without you. Do not live without me.
Let us share the joys.
We are word and meaning, united.
You are thought and I am sound.
I am the words and you are the melody. I am the melody and you are the words.

Selection 6 (an Eskimo love song)

You are my husband/wife.
My feet shall run because of you.
My feet dance because of you.

My heart shall beat because of you.
My eyes see because of you
My mind thinks because of you.
And I shall love, because of you.

Selection 7 (from the I Ching; to be spoken by the celebrant at the taking of the vows)

When two people are at one in their inmost hearts, they shatter even the strength of iron or bronze.

And when two people understand each other in their inmost hearts, their words are sweet and strong, like the fragrance of orchids.

Selection 8 (from the Sufi poet Rumi; this also works well recited by the celebrant immediately after the exchanges of vows and rings)

The tender words you have said to one another are stored in the secret heart of heaven. One day like rain they will fall and spread, and your mystery will grow green over the world.

Pronouncement

At last, the grand finale—the pronouncement of the couple as husband and wife, followed by the kiss! You may wish to suggest one of the following pronouncements to your celebrant.

Nobody has ever measured, not even poets, how much the heart can hold.

—*Zelda Fitzgerald*

Selection 1

[Bride] and [groom], you have been brought together by love and commitment. You have exchanged solemn and sacred vows. By this integrity and truth, in the beloved company of family and friends, it is my honor—and with absolute delight—that I now pronounce you husband and wife.

Selection 2

[Bride] and [groom], you have committed yourselves to each other through sacred vows and honored each other with the gift of eternal love. Your life is now one. Therefore, it is now by the grace of God, in the blessed company of your family and friends, that I am able to pronounce you husband and wife.

Selection 3 (from Celebrating Interfaith Marriages *by Rabbi Devon Lerner)*

Your friends and family, all of us here, rejoice in your happiness and we pray that this day marks only one of many more blessings you will share in the years ahead. And now that you have spoken the words and performed the rites that unite your lives, I do hereby, in accordance with your beliefs and the laws of this state, declare your marriage to be valid and binding, and I now declare you, [groom] and [bride], husband and wife.

Kiss

Not that words are necessary! However, you may want your celebrant to frame the moment with a bit of verse.

Selection 1

It is said that an entire universe exists in the hold of a kiss. You may kiss.

Selection 2

Legend holds that a nuptial kiss unleashes great power in heaven and on earth. You may kiss.

Selection 3

The bride and groom kiss, and all of creation sings for them.

Chapter Eight

Religions and Their Marriage Practices

I n this chapter you will find an overview of the world's main religions and their beliefs. It is my hope that as you hear the voices of their great founders, you will discover the threads that bind us all one to another: the awareness of that which is unseen, the realization of something that is beyond knowing in the manner by which we know what it feels like to eat and drink, to hear the rain, to love a child; the human need to reach toward a greater, more profound experience than ourselves; the summons to the upright life, the golden rule, and the power of love.

Estimates of the numbers of people adhering to each religion are taken from the *World Almanac 2001*.

We summarize here the marriage practices and ceremonies particular to specific religions and demonstrate how their core elements can be adapted for a contemporary ceremony. The passages following ∾ are to be spoken by the celebrant.

■ ■ ■

The earth is but one country and mankind its citizens.
—Baha'u'llah, founder of the Baha'i faith; from *Gleanings from the Writings of Baha'u'llah*

Baha'i

The beliefs of the Baha'i faith are eminently noble. Baha'is envision the birth of a universal civilization where all creeds, classes, races, and nations will eventually embrace their oneness. The Baha'i faith focuses, in part, on the social order of things, including the nature of relationships between people and the meaning of right living. Among its principles are these:

Racial and other forms of prejudice are to be eliminated, as are extremes of wealth and poverty. Women and men are to share absolute equality of opportunity. Since God is one, the unity of all religions is acknowledged, while various expressions of religious truth are to be respected. To be genuinely religious is to know that faith exists simultaneously with reasoned thinking and the pursuit of scientific knowledge. Baha'is are promoters of lasting world peace.

> Truth is one; the sages call it by many names.
>
> —*The Vedas*
>
> *(Hindu scripture)*

Baha'u'llah, the founder of the Baha'i faith, lived and taught in midnineteenth-century Persia (now Iran). He stated that God himself conveyed the universal message, and that he has revealed himself to human beings in stages by inspiring a series of Divine Messengers throughout the course of history. They include Abraham, Buddha, Jesus, Krishna, Moses, Muhammad, Zoroaster, and Baha'u'llah, who is considered by the faithful to be the most recent messenger, or Manifestation of God. The messengers constitute an unbroken line that stretches back through millennia. Baha'u'llah taught that the Divine Messengers all speak the same language. That language urges us toward spiritual and moral maturity, the ways one lives a truly civilized life in which all are treated equally.

The Baha'i faith, the youngest of the world's independent religions, has no clergy. Rather, it is organized and administered by annually elected bodies called upon to study and explore religious writings and tenets. The Baha'i faith is considered one of the fastest growing and most geographically widespread religions; estimates place the number of Baha'is today at close to 7 million worldwide.

Marriage in the Baha'i Faith

Marriage, said Baha'u'llah, is "a fortress for well-being and salvation." It is said that a married couple should be "loving companions and comrades and at one with each other for time and eternity." But the couple should receive and accept the guidance and support of their families. A man and woman are free to choose each other, but the permission of all living parents is required before the marriage can take place. In this way, mothers and fathers and bride and groom will all arrive at the wedding day confident in the rightness of this particular joining of hands and hearts.

Husband and wife are to remain faithful to each other throughout their marriage; while divorce is permitted, a couple is encouraged to allow enough time to be sure of their decision to end their union. They are to take "a year of patience"—a year of living separately, during which they discuss their difficulties, seek the guidance of their Baha'i council, and make every effort to reconcile.

Practical Wedding Considerations and Customs

The core requirements of a Baha'i wedding are very simple: Before two witnesses approved by the Local Spiritual Assembly, the bride and groom each recite the verse "We will all, verily, abide by the will of God." Aside from that, the couple may create a ceremony to their liking. Typically, witnesses or family members read Baha'i prayers and writings. If the couple marry in the temple, the bride may not wear a veil, nor may the couple exchange rings during the ceremony. If the wedding is held elsewhere, these restrictions do not apply.

For the Ceremony: A Menu of Elements

If you wish to incorporate Baha'i elements in your ceremony, you may like the following readings. Your celebrant may include them in her remarks, or a guest may offer them at points in the service.

- The world of humanity is possessed of two wings—the male and the female. As long as these two wings are not equivalent in strength the bird will not fly. [A Baha'i wedding quotation, Abdu'l-Baha, in *The Promulgation of Universal Peace*]
- It is, therefore, evident that in the world of humanity the greatest king and sovereign is love. If love were extinguished, the power of attraction dispelled, and the affinity of human hearts destroyed, the phenomena of human life would disappear. [From Abdu'l-Baha, in *The Promulgation of Universal Peace*]
- Love gives life to the lifeless. Love lights a flame in the heart that is cold. Love brings hope to the hopeless and gladdens the hearts of the sorrowful. [From Abdu'l-Baha, *Paris Talks*]
- The friends of God must so live and conduct themselves, and evince such excellence of character and conduct, as to make others astonished. The love between husband and wife should not be purely physical, nay, rather it must be spiritual and heavenly. These two souls should be considered as one soul. How difficult it would be to divide a single soul! [Abdu'l-Baha, *Divorce: A Compilation*]

■ ■ ■

"Are you a god?"
"No."
"An angel?"
"No."
"A saint?"
"No."
"Then what are you?"
Buddha answered, "I am awake."
—from Huston Smith, *The World's Religions*

Buddhism

Buddhism began with one man, Siddhartha Gautama, the son of a king, born around 588 B.C.E. in a place now known as the kingdom of Nepal. The story of Siddhartha's birth and his transformation from prince to ascetic to the Buddha (meaning "the Enlightened One") has been told and retold throughout the centuries. Upon Siddhartha's birth, it was predicted by seers that if he stayed in the world, he would become a king and a great conqueror; if, however, he forsook the world, he would become a great redeemer. His father went to extreme lengths to prevent him from witnessing the hardships of life so that he would remain in the world. Siddhartha grew up secluded in exquisite palaces, married, and had a child.

One day he convinced his father to allow him to journey outside the palace to see his future realm. On his journey he observed a frail and bent man, a very ill man lying on the roadside, and a corpse being carried to its funeral pyre. Thus Siddhartha discovered old age, sickness, and death. On his return to the palace he passed a monk with a shaved head, who radiated peacefulness and carried his only earthly possession, a single bowl. At that moment Siddhartha learned of renunciation. After this journey he became moved by the reality of suffering. At the age of twenty-nine, the wealthy and handsome prince left all behind in search of answers as to how to alleviate suffering.

Taking on the life of the ascetic, he put himself through many trials and ate so little that he came close to death. But asceticism failed to bring enlightenment, and Siddhartha then embarked on the Middle Way, a life of neither indulgence nor deprivation. At the age of thirty-five, seated in meditation under a Bodhi tree, he attained Enlightenment and became the Buddha. For forty-nine days he remained transcendent in the blissful rapture; for the following forty-five years of his life, he traveled throughout northern India sharing his message.

His teachings spread to China, Tibet, Mongolia, Siberia, Korea, Japan, Sri Lanka, Burma, Thailand, Laos, Kampuchea, and Indonesia. Today, there are somewhat over 356 million Buddhists in the world, about 2.5 million living in North America. Besides the Enlightened One, the Buddha has been called a rebel saint, silent sage, supreme teacher, and—indeed—a redeemer. He is not, however, considered a god.

INDIVIDUAL CONSCIENCE OVER DIVINITY. Interest in Buddhism in the West is increasing tremendously, perhaps because it is a religion that emphasizes conscience over divinity. Buddha taught self-knowing rather than blind reliance on authority, and that right action is more ennobling than ritual. Because of its pragmatic, psychological, yet nonjudgmental approach to life, Buddhist thought appeals to many in the West. Buddha summarized his message as follows: "To refrain from all evil. To achieve the good. To purify one's own mind. This is the teaching of all awakened ones."

Buddha did not focus on an afterlife. His teachings instead point the way to the cessation of suffering, which brings Nirvana, a state of ultimate peace and tranquillity. Nirvana is freedom and bliss. It is beyond name or form. Here we find the transcendent in Buddhism! Without mention of a creator God, there lies a sense of the eternal in ultimate peace. And to point the way to freedom and Nirvana, Buddha created a set of guidelines to be found in the Four Noble Truths.

THE FOUR NOBLE TRUTHS AND THE EIGHTFOLD PATH. In Buddhism, the First Noble Truth is *dukkha:* Life is suffering; each of us will experience loss and pain in our lifetime. The Second Noble Truth is *tanha,* the origin of suffering, which is ego, desire, and selfish cravings. The Third Noble Truth, *nibbana,* states that in order to end suffering we must let go of such desires and cravings. The Fourth Noble Truth—laid out in the teachings of the Eightfold Path—shows the way to enlightenment and the cessation of suffering. The Eightfold Path consists of Right Views, Right Intention, Right Speech, Right Action, Right Livelihood, Right Effort, Right Mindfulness, and Right Meditation. The path is not easy. It requires rigorous practice and constant mindfulness. As the lotus grows in a muddy swamp yet remains pure and undefiled, so the enlightened mind is not influenced by worldly desires or conditions.

THE BRANCHES OF BUDDHISM. As with most religions, Buddhism expanded into numerous orders and traditions. Tibetan Buddhism has become well known in the West in great part because of its present spiritual leader, His Holiness the Dalai Lama, who was awarded the 1989 Nobel Peace Prize. It was he who stated, "There is no need for temples; no need for complicated philosophy. My own brain, my own heart is my temple; the philosophy is kindness."

Marriage in the Buddhist Tradition

Traditionally in Buddhist countries, marriage was regarded as a cultural affair, a contract between two people and their families. Blessings and guidance from the monks are considered important parts of the ceremony and of a successful family life.

In the wedding ceremony the couple is encouraged to uphold Buddhist teachings as a guide to live harmoniously, be respectful to their elders and kind to the young, and to attempt to solve marital problems that may arise. Buddhism encourages relationships based on mutual compassion and kindness, fidelity and trust. Marriage should not be anticipated as always pleasurable, since suffering is a reality of life.

Practical Wedding Considerations and Customs

THE CELEBRANT. Buddhist monks will perform interfaith weddings using a traditional Buddhist format. Some ordained Western Buddhist monks will perform a Buddhist ceremony modified for a Western congregation. However, if you are drawn to Buddhist principles but would like to incorporate them in a Western-style ceremony, you may wish to have your wedding celebrated by an interfaith minister, judge, or other officiant. One of the sample ceremonies in Part III is the wedding of Mercedes and Jack. Mercedes was raised Catholic and converted to Buddhism; Jack, raised Jewish, considered himself a humanist. They came to me wanting an essentially Buddhist ceremony that would not "feel too strange" for either family.

THE SETTING. A Buddhist ceremony typically takes place at the couple's home or at a local temple, but your ceremony can be held in any appropriate setting. You may need to set up a table to serve as an altar, which may include candles, incense, flowers, water, fruit, sweets, and perfumed water. Or you may elect to have no offerings at all. If you wish to open and close the ceremony with the traditional ringing of bells, bells can be placed on the altar; any clear sounding bells will do, though Tibetan bells work quite nicely.

THE PROCESSION. In Buddhism, there is often no formal procession, or the procession is based on local cultural tradition. You may have your procession however you wish.

For the Ceremony: A Menu of Elements

RINGING OF BELLS. *Three distinct bells are sounded to commence the ceremony.*

LIGHTING OF CANDLES AND OFFERING OF FLOWERS. *The ceremony may begin with the bride and groom each placing flowers on the altar (flowers may be set to one side beforehand, then brought to the altar once the couple have taken up their places before the celebrant); then lighting candles and incense, if desired. Traditionally, one candle is lit for the Buddha and the other for the community of monks. You may make the symbolism your own, however, and have your celebrant explain the significance of the ritual to your guests in the following manner:*

∿ In Buddhism it is traditional for the bride and groom to begin the ceremony by lighting candles and incense. [Bride] and [groom] have lit two candles. One candle represents the light of their love; the other signifies their commitment to share that love with their family and friends and with the community at large. They will light incense, two sticks to represent their individual selves and a third symbolizing the new life they are creating in marriage.

The flowers they have placed upon the altar are offerings representing beauty, love, compassion, and peace.

[The celebrant may pour some water on the ground, if the ceremony is outdoors, and sprinkle flower petals; indoors, he may pour some of the perfumed water into a separate bowl, strew flower petals on it, and explain the ritual.]

∿ This is the ground anointed by scented water, bestrewn with flowers, and beautified by love and compassion.

OPENING WORDS. *You may wish to have your celebrant include one of the following selections, all of which are infused with Buddhist philosophy.*

∿ Marriage begins with the giving of words. This is an unconditional giving to join yourselves to each other, which really joins us to the unknown future. You must have faith in yourselves to make these vows, and in each other to keep them. As friends we must all help them do that. The condition of marriage is worldly, its meaning is communal. You do not know the road; you are committing your life to a way. The word-keeping, standing by one's vow, is a double fidelity—to the community and to oneself. In the Buddhist wedding we are joined mind to mind, body to body, nature to nature, and true nature to true nature. [Adapted from the wedding rite provided by Reverend Tozan Hardison of the Seidoan Zen Temple, Blowing-Rock, North Carolina.]

∿ We have come together to bless the marriage of [bride] and [groom]. This day is possible through the grace of your ancestors, your parents, your friends and society, and indeed of the earth and all creation. We, your family and friends, are here to witness and celebrate your love. You are not alone. All that lives, all that is, abides within this moment. The past and future are also here. As you confirm your relationship in the eyes of this greater community, you are also confirming that this community lives in your love for each other. May your life as one be dedicated to the well-being of all creation. [From the website of the Zen Peacemaker Order]

∞ We are gathered here with deepest reverence to bring together into perfect matrimony [bride] and [groom]. May this couple be lastingly true to their vows. May they love and respect each other. May they help each other in stress and woe. May they keep themselves pure in mind and body and encourage each other in the promotion of all virtues. Thus spoke Buddha: "The greatest happiness which a mortal man or woman can imagine is the bond of marriage that ties together two loving hearts. But, there is a greater happiness still: it is the embrace of Truth." [Adapted from the wedding rite "Manual of Shin Buddhist Services (Seiten)" of the Buddhist Churches of America in San Francisco, provided by Reverend Don Castro]

THE THREEFOLD REFUGE AND THE PRECEPTS

∞ Now, will you take the Threefold Refuge?

[The couple answer, "Yes we will," and they repeat the words after the celebrant.]

With great devotion of body, voice, and mind, we take refuge in the Source of all being. This is our unconditional nature and the nature of all things.

With great devotion of body, voice, and mind, we take refuge in our Seeking and in our Life Lessons. This is the path of the heart and the enlightened mind.

With great devotion of body, voice, and mind, we take refuge in our Humanity and in the Boundless Interconnection of all Beings.

[Bride] and [groom], are you able to accept these as guidelines for your life?

[The couple answer, "Yes, we are."]

I will now ask the bride and groom if they are willing to observe the five basic Buddhist precepts for sacred living.

Will you keep from destroying living beings?

Will you keep from taking things not given?

Will you keep from sexual misconduct?

Will you abstain from false speech?

Will you abstain from substances causing intoxication and heedlessness?

Do you undertake to do this to the best of your ability?

[The couple reply in the affirmative—"We will" or "We do"—to each question.]

[Adapted from Reverend Tozan Hardison]

➥ We nourish ourselves and each other in living by the following five precepts:

In every way we can, we allow our deepest self to appear.

We take full responsibility for our own life in all its infinite dimensions.

We affirm our trust in the honesty and wisdom of our own body, which with our love and reverence always shows us the true way.

We are committed to embrace all parts of ourselves, including our deepest fears and shadows, so that they can be transformed into light.

We affirm our willingness to keep our hearts open, even in the midst of great pain.

[An alternative selection of precepts, provided by the Zen Center of San Francisco, adapted by Vicki Chang; the couple may say them jointly]

CELEBRANT'S ADDRESS. *You may wish to ask your celebrant to include the following passage, a Buddhist marriage homily, in the address to the couple.*

➥ Nothing happens without a cause. The union of this man and woman has not come about accidentally. This tie can therefore not be broken or dissolved. In the future, happy occasions will come as surely as the morning. Difficult times will come as surely as night. When things go joyously, be compassionate. When things go badly, be compassionate. Compassion and meditation must guide your life. To say the words is easy. But to accept that love and compassion are built upon patience and perseverance is not easy. Your marriage will be firm and lasting if you remember this. [Adapted from *Wedding Readings* by Eleanor Munro]

READINGS. *Here is a lovely Buddhist reading.*

➥ I offer to you my body, transformed into a celestial mansion, adorned by an ocean of understanding, wreathed about by the flowers of virtue. In it shines the lamp of wisdom and there, too, lies a lake of faith's perfume. The food of meditative bliss I offer you with the sweet music of songs of praise; a canopy fashioned from my compassion for others; a banner that consists of discernment and a sign of courage held high. This I offer to you, who dwells always in the lotus of my heart. From the deep recesses of my mind I pray you will always be pleased with me. [Adapted from *Dharma Recitations, Tho pa Gya ts' oMa,* provided by Lama Pema Wangdak, New York City]

THE METTA SUTTA. *A favorite reading at Western Buddhist weddings is the Metta Sutta, or the Buddha's Discourse on Loving Kindness. The sacred book of*

Buddhist scriptures, or suttas, written around 100 B.C.E., *preserved from an oral tradition hundreds of years old, is treasured by Buddhists—not as divine revelation but as the guided words of a great teacher. Millions love the Metta Sutta for its profound and moving message of love, kindness, and peace, which can be read by your celebrant or an honored guest. The message is universal.*

∾ This is what should be done by the man and woman who are wise, who seek the good, and who know the meaning of the place of peace. Let them be fervent, upright, and sincere, without conceit of self, easily contented and joyous, free of cares; let them not be submerged by the things of the world; let them not take upon themselves the burden of worldly goods; let their senses be controlled; let them be wise but not puffed up, and let them not desire great possessions even for their families. Let them do nothing that is mean or that the wise would reprove.

May all beings be happy and at their ease. May they be joyous and live in safety.

All beings, whether weak or strong—omitting none—in high, middle, or low realms of existence, small or great, visible or invisible, near or far away, born or to be born: may all beings be happy and at their ease.

Let none deceive another or despise any being in any state. Let none by anger or ill-will wish harm to another.

Even as a mother watches over and protects her only child, so with a boundless mind should one cherish all living beings, radiating friendliness over the entire world, above, below, and all around without limit. So let them cultivate a boundless good will toward the entire world, unlimited, free from ill-will and enmity.

Standing or walking, sitting or lying down, during all their waking hours, let them establish this mindfulness of good will, which is the highest state. [From *Into the Garden* by Robert Hass and Stephen Mitchell; translation by Edward Conze]

HANDFASTING AND/OR WATER POURING. *Handfasting—loosely binding together the hands of the bride and groom (described in Chapter 6)—is a feature many couples love. Your celebrant will do it or you may want to have him invite your parents to come forward and participate. The binding can take place with a sash of silk fabric, or you may wish to use a Buddhist rosary, a 108-bead mala. Water pouring is another optional ritual, and a ceremony of purification and blessing. The celebrant pours water over the couple's joined hands; the water flows into a bowl containing flower petals as he offers a blessing.*

BLESSING AND EXCHANGE OF RINGS. *After the couple has exchanged rings (see Chapter 6 for suggested words) and simple vows (see Chapter 7 for suggestions), the celebrant places his hand upon their joined hands, and says,*

∽ This marriage is sealed in devotion. By this truth let there be happiness.

EXCHANGE OF WHITE SILK SCARVES. *In some Buddhist cultures, the celebrant places white silk scarves, representing the spiritual purity of the marriage, around the necks of the bride and groom. The ritual indicates that the marriage rite has been completed. In a modern adaptation, couples sometimes opt to exchange the scarves themselves.*

CLOSING BLESSINGS. *Following are Buddhist blessings, each a fitting way to close your ceremony. You may wish to have a guest or family member read "The Blessings of Unknowing" (see page 129 for the text), and your celebrant close with one of the following selections.*

∽ Let us vow to remember the causes of suffering and to practice an end to suffering. I shall accept all that I cannot change and let my heart be broken. May we be gentle for all our days, here, there and everywhere.

Let us vow to bear witness to the wholeness of life, realizing the completeness of each and every thing. Embracing our differences, I shall know myself as you, and you as myself. May we serve each other for all our days, here, there and everywhere.

Let us vow to open ourselves to the abundance of life. Freely giving and receiving, I shall care for you, for the trees and stars, as treasures of my very own. May we be grateful for all our days, here, there and everywhere.

Let us vow to forgive all hurt, caused by ourselves and others, and to never condone hurtful ways. Being responsible for my actions, I shall free myself and you. Will you free me, too? May we be kind for all our days, here, there and everywhere.

Let us vow to remember that all that appears will disappear. In the midst of uncertainty, I shall sow love. Here! Now! I call to you: Let us together live the Great Peace that we are. May we give no fear for all our days, here, there and everywhere. ["A Blessing for the Journey," by Wendy Egyoku Nakao]

∽ May all beings have happiness and the cause of happiness. May all be free from suffering and the cause of suffering. May all never part from the happiness of no suffering. May all remain in equanimity, free from partiality, attachment and aversion. [The Four Boundless Meditations, provided by Lama Pema Wangdak]

∽ Gift of Dharma. May you, [bride] and [groom], always uninterruptedly hear the sound of Dharma issuing from birds and trees, beams of light, and even space itself.

Gift of Kindness. May you always be free from unease, and be endowed with faith, wisdom, and kindness; with right livelihood and excellent conduct. May you be mindful throughout your lives.

Gift of Fearlessness. May you never suffer, effected by evil, or never fall ill. May you never be afraid or belittled, or your minds be unhappy.

Gift of Material. May you always be prosperous, just like the treasure of space, and free of strife or harm, may you always enjoy it as you wish. [Auspicious Prayer, provided by Lama Pema Wangdak, adapted from *The Bodhisattva's Way of Life*]

THE PRONOUNCEMENT.

∽ You are now pronounced husband and wife. Go now in loving kindness and compassion.

RINGING OF BELLS. *The ceremony may conclude with the ringing of three bells.*

■ ■ ■

Ye have heard that it hath been said, Thou shalt love thy neighbor and hate thine enemy. But I say unto you, Love your enemies, and bless them that curse you, do good to them that hate you, and pray for them which despitefully use you and persecute you.
—*Jesus Christ*

Christianity

It is awe-inspiring to think how the life and teachings of one poor Jewish carpenter born in a stable over two thousand years ago have affected and transformed much of the world. However Christian practices may vary—from a ritualistic High Catholic Mass to a simple Quaker assembly, in temples of worship that range from elaborately ornate and majestic cathedrals to unadorned wooden meeting houses—all hold in common the teachings of Jesus of Nazareth. He lived for only thirty-three years, he wrote nothing, he traveled little, he was crucified by the political leaders of his culture. Very little is known with absolute certainty about this historical Jesus, and scholars continue the debate over whether Jesus' sayings were actually his. Still, there is no denying that the power of those words have inspired for centuries.

WHAT JESUS TAUGHT. Jesus was a healer, a teacher, a miracle worker, a man who emerged from forty days of fasting and praying in the wilderness to spend his remaining few years talking to his followers and to the crowds that gathered around him. His message, in essence, was simple: God loves you, and you can best embrace his love by practicing love and forgiveness among your fellow human beings. We hear his message as he describes the last judgment (Matthew 25:40): "Inasmuch as ye have done it unto the least of my brethren, ye have done it unto me."

The words of Jesus of Nazareth electrified those who heard him and remain at the ethical foundation of much of modern civilization. Many of his teachings came in the form of startling images:

"Why do you see the speck in your neighbor's eye, but do not notice the log in your own eye?"
"If you have faith the size of a mustard seed, you will say to this mountain, 'Move from here to there,' and it will move."
"It is easier for a camel to go through the eye of a needle than for someone who is rich to enter the kingdom of God."
"Let anyone among you who is without sin be the first to throw a stone."
"Unless you change and become like children, you will never enter the kingdom of heaven."

A personal note: I was raised Christian. To me, one of the most astonishing teachings of Jesus was this powerful cornerstone of the Christian faith: "But if anyone strikes you on the right cheek, turn the other also; and if anyone wants to sue you and take your coat, give your cloak as well; and if anyone forces you to go one mile, go also the second mile." And, perhaps it was at his crucifixion, with death near, that Jesus gave his most compelling lesson: "Father, forgive them, for they know not what they do." Such unconditional love for all humanity is what so many millions find uplifting and transforming.

> Whosoever comes to Me, through whatsoever form, I reach him: all men struggling through paths, which in the end lead to Me.
> —*Bhagavad-Gita*

FROM THE HISTORICAL JESUS TO THE CHRIST OF FAITH. Jesus' life, ministry, death, and the belief in his resurrection have become enduring symbols of life and the liberation from its pain. Indeed, it is faith in his resurrection that is at the foundation of the Church. For Christians, it is synonymous with their own resurrection, signifying a spiritual rebirth. When speaking of Christ and the Church, Christians are referring to the mystical body of Christ—a body of light, love, and compassion, available to all humankind.

Estimates put the number of Christians at about 2 billion, making Christianity the largest religion in the world today. Its divisions include Roman Catholicism; Protestantism (including Episcopalian, Anglican, Methodist, Lutheran, Presbyterian, Baptist, and Quaker denominations, and the Evangelical and Pentecostal movements); Eastern Orthodoxy (including members of the Russian Orthodox and Greek Orthodox Churches); and the Church of Jesus Christ of Latter-day Saints, or the Mormon Church.

Christianity's scripture is the Bible: the thirty-nine books of the Old Testament and the twenty-seven books of the New Testament. It is there that we read the message of love that underscores all the branches and denominations we call Christianity.

Marriage in the Christian Tradition

In Christianity, marriage is considered a sacrament. For Roman Catholics, Anglicans, and those of the Eastern Orthodox faith, Holy Matrimony is one of the seven great sacraments that define a life, from Baptism at birth to Anointing of the Sick at death.

It is the joining of a man and woman in a permanent state of unity. Both parties must enter into marriage seriously, and neither may be coerced. Together, husband and wife are expected to endure whatever life may bring— whether happiness or sorrow, sickness or health, abundance or hardship. Because of the separation of church and state, it remains up to the various Christian sects and churches whether to accept or reject divorce. Catholicism rejects divorce, though in some cases annulments may be obtained.

Practical Wedding Considerations and Customs

THE USE OF LANGUAGE. In an interfaith ceremony, when one is a Christian and the other is not, referring to Jesus may be inappropriate. For example, as a general rule one does not mention Jesus Christ in a Jewish-Christian ceremony, because doing so would be uncomfortable for the Jewish family. Jews acknowledge Jesus as a prophet and a teacher but not as the Messiah or God. Before one ceremony I conducted, the Born-Again Christian groom, marrying a Jewish woman with observant parents, declared, "I don't care if we have an all-Jewish ceremony as long as I can state that Jesus Christ is my Lord and Savior." Since he told me he did not wish to offend his in-laws, I suggested that he affirm Jesus silently in his own heart.

If yours is a Christian-Muslim union, it is probably wise to eliminate mention of Jesus or Allah in the course of the service. Muslims do recognize Jesus as a prophet of God, but they accept Muhammad as the final prophet. In a Christian-Hindu service the potentially troublesome words would be Jesus, Ganesh, and Vishnu.

THE ALTAR OR TABLE. Most Christian weddings have an altar. The altar may hold the unity candle, wine, and bread. If you are Greek Orthodox, your altar may hold the wreaths—the stephana—and perhaps a tray of sugared almonds and rice, symbolizing fertility and good luck.

For the Ceremony: A Menu of Elements

OPENING WORDS. *The celebrant may wish to include in her opening words an invocation—a direct call to God—or a general convocation acknowledging God's presence. Here are several versions.*

~ Almighty God, you have made the bond of marriage a holy mystery. Hear our prayers for [bride] and [groom], who have come here today to be united in marriage. With faith in you and in each other, they pledge their love today. May their lives bear witness to the reality of that love. [A Catholic invocation, adapted]

~ O eternal God, you have brought this bride and groom to unity. Bless [bride] and [groom], who now plight each other their troth. May their love be an indissoluble union. Guide them unto every good work. Send down upon them perfect and peaceful love. Preserve them in oneness of mind and steadfastness of faith. Bless them with a blameless life. O eternal God, grant them peace. Amen. [An Eastern Orthodox invocation, adapted]

~ We are gathered together in the sight of God to join this man and this woman in marriage. Let all who enter marriage know it as a sacred and joyous covenant, a way of life ordained by God from the beginning of creation. God blesses the covenant of marriage: that husband and wife may give to each other companionship, help, and comfort, both in prosperity and in adversity; that he may hold sacred the expression of natural affections; that children may be born and nurtured in families; and that human society may stand on firm foundation. Let us therefore invoke the blessing of God on this marriage between [bride] and [groom]. [A Protestant convocation, adapted]

PASSING THE SIGN OF PEACE. *A common element in many Catholic services, this ritual typically comes later in the ceremony. I prefer to include it toward the beginning, after the opening words; it then becomes the ritual enactment of the unity the celebrant is seeking to encourage among the families and guests. The celebrant may use the following words:*

~ In the spirit of love and unity, the bride and groom have asked that we pass the sign of peace. For those of you not familiar with this ritual, simply offer a handshake to your neighbor, with the words "Peace be with you." If you feel so inspired, a hug or a kiss would be most appropriate as well!

READING(s). *You may include a selection from the Bible or a piece of poetry, or one of each as readings. Again, take care that each reading is universal and reflective of both traditions, as well as of your love and your beliefs. Here are Christian readings appropriate for an interfaith ceremony. These selections are very popular with couples.*

∽ If I speak in the tongues of mortals and of angels, but do not have love, I am a noisy gong or a clanging cymbal. And if I have prophetic powers, and understand all mysteries and all knowledge, and if I have all faith, so as to remove mountains, but do not have love, I am nothing. If I give away all my possessions, and if I hand over my body, but do not have love, I gain nothing.

Love is patient; love is kind; love is not envious or boastful or arrogant or rude. It does not insist on its own way; it is not irritable or resentful; it does not rejoice in wrongdoing, but rejoices in the truth. Love bears all things, believes all things, hopes all things, endures all things. Love never ends.

Prophecies will cease, tongues will be silent, knowledge will pass away. . . . There are in the end three things that last: faith, hope and love, and the greatest of these is love. [From 1 Corinthians 13. This is the most common Christian Bible reading at weddings.]

∽ My Beloved lifts up his voice; he says to me: Come then, my love, my Lovely, come. My dove, hiding in the clefts of the rock, in the coverts of the cliff, show me your face. Let me hear your voice; for your voice is sweet and your face is beautiful.

My Beloved is mine and I am his. He said to me: Set me like a seal on your heart, like a seal on your arm. For love is infinitely strong. . . . A flame of the Lord himself. Love no flood can quench, no torrents drown. [From the Song of Songs]

∽ Blessed are the man and the woman who have grown beyond themselves and have seen through their separations.

They delight in the way things are and they keep their hearts open, day and night. They are like trees planted near flowing rivers, which bear fruit when they are ready. Their leaves will not fall or wither. Everything they do will succeed. [From Psalm I, adapted by Stephen Mitchell]

∽ Love flies, runs, and rejoices; it is free and nothing can hold it back. It gives all for all, and has all in all, because it rests in the highest good, from whom all goodness originates and flows. It doesn't look to the gifts but to the giver of all good things. Love often knows no limits, but burns beyond every limit. Love feels no burden, shrinks from no effort, aims beyond its strength, sees nothing as impossible, for it believes that all things are possible and allowable to it. Thus it is capable of everything and it succeeds because it is confident of the result, while someone without love loses courage and gives up.

Love keeps watch and is never unaware, even when it sleeps; tired, it is never exhausted; hindered, it is never defeated; alarmed, it is never afraid; but like a living flame and a burning torch it bursts upward and blazes forth.

Whoever loves, knows what this voice cries out; a mighty cry in the ears of God is the burning desire of the soul, which says:

"My love, you are all mine and I am all yours. Let me grow in love, so that I may learn to taste in my innermost heart how sweet it is to love, to be dissolved and to plunge into the ocean of love. Let love possess me; let me pass beyond myself in fervor and astonishment; let me sing love's song; let me follow my beloved into the heights; let my soul, rejoicing in love, lose itself in your praise. Let me love you more than myself, and myself only for you; and in you, all who truly love you, as love's law, shining from you, commands." [The Imitation of Christ, by Thomas A'kempis; from *Into the Garden*. This is one of the most frequently read pieces in Christendom.]

THE BREAKING OF BREAD AND DRINKING OF WINE. *The celebrant holds the bread high. After speaking the following words, he breaks the bread and offers it to the bride and groom, and, perhaps, the bridal party.*

◆ The breaking of bread among family and friends is an ancient tradition. It symbolizes that we are all nourished and sustained by the very same love that brought our bride and groom together.

Next, the celebrant holds up the cup of wine, offers the following explanation, and gives the cup to the bride and groom.

◆ This goblet represents the cup of life. As bread represents the sustenance of life, wine represents all that is good and sweet. [Bride] and [groom], before you take your vows, we ask you to drink from the cup of mirth and abundance. As you share this cup of wine, you undertake to share all that the future may bring. As wine is sweet, so we pray that your future be sweet. Whatever bitterness life may bring will be less bitter because you share it.

THE DECLARATION OF INTENT. *Here are two versions appropriate for a Christian interfaith ceremony.*

◆ The covenant of marriage is sacred. It is not to be entered into unadvisedly or lightly but reverently, discreetly, advisedly, and soberly. Into this holy estate, [bride] and [groom] come to be joined. Is it your desire now to continue in this sacred ceremony, and do you solemnly promise that the vows you are about to take reflect your true inner feelings?

◆ [Bride] and [groom], have you come here to offer yourselves to each other in the presence of a gracious and loving God who has brought you to this day and this holy moment? Have you come here freely and without reservation to give yourselves to each other in the holy state of matrimony?

THE VOWS AND THE EXCHANGE OF RINGS. *Here is the most crucial element of the Christian ceremony. Though marriage is considered a sacrament, technically the priest or minister is a witness to the actual marriage of the bride and groom. Vows can range from the most traditional to highly personal statements* *written by the couple. In Chapter 7 you will find a selection of vows as well as words to accompany the exchange of rings.*

LIGHTING OF THE UNITY CANDLE. *Here is perhaps the most popular and best loved Christian wedding ritual other than the exchange of vows and rings. Chapter 6 provides a selection of passages that may accompany this ritual. Here are additional passages appropriate for a Christian ceremony.*

⌇ [Bride] and [groom], you have pledged yourselves to each other through solemn vows. Will you jointly now light the candle symbolizing this sacred union?

[After they have lighted the candle]:

What God has joined together, let no one separate.

⌇ [Bride] and [groom], you have exchanged sacred vows. Your lives are now one. The side candles symbolize the light of your individual souls. The center candle symbolizes the light of your marriage. We now ask you to light this unity candle, and as you do, we pray that the flame in your hearts will never be extinguished.

AN ORTHODOX RITUAL: THE EXCHANGE OF CROWNS. *A crucial element in an Eastern Orthodox ceremony is the exchange of crowns (also called the crowning), two wreaths of flowers connected by a single cord or ribbon. Typically, the bride's or groom's godfather or another close male member of either family comes forward to perform the crowning and offer a brief blessing to the couple.*

The individual who will do the crowning stands behind the bride and groom. He holds one wreath in each hand, just above the couple's heads; then he crisscrosses them three times, before lying the wreaths on their heads. He may state a personal blessing at the same time or wait until the crowns are placed on the couple's heads. In an Orthodox service the couple, still bearing the crowns, are then led around the altar three times by the priest, who carries an ornate Bible. In most of the interfaith services I have conducted, the crowns are laid on the couple's heads for a few moments after the blessings are completed, then placed back on the altar or ceremonial table.

Here are two selections for the celebrant to speak—one for an Eastern Orthodox ceremony and one specifically for a Greek Orthodox ceremony.

⌇ [In the Eastern Orthodox tradition]

It is the tradition in an Eastern Orthodox service for the bride and groom to be crowned with floral wreaths, signifying that they are to be king and queen in their own home. The wreaths are bound by a single cord, the cord of love and commitment. The flowers represent romance and life's sweet blessings. As they are crowned, they are forever united.

We now call forth [honored guest], who has the honor of exchanging the wreaths three times, as is the custom. He shall also bestow a personal blessing.

∞ [In the Greek Orthodox tradition]

For thousands of years, people in Greece have been crowned with floral wreaths, signifying achievement. At weddings the wreaths signify mastery of the bride and groom's home. These wreaths, the stephana, are bound by a single cord, a cord of love and commitment. The flowers represent romance and life's sweet blessings. As they are crowned, they are forever united. We now call upon [honored guest], who will exchange the stephana three times as is custom and offer a personal blessing.

PRAYERS. *Common to all Christian denominations is the Lord's Prayer. Another familiar reading is the prayer of Saint Francis of Assisi, the second selection here.*

∞ O God [in Christian services, one may retain the words "Our Father"], who art in heaven, hallowed be thy name. Thy kingdom come; thy will be done, on earth as it is in heaven. Give us this day our daily bread, and forgive us our trespasses as we forgive those who trespass against us. And lead us not into temptation but deliver us from evil. [Protestants add: For thine is the kingdom and the power and the glory forever and ever.] Amen.

∞ Lord, make me an instrument of your peace. Where there is hatred, let me sow love. Where there is injury, pardon. Where there is doubt, faith. Where there is despair, hope. Where there is darkness, light. Where there is sadness, joy.

O Divine master, grant that I may not so much seek to be consoled as to console, to be understood as to understand, to be loved as to love with all my soul.

For it is in giving that we receive. It is in pardoning that we are pardoned. It is in dying that we are born to eternal life.

THE KISS. *The celebrant may announce the kiss in various ways; here is a version, adapted from the Bible, that might be appropriate.*

∞ The Song of Songs states: "Let him kiss her with the kisses of his mouth. For love is better than wine." You may kiss!

CLOSING BLESSING. *We have presented a number of well-liked universal blessings in Chapter 7. Here is a selection of blessings of a religious nature.*

∞ May Almighty God unite your hearts in the never-ending bond of pure love. May your children bring you happiness, and may your generous love for them be returned to you many times over. May peace live always in your hearts and in your home. May you have true friends to stand by you, both in joy and in sorrow. May you be ready and willing to help and comfort those who come to you in need. May you find happiness and satisfaction in your work. May daily problems never cause you undue anxiety. May your hearts' first desire be always toward good things. And may God bless you with many happy years together. [Adapted from a Catholic prayer]

∞ Eternal God, creator and preserver of life, author of salvation and giver of grace: Look with favor upon this man and this woman. Give them wisdom and devotion in the ordering of their common life, that each may be to the other a strength in need, a counselor in perplexity, a comfort in sorrow, and a companion in joy. Grant that their wills may be so knit together in your will, and their spirits in your spirit, that they may grow in love and peace with you and one another all the days of their life. Give them grace. Amen. [Adapted from the Episcopal Book of Common Prayer]

∞ Most gracious God, we give thanks for your tender love. We thank you also for consecrating this union. Pour out the abundance of your blessing upon this man and this woman. Defend them from every enemy. Lead them into all peace. Let their love for each other be a seal upon their hearts, a mantle on their shoulders, and a crown upon their foreheads. Bless them in their work and in their companionship; in their sleeping and in their waking; in their joys and in their sorrows; in their life and in their death. Finally in your mercy, bring them to your heavenly home. Amen. [A Protestant blessing, adapted]

∞ O God, bless [bride] and [groom], who through your good providence are now united together in wedlock. Bless their going out and their coming in; replenish their life with good things; receive their crowns into your kingdom, preserving them spotless, blameless, and without reproach, unto ages and ages. [Bride] and [groom], may God grant unto you length of days, fair children, prosperity of life, and faith; and fill you with abundance of all earthly good things. Amen. [An Eastern Orthodox blessing, adapted]

∞ May God bless you and keep you.
May God's face shine upon you.
May God look upon you with favor and give you peace.
[A Protestant blessing, adapted from Numbers 6:24–26. This is referred to as the priestly blessing and is also used in Jewish services.]

∞ O God, you have so consecrated the covenant of marriage. Send therefore your blessing upon these your servants, that they may so love, honor, and cherish each other in faithfulness and patience, in wisdom and true godliness, that their home may be a haven of blessing and peace. [A Protestant blessing, adapted]

∞ May God give you his joy and bless you. May God have mercy on you and help you in good times and in bad. May God's spirit always fill your hearts with love. [A Catholic blessing, adapted]

■ ■ ■

To find the central clue to our moral being which unites us to the universal
order, that indeed is the highest human achievement.
—Confucius

Confucianism

Confucius's teachings are devoted to the ethical, moral, and social life of the
individual and society. Although most studies of comparative religions discuss Confucianism, it's difficult to perceive this tradition as a religion in the
usual sense. Confucius did not negate heaven, or what is unseen or unknow-
able. In fact, his writings at times refer to "heaven" and "gods." But the concerns of this powerfully influential thinker, teacher, and reformer lay
primarily in the quest for "the central clue to our moral being," and for that
which would bring the individual into harmony with the rest of society. His
emphasis was life here on earth.

Born around 551 B.C.E. in northeastern China, Confucius—his actual
name was Kung Fu-Tzu, or Kung the Master—came from a modest upbringing. At about age fifteen he committed himself to learning. History in
particular caught his interest; he continued to
study, edit, and reinterpret Chinese classics and
tradition throughout his life. For many years he
traveled around the country, attempting to advise
provincial rulers on how to improve what was at
the time a fractured and chaotic social order.

There are many paths
to the top of the
mountain, but the
view is always
the same.

—*Chinese proverb*

In this Confucius had little visible success.
Nevertheless, he gathered an ever larger band of
disciples and was recognized as a brilliant teacher
by those who heard him. A modest man of high
integrity, he presented himself to his students as
"a fellow traveler." Still, it was not until after his
death that his real fame began. His philosophy shaped the fabric of Chinese
life for two thousand years and has also contributed to the cultures of Japan,
Korea, and other East Asian countries.

"HUMAN BEINGS ARE BY NATURE GOOD." This saying from the Analects,
the collection of Confucius's teachings, anecdotes, and rules of conduct, was
learned by generations of Chinese schoolchildren, and it was the starting
point of his thinking. However, he believed that people must be persuaded
to act on those good instincts, because moral behavior doesn't always come
naturally. His Analects aim to educate.

JEN. Central to Confucius's thinking was the concept of *jen,* or, broadly speaking, "human benevolence." It is a humane and perfect love that encompasses dignity and respect for oneself and for others. It prompts unselfish conduct, kindness, and empathy. Confucius exalted *jen* as the highest virtue, the ideal state of mind and heart. And it is toward *jen,* in attitude and deed, that we must always strive. "What you do not wish done to yourself," he said, "do not do to others." He wrote, "If you can practice these five things with all the people, you can be called jen. Courtesy, generosity, honesty, persistence, and kindness."

CONFUCIUS'S LASTING LEGACY. Until Communism took hold in China, each classroom bore a plaque bearing the name of Confucius. In New York City's Chinatown today, in the heart of Confucius Square, stands a large sculpture of this modest man. His Analects have filtered down to the illiterate and even penetrated Western society. The world considers Confucius one of the great teachers, in the same league as Socrates.

Marriage in the Chinese/Confucian Tradition

Traditionally, the marriage of a Chinese bride and groom was arranged through negotiation between the family members and a matchmaker. To signify the young pair's engagement, the two families exchanged documents containing the "eight characters" of a son and daughter, including the hour, day, and year of each child's birth. The boy's father wrote a formal proposal of marriage to the girl's father, who then wrote back a letter of acceptance. Gifts were exchanged; a wedding date was selected. At the family altar, the bride-to-be honored the gods and spirits of her ancestors.

For the Ceremony: A Menu of Elements

In a Western-style ceremony in which one or both members are Chinese, I often choose Confucian Analects to preface my opening words, to come before a reading or blessing, or to use at another interval. Chinese families, who are generally extremely tolerant of other religious and philosophical ideas, may include Taoist, Confucian, Buddhist, and Christian members; all find these sayings appealing. Occasionally, a non-Chinese bride or groom has revealed on the questionnaire a deep appreciation for Confucian or Taoist thought, and in that case I also try to include an Analect.

You might wish to incorporate one or more of the following Analects in your ceremony, each of which suggests something about the nature of marriage:

✑ Confucius, when talking with the Grand Music Master of Lu, said the following words, which can be taken as a wonderful metaphor for marriage: "In my understanding of music, the piece should be begun in unison. Afterwards, if it is pure, clear, and without break, it will be perfect."

∽ Fan Chih asked the Master about the meaning of jen, which can be translated as human benevolence or human-heartedness. Confucius replied simply: "Love others." Asked about the meaning of knowledge, his answer was equally eloquent: "Know others."

∽ When asked how to increase virtue and dispel confusion, Confucius said, "Base yourself in loyalty and trust and permeate yourself with righteousness, and your virtue will be paramount."

∽ [At the exchange of rings]:

I hold in my hand two beautiful rings, symbolic of a binding contract. They are circles of life and circles of love. The circle represents the wholeness of your love, unbroken and eternal. I give you the words concerning marriage of the great Chinese master Confucius: "The moral man and woman will find the moral law beginning in the relation between husband and wife, but ending only in the vast reaches of the universe."

■ ■ ■

The mind of India has never tired in the search of Light.
—Juan Mascaro

Hinduism

Hinduism, the world's third largest religion, grew gradually in India over a period of five thousand years. There are approximately 800 million Hindus in the world today; about 1.3 million live in North America. Hinduism's major scriptures are the Vedas, the Upanishads, and the Bhagavad Gita. Mahatma Gandhi, perhaps the world's most famous Hindu, described the Bhagavad Gita as "the book par excellence for the knowledge of truth."

Hinduism believes that all religions are valid paths to God. The Vedas state: "Truth is one; the sages call it by many names." Or we can look to the words of Ramakrishna: "My dear friend, when you hear one of the glorious Divine Names—be it Allah, Tara, Krishna, or whichever revealed Name is closest to your heart—if tears of ecstasy come spontaneously to your eyes or if the sensation of weeping springs forth secretly in your heart . . . this is authentic confirmation that you are awaking."

Hinduism teaches of one ultimate reality, one Supreme God who is behind the universe—Brahman. This reality is then manifested in various gods and goddesses. The Bhagavad Gita points to the nature of the Supreme God with these words: "And know, Arjuna, that I am the seed of all things that are; and that no being that moves or moves not can ever be without me. . . . Know thou that whatever is beautiful and good, whatever has glory and power is only a portion of my own radiance. But what help is it to thee to know this diversity? Know that with one fraction of my Being I pervade and support the Universe, and know that I AM."

To be one with Brahman is to reach an eternal state of perfect knowledge and bliss. This is the soul's objective and the path to liberation. The Bhagavad Gita tells us: "And when a man sees that the God in himself is the same God in all that is, he hurts not himself by hurting others: then he goes indeed to the highest Path." Brahman's existence within the inner soul of a man or woman is known as Atman. The experience of Atman is expressed in the Chandogya Upanishad as a "Spirit which is mind and life, light and truth and vast spaces." Brahman "enfolds the entire universe, and in silence is loving to all." Brahman is "greater than all worlds" yet resides in every living thing and within each human heart.

Hinduism believes in reincarnation and karma, the moral law of cause and effect. Through the spiritual disciplines known as yogas, the soul tries to release the hold of ego in order to realize unity with God, to become one with Brahman. The word *yoga* is derived from the same root as the English word *yoke;* yoga yokes us or unites us back to God. Hinduism categorizes four well-developed systems of yogas or paths to God: jnana yoga—the path of knowledge; bhakti yoga—the path of love; karma yoga—the path of work-action; and raja yoga—the path through psychophysical exercises. In recent decades the West has become familiar with yoga. Consequently, many people from various backgrounds and traditions have discovered the benefits of yogic practices, which can range from increased physical well-being to inner peace, or even to a direct experience of God.

A personal note: It is through the discipline and practice of Hindu meditation that I have had the mystical experience of God, known as samadhi. I began to practice meditation seventeen years ago; I have been meditating daily for fifteen years. The practice of meditation—withdrawing into silence, becoming the witness, then becoming awareness itself—has not only profoundly affected my life, but transformed it. All barriers truly dissolve. In the state of divine oneness, utter joy permeates and envelopes one's being. During meditation, tears sometimes run down my face; other times the experience is too sublime for tears—one simply basks in the light, and is grateful.

Marriage in the Hindu Tradition

Of the sixteen Hindu sanskaras, or sacraments, that make life noble and prosperous, marriage is the most important. It is conceived as a spiritual union within which two individuals can direct their instincts toward the progress of their souls. The couple become one, united spiritually, mentally, emotionally, and physically. Marriage is a lifelong commitment and the strongest social bond between a man and woman. In fact, it is believed that an individual has not attained his or her complete self unless he or she is married. For parents, the giving of one's child in marriage is the ultimate gift.

Practical Wedding Considerations and Customs

In India weddings are elaborate celebrations steeped in sacred rites and cultural traditions. The wedding process—including preparation rituals, the ceremony, and the banquet—usually lasts for three or more days, with the actual ceremony taking about two and a half hours.

THE CELEBRANT. A Hindu pandit will usually perform a traditional Hindu ceremony for an interfaith couple. Some couples choose to have two ceremonies—one Hindu and one Christian, for example. However, you may find it difficult, or impossible, to find a priest, imam, or rabbi to officiate at your interfaith union. An interfaith minister, a Unitarian Universalist minister, or a judge will certainly perform your ceremony.

THE SETTING. Hindu interfaith weddings in the West can be held in any appropriate setting, such as a private home, banquet hall, or catering facility.

THE MANDAP AND THE ALTAR. Hindu marriage ceremonies take place under a mandap, a wedding canopy or pavilion that has four pillars or poles and is often beautifully decorated. On a table or altar within the mandap there is the Sacred Fire (Agni), symbolizing eternal light, wisdom, and purity. There are offerings of fresh flowers (for beauty), coconut (for fertility), ghee (oil, to feed the fire), and kum kum (red powder for good luck). Water, the life-nourishing element, is also used during the ceremony. Customarily the bride and groom sit on two thronelike chairs.

LANGUAGE. Hindu ceremonies are generally performed in Sanskrit, the ancient language of India and of the Vedas. Though it is the Hindu priest, the pandit, who will be fluently versed in Sanskrit, most Hindus know basic mantras. We have included some Sanskrit passages, with English translations. If you wish, an honored family member—perhaps a father or an uncle—can recite the mantras.

THE ORDER OF ELEMENTS. In a traditional wedding, the bride and groom and their parents participate in various welcoming rituals, depending on local custom. In a Western-style ceremony, you may arrange the procession in the style you find most comfortable.

The circling of the sacred fire and the seven steps (described in the next section) remain at the center of the ceremony. Among the other elements, choose the ones you like and arrange them as you wish. For example, garlands are sometimes exchanged at the beginning of the ceremony or after the seven steps. Rose petals are sometimes showered in welcoming the bride and groom and sometimes at the conclusion of the ceremony. Rely on your good instincts and on the experience of your family in creating a pleasing flow to your service. Logistics and plain common sense are important too!

For the Ceremony: A Menu of Elements

THE WELCOME CEREMONY AND THE GIVING AWAY OF THE BRIDE. *Traditionally, the groom arrives with his family, is greeted by the bride and her family, and is treated to a ritual welcome. Depending on local custom, the bride's mother may welcome the groom by marking his forehead with red powder and offering him honey, sweets, and water or pouring rice and flowers upon him. In India the farewell to the bride from her family and friends is usually highly emotional, with tears of joy and sorrow. In an interfaith ceremony, these traditional Hindu welcoming rituals can be combined with a Western-style procession. Once the bride and groom take their places under the mandap, the celebrant can offer one of the following explanations. (If yours is a Jewish-Hindu ceremony, you may want to point out the correlation between the chuppah and the mandap. The meaning is similar.)*

⁓ Today we bless this union under a mandap. In Hindu tradition, it represents sanctity, shelter, and peace. The four poles correspond to the four directions, as the couple's love will span to the four corners of the earth. The sides of the mandap are open, as the couple's home and arms will remain open to family and friends.

⁓ Today we celebrate this marriage under a canopy called the mandap. It symbolizes the sanctity of the home. May the bride and groom find peace, refuge, and strength here. May they be brought together heart, mind, body, and soul.

⁓ Today we bless this marriage under a mandap. It is under this sacred canopy that Hindu marriages and other religious acts are celebrated. The mandap represents a home supported by four pillars—truth, humanity, meditation, and purity.

INVOCATION

⁓ In Hinduism every auspicious occasion begins with an invocation to God. Blessings are sought for a ceremony that will be free from impediments and for a marriage free from all hardships and obstacles. God's grace is invoked for the health, happiness, prosperity, and peace of the bride and groom and their families.

At this time [family member] will recite the Ganesh Pooja, and I will
 provide the English translation.

Ajam nirvi kalpam niraa kaara mekam
Niraa nandam anandam advaita purnam
Param nir gunam nirvi shesham nireeham
Para bhrama rupam ganesham bajemam

Unborn, absolute, and formless Thou art,
Beyond bliss and yet infinite bliss Thou art,
From attributes and desires Thou art free.
O Supreme Spirit, we worship thee. [Provided by Pandit Harkishin
 Sharma]

KANYADHAN, THE OFFERING OF THE BRIDE. *The bride's parents come forward and place their daughter's right hand in the groom's hands. This ritual may
include the pouring of water on their joined hands. The celebrant explains.*

⟋ In the kanyadhan, the bride's family gives their daughter to the
groom by placing her right hand in his hand. In Hinduism it is believed this
is the greatest gift they can give. We celebrate with the pouring of water,
which flows from the hands of her parents to the bride's hands, to the
groom's hands. The words of the Bhagavad Gita: "He who offers to me with
devotion only a leaf, or a flower, or a fruit, or even a little water, this I accept
from the yearning soul, because with a pure heart it was offered with love."

THE TYING OF HANDS. *This ritual is performed in various ways, according to
local customs. Most simply, you may have your officiant bind your hands loosely
with a cloth or thread used specifically for that purpose. You or your officiant can
then remove the thread before going on to the next ritual. In addition, the corner
of the bride's sari may be tied to a scarf worn by the groom. Your officiant can
give one of the following explanations:*

⟋ The couple's hands are joined together, representing their eternal
bond. [Bride] and [groom], we pray that you may forever look upon each
other with love and compassion.

⟋ The bride and groom are tied together with a cloth that is worn by
the bride. A single thread is easily broken, but interwoven strands form a
very strong bond. So will the individual abilities and virtues of our bride and
groom combine to form a stronger bond.

⟋ The corner of the bride's sari is tied to a scarf worn by the groom.
The hands of the couple are then tied with a thread. The tying of the hands
signifies an eternal bond that will join them forever.

*The following verse may be recited or chanted in Sanskrit, after which the
officiant offers the English prayer.*

∾ *Grnhaami te suprjaastvaaya hastam mayaa patyaa*
  jaradhashtiryayaaasah
Bhago Aryamaa Savitaa Purandhirmahyam tvaadhur gaarhapatyayaaya
  devaah
Bhaga, Aryamaa, Savita and Purandhi. [Provided by AVM S.
  Lakshminarayanan (AVSM)]

God whom all scripture praises
Has willed that [groom] and [bride] become husband and wife.
May the Divine Spirit bear witness to this
Now by holding hand in hand.
May they live together in happiness and have fine healthy children.
May they keep one another company and grow old together with happiness
  and peace.

VIVAHA HOMA, THE LIGHTING OF THE SACRED FIRE. *The sacred fire—symbolizing the Radiant One and serving as the representation of divine witness as the couple take their vows—is lit. Family members are invited to participate. The celebrant may explain the rite like this:*

∾ At this time we light the sacred fire and make offerings in a ritual known as the vivaha homa. Fire is a symbol of the illumination of the mind and also serves as a pure, holy witness to the marriage ceremony. The fire represents eternal light. The offerings you see before you include flowers for beauty, coconut for fertility, rice for sustenance, and sweets to ensure a sweet life! [Bride's] and [groom's] parents will come forward and help the bride and groom light the fire.

[As the family lights the fire]

∾ First Created Being, give food and drink to this household. O God, who reigns in richness and vitality over all the worlds, come take your proper seat in this home. Accept the offerings made here, be their protector on this day. O you who see into the hearts of all created beings, bring them together as one.

MANGAL FERA, THE CIRCLING OF THE SACRED FIRE. *The groom leads his bride by the hand in the first two circles; she leads him in the following two. After each round a member of the bride's family may place an offering of rice and flowers in the fire.*

∾ According to Hindu philosophy, there are four essential aspects to a full life. These are Dharma—religion, moral values, and the wisdom to lead a good life; Artha—prosperity, to make life as happy as possible; Kama—energy and passion in life, family, and children; and Moksha—unity with God and the attainment of the state of completeness. The bride and groom will now circle the fire four times, in a prayer for a good and long life permeated by God, and filled with abundance, family, and peace. The four rounds also correlate to the four stages of human life: childhood, youth, middle age, and old age.

SHILAROHANA, THE STEPPING ON THE STONE. *One of these two variations may be used.*

∽ The bride places her foot on a stone, as if to say, "May our marriage be as firm and steadfast as the stone. May our commitment be strong and faithful." [The bride steps on the stone.]

∽ We now request that the bride and groom take part in the stepping on the stone or shilarohana.

[Groom] Come, my love, step on the stone. May our marriage be forever strong.

[Bride] As the heavens are stable, as the earth is stable, as the mountains are stable, as the whole universe is stable, so may our union be permanently settled.

SATAPADI, OR THE SEVEN STEPS. *In this most important rite, bride and groom, hand in hand with groom leading, take seven steps together around the fire as they make seven promises to each other. These vows are sacred prayers; after the seven steps, the couple are considered married. The celebrant introduces the ritual; the couple, together, then recite the vows, which can be read from a printed card. Three versions of the seven steps are given here. After the vows are recited, you may elect to say together the Hindu mantra here, the last two lines of which are well-known.*

∽ [The first version]

In Hindu tradition, the bride and groom take seven steps to symbolize the beginning of their journey though life together. These steps represent seven principles and promises to each other. It is said that if the bride and groom walk seven steps together, they will become lifelong friends.

[Bride] and [groom], take the first step. [The celebrant continues after each promise, "Take the second step," and so on.]

We shall cherish each other in sickness and health, in happiness and sorrow.

We shall be lifelong friends.

Together we shall share each other's ideals.

We shall nurture each other's strengths, talents, and aspirations.

Together we shall make each other happy.

Together we shall love and care for our children and our families.

Together we will look toward the mysteries of the future with awe, open-mindedness, and inspiration.

∽ [The second version]

Sacred and central to the Hindu wedding ceremony is the satapadi. In this ancient ritual, the bride and groom shall take seven steps and, with them, seven eternal vows. Through the seven steps the couple become united in spirit, commitment, and purpose. [Bride] and [groom], please take the seven steps.

[Bride and groom in unison]

We vow to remain together through happiness and sadness, united
    through whatever life may bring.

We promise to embrace each other's families.

We commit to remaining forever faithful.

We promise to love, comfort, and nurture each another.

We shall come together spiritually, mentally, emotionally, and physically.

We acknowledge God's presence in our marriage and in our lives.

We resolve to share all spiritual, moral, and financial activities.

∞ [The third version, begun by the celebrant]

[Bride] and [groom], please take the first step. [The celebrant continues after each promise, "Take the second step," and so on.]

With God as our guide, we shall nourish and sustain each other.

With God as our guide, we shall grow in strength.

With God as our guide, we shall prosper.

With God as our guide, we shall share our joys and sorrows.

With God as our guide, we shall cherish and care for our children.

With God as our guide, we shall be together forever.

With God as our guide, we shall remain lifelong friends. [Adapted from
    www.vivaaha.org, a global Hindu electronic networks website
    (GHEN)]

[The mantra] We have taken the seven steps. You have become mine forever. Yes, we have become partners. I have become yours. Hereafter, I cannot live without you. Do not live without me. Let us share the joys. We are word and meaning, united. You are thought and I am sound. I am the words and you are the melody. I am the melody and you are the words.

TOUCHING OF THE HEARTS. *This ritual is not crucial, but I think it is quite moving—and very romantic! The touching of the hearts may take place after the exchange of vows, rings, or garlands. Bride and groom place their hands upon each other's hearts and alternately recite one of the following phrases.*

∞ May our hearts be joined as one.

∞ May my heart be forever yours and your heart forever mine.

∞ I give you my heart.

EXCHANGE OF GARLANDS. *The exchange of flower garlands, worn around the neck, signifies that both bride and groom accept the marriage. In an interfaith service, you may wish to combine this ritual with the Western exchange of* rings. *The ritual can be done in silence, or the celebrant may say a few words. After the following explanation, he hands the garlands to the couple, who in turn exchange them.*

➦ The bride and groom will now exchange garlands, indicating that both parties accept the marriage. From the earliest times, the circle has been a symbol of committed love. It is unbroken and has no end. The circle also represents wholeness, the state in which nothing is missing and everything is possible. Let these garlands remind you of the coming around of an eternal cycle—from want to plenty, from despair to joy, from failure to possibility, from loneliness to love.

THE MANGAL SUTRA

➦ The groom will now place a beaded chain, the mangal sutra, around the bride's neck, signifying his abiding love, integrity, and devotion. Symbolizing marriage in the Hindu tradition, the mangal sutra represents the groom's commitment to uphold the sanctity of their union, and a welcoming of the bride by the groom's parents.

MARKING OF THE BRIDE'S FOREHEAD. *The groom or female relatives, depending on local custom, put sindhoor, a vermilion powder, on the bride's forehead, symbolizing her new status as a married woman. Red, the most auspicious color, indicates the hope of a good and long life.*

BLESSING. *The celebrant pronounces the couple husband and wife and offers a blessing. A well-known mantra is the Om Shanti mantra, the prayer for peace. Again, you may wish to have a family member recite the mantra in Sanskrit, with the celebrant supplying the English translation.*

➦ *Aum sarveshaam swasthir bhavatu*
sarveshaam shaanthir bhavatu
sarveshaam poornam bhavatu
sarveshaam manglam bhavatu
om shaanti, shaanti, shaanti

May perfection prevail on all.
May peace prevail on all.
May contentment prevail on all.
May auspiciousness prevail on all.
Peace, peace, peace. [Provided by Pandit Harkishin Sharma]
[The celebrant may also add one of the following.]
Peace be in the heavens, in the sky, and on earth.
May life grow in peace.
May peace come to this couple and to us all.

SHOWERING OF ROSE PETALS

∞ In India the bride and groom are showered with flower petals by family and friends, as if to say, through the extravagance of spilled flowers: May your life together be filled with the beauty and romance of flowers. May you want for nothing. [Adapted from *Weddings from the Heart* by Daphne Rose Kingma]

■ ■ ■

> God is most great. God is most great. I testify that there is no god but God.
> I testify that Muhammad is the Prophet of God. Arise and pray; God is
> most great. God is most great. There is no god but God.
> —Prayer that can be heard from the minaret

Islam

"We believe in Allah [God] and that which has been sent down to us and that which has been sent down to Abraham, Ishmael, Isaac, Jacob, and the tribes, and that which has been given Moses and Jesus and to all prophets by their Lord. We make no distinction among any of them, and to Him we have committed ourselves." These lines from the Koran point to the Muslims' belief in the common origin of Jews, Christians, and Muslims. A bit of religious history: God created Adam and Eve; among Adam's descendants was Abraham, married to Sarah. Since Sarah could not provide a son, Abraham took a second wife, Hagar, and with her had Ishmael. Sarah then herself gave birth to a son, Isaac.

Isaac's descendants, who remained in Palestine, were the Hebrews, or Jews; Ishmael settled in what was eventually called Mecca, in Arabia; his people became the Muslims. Though the Bible and the Koran tell the story somewhat differently, it's important to note that in Jewish-Christian Scripture (Genesis), God specifically tells Abraham that he will make "a great nation" from Ishmael as "he is thy seed." Muslims, Christians, and Jews all belong to the "Abrahamic" family of religions, and the concept of one almighty creator God of Jews and Muslims is identical. Christians and Muslims actually share some beliefs about Jesus: both believe in his miraculous birth without human intervention, that he was the Messiah as predicted in the Bible, and that he will return in the Last Days. Muslims, however, do not consider Jesus to be God, nor do they worship him. They believe he is a true prophet of God.

Today there are more than a billion Muslims throughout the world, of various races, ethnic groups, and nationalities. The vast majority of Muslims are not Arabs but live in Indonesia, India, Pakistan, China, Africa, Turkey, the former Yugoslavia, the former Soviet Union, and other countries, including the United States, where (according to statistics compiled by the National Congress for Community and Justice) about 6 million Muslims live. All are united in worship of Allah and in great admiration of Muhammad, the founder of the Islamic religion.

MUHAMMAD: THE FINAL PROPHET, THE LAST MESSENGER OF GOD. Born in Mecca in the late sixth century C.E., Muhammad, a poor boy orphaned early in life, became a shepherd and a camel driver—a simple man living in the manner of his time. But he was respected and loved by those who knew him for his goodness, insight, and charity. While meditating in a cave at Mount Hira, Muhammad came to an understanding of the truth through divine revelation: There was but one God, who was Allah (the Arabic name for Almighty God); and he was loving, compassionate, and merciful. At Mount Hira the angel Gabriel appeared to Muhammad, charging him to proclaim this great revelation to the world. Though Muhammad protested, he did finally go forth with God's message.

Muhammad went on to become a mystic, prophet, merchant, soldier, statesman, magistrate, and leader; he established a colony of believers at Medina (today, with Mecca, one of the holy cities of Islam). He fought persecution and ignorance, spread a message of justice, mercy, the equality of all people, and rights for women, and united the Arab world.

Muhammad is not to be considered divine. Indeed, Muhammad himself taught his followers to think of him as "God's Messenger and His Slave." But so revered is this humble man—who continued to live simply in a clay house and was often seen milking his goats—that each time Muslims say his name they follow it with the words "peace be upon him."

THE LIVING MIRACLE. To Muslims, the Koran is a living miracle. Although it was conveyed by Muhammad, an illiterate man, it is expressed with exquisite rhythm, more sublime than the finest poetry. And it is considered divine speech, the finite manifestation of the infinite reality. "It is not about the truth," wrote one translator, "it is the truth."

The Koran was given to Muhammad over a period of twenty-three years; he would enter a trancelike state at those times and repeat what he was hearing to his followers. In the revelations, God speaks directly, referring to himself interchangeably as I, He or We. According to Muslims, God gave the Koran as the final scripture following the Old and New Testaments, and "it confirms the Scriptures which came before it and stands guardian over them." Though Islam recognizes Abraham, Noah, Moses, and Jesus as among the prophets, Muhammad is the final one. Many believe that only when the Koran is read in Arabic can its true beauty be fully appreciated. For Muslims, it remains the holiest of books. God's very presence is believed to be within its letters and sounds, and it is said that every verse holds up to seventy hidden meanings.

All knowing, all powerful, and awesome, God is also—the Koran tells us—closer than our jugular vein.

THE FIVE PILLARS AND THE LAWS OF ISLAM. The Muslim is enjoined to act in particular ways, and the Koran and the Hadith—the sayings and deeds of Muhammad himself, recorded by those who knew him—provide an explicit list of what is expected. Five requirements, the Five Pillars, are prominent, beginning with the individual's need to confess his faith: "Al ilaha illa 'llah!"—"There is no god but God." This is the foundation of Islam, the call from the minaret, a reminder to the Muslim of what is at the core of life. Implicit in that reaffirmation is the notion of submission to God's will. Indeed, the word Islam, from the same root as the Arabic word *salaam,* means "surrender" or "peace." Muslims believe that only after total and unconditional surrender to God comes true peace of mind.

Muslims are called to pray five times a day; to support and care for the poorest among them; to make a pilgrimage to the holy city of Mecca at least once in a lifetime; and to fast from dawn to sundown during the holy month of Ramadan. They believe there will be a Day of Judgment. As explained in *A Quick Introduction to Islam,* by Abu Yusuf Daniel Masters, Abu Maryam Isma'il Kaka, and Abu Iman Robert Squires: "Islam teaches that life is a test, and that all human beings will be accountable before God. A sincere belief in the life hereafter is key to leading a well-balanced and moral life."

Whereas the Koran was divine revelation, the Hadith are Muhammad's own words, and many of those words are simple and universal. They speak of peace, gentleness, and forgiveness. In the Hadith we read:

> Kindness is a mark of faith: and whoever hath not kindness hath not faith.
> Follow up an evil deed by a good one which will wipe [the former] out, and behave good-naturedly to people.
> The ink of a scholar is more holy than the blood of the martyr.
> Shall I not inform you of a better act than fasting, alms and prayers? Making peace between one another: enmity and malice tear up heaven's rewards by the roots.
> The rights of women are sacred. See that women are maintained in the right assigned to them.

Marriage in the Muslim Tradition

Marriage in Islam is seen as a comfort, a fulfillment of social responsibility, a human necessity, and a gift from God. States the Koran: "Just as garments are for protection, comfort, show and concealment for human beings, Allah expects husbands and wives to be for one another." Divorce is not prohibited, but it is a serious decision, to be reached only as a last resort after attempts to resolve problems and differences. Muhammad himself, it is believed, urged: "Get married, and do not divorce; indeed, divorce causes the Throne of God to shake!"

Muslim men may marry "people of the book"—that is, Christian and Jewish women who are religious, as well as women of the Islamic faith. A non-Muslim wife cannot be forced to convert, although it is hoped that she will willingly come to embrace Islam. In fact, it is stated in the Koran: "Let there be no compulsion in religion." A Muslim woman, however, is not to marry a non-Muslim.

Practical Wedding Considerations and Customs

THE CELEBRANT AND THE SETTING. The man and woman must each freely consent to the marriage, which is to be declared publicly, but there are no hard-and-fast rules concerning where the ceremony is to take place. A wedding can be held in a mosque, but this is not required. Private homes, banquet ballrooms, courtrooms, and other settings are permitted, although Muslim custom decrees that the celebration must not be excessively lavish and no liquor should be served. An imam, an Islamic religious leader, typically leads the ceremony; however, any Muslim who understands the traditions of Islam may perform a marriage, in the presence of at least two witnesses. An interfaith or Unitarian Universalist minister, a humanist celebrant, or a civil judge will officiate Muslim interfaith marriages.

THE MEHR (OR MAHER). The mehr is a token gift from the groom to the bride, symbolizing the fact that he's willing and able to assume responsibility for the family they will form. Traditionally, this might have been an assured sum of money, a piece of property, jewelry, or the price of an education. There is no prohibition against the bride's working and earning a living as well, but providing for the family is considered primarily the Muslim man's responsibility.

WEDDING FORMS AND RITUALS. Although the Koran spells out rules concerning marriage, the ceremony is not considered a religious event. A traditional Muslim ceremony is simplicity itself; it takes about five minutes.

Consequently, ceremonies often are most noted for the cultural traditions of the country. In India, Pakistan, and Morocco, for example, weddings may go on for days. Iran has the visually sumptuous sofreh—literally translated, "the marriage spread"—that dates to before the Zoroastrian era.

Here I have listed a number of sayings and quotations that have particular beauty and meaning in the Islamic faith and would be appropriate in an interfaith ceremony. You may wish to have your celebrant incorporate one or another at the parts of the service I have indicated. I'd also suggest you look at the section on Sufism, a mystical tradition that bases its teachings on the Koran and the Hadith.

For the Ceremony: A Menu of Elements

OPENING WORDS

∞ Legend says: "When a man and a woman join in marriage, God himself opens wide the heavens. He then commands legions of angels to go forth and bear witness. For all heaven rejoices in the union."

∞ In the Koran we read these words: "And of His signs is this: that He has created mates for you from yourselves that you might enjoy blissful tranquility in their company. He promotes between you love and compassion. Surely there are signs in this for those who reflect."

∞ At this precious moment we are uniting [bride] and [groom] as husband and wife in the sacred bond of marriage. May this union be blessed by God and filled with His divine benevolence. May God fill their life with joy and grant them peace, health and prosperity. May they always live together in an atmosphere of tranquility and never-diminishing love and tender regard for one another. [Adapted from *Marriage in Islam,* by Muhammad Abdul-Rauf.]

∞ Praise be to Almighty God, the Merciful, the Compassionate. He created male and female, each in need of the other, and established the institution of marriage as a means of uniting two souls in a blessed bond of love. [Adapted from *Marriage in Islam,* by Muhammad Abdul-Rauf.]

SURA AL-FATIHA. *The following passage has been called the very essence of the Koran. It's often read at an Islamic wedding. For an interfaith ceremony, I have translated the word Allah, which means "God."*

∞ In the Name of God, the merciful Lord of mercy. Praise be to God, the Lord of all Being, the merciful Lord of mercy, Master of the Day of Judgment. You alone we serve and to You alone we come for aid. Guide us in the straight path, the path of those whom You have blessed, not of those against whom there is displeasure, nor of those who have gone astray.

CELEBRANT'S ADDRESS

∞ From the Hadith, sayings attributed to Prophet Muhammad: "If you would put your faith completely in God, He would provide for your needs in the same way He provides for the birds. They go out in the morning with their stomach empty and return filled in the evening."

∞ From the Koran, Sura al-Ahzab: "He it is who bestows His blessings upon you, with his angels, so that He might take you out of the depths of darkness into the light. And, indeed, a dispenser of grace is He unto the believers. On the day when they meet him, they will be welcomed with the greeting 'peace' [salaam]; and He will have prepared for them a most excellent reward."

∞ From the sayings of the Prophet: "When a man looks upon his wife and she upon him, God looks mercifully on them. When they join hands together, their sins disappear in the interstices of their fingers. When they love, the angels encircle the earth." [From *One River, Many Wells,* by Matthew Fox]

Vows. *Often the couple join their right hands and the celebrant places a white cloth, symbolizing spiritual purity and protection, over their hands. Vows in Islam can be as simple as the following:*

∞ I sincerely and honestly pledge myself to be a faithful wife/husband to you.

CLOSING BLESSING

∞ O God, bless this gathering. Bless us all. Bless our bride and bridegroom. Grant them health, success, and prosperity. Amen. Ma' Salaama—God's peace go with you.

■　■　■

Ahimsa, Anekantwad, Aparigraha
[nonviolence, nonabsolutism, nonpossessiveness]
—Jain Code of Conduct

Jainism

The core of Jainism is ahimsa, or the principle of nonviolence and reverence for all life. Mahatma Gandhi, the great Indian nationalist leader and social reformer, himself a Hindu, was deeply influenced in his life and politics by ahimsa. The Rev. Dr. Martin Luther King, Jr., in turn, was inspired by Gandhi and carried on his ideals of nonviolent protest. And so we see how this fundamental Jain belief has rippled through our contemporary world in powerful ways.

Considered one of the oldest religions in India, Jainism evolved through twenty-four Tirthankaras, "pathfinders" or spiritual leaders, individuals who first achieved spiritual liberation themselves through meditation, then spread their teachings. The last of these was Lord Mahavira, a contemporary of Buddha, who is believed to have died around 526 B.C.E. Jain temples are among the most beautiful in India; Jain temples are also found in Europe, North America, Africa, and the Far East. Today there are somewhat over 4 million Jains worldwide, the majority living in India.

Both a religion and a way of life, Jainism shares with Hinduism and Buddhism a belief in the cycles of life, death, and rebirth, and in karma—our actions affect the course of our lives and of our future lives. In Jainism this karma subtly weighs down the soul, the jiva, and so the Jain is careful not to accumulate karma. Jains try to lift the veils of karma through self-control, nonattachment, and overcoming the passions of the ego. In its true state, the jiva is pure, omniscient, and one with all beings. The highest state of perfection is known as kevala, in which one is infinitely virtuous, in perfect harmony.

The Jain is called upon to harm no living thing, in thought, word, or deed. We are all mutually dependent; life is a gift to be cherished in all its diversity, no matter how large or small. Strict vegetarians, practitioners of Jainism even avoid lines of work that in any way endanger animal life. To preserve the natural environment; to serve others through peace, goodwill, and friendliness; to be forgiving and to pray for forgiveness; to live simply in a nonpossessive manner—these are among the principles that guide life for the Jain. One is considered a Jain by conduct, not by conversion or birth. And each individual has within himself or herself the potential to achieve freedom and spiritual perfection.

Practical Wedding Considerations and Customs

Marriage is a public declaration of a couple's intent to be together for life, and a declaration of the community's support for the new bride and groom. Because Jains and Hindus have shared the same subcontinent for centuries, it is not surprising that their marriage traditions are similar.

If you plan to honor your Jain heritage, I suggest you read the description of the Hindu marriage ceremony in this chapter, many of whose elements will apply. Two elements for your ceremony will be the mandap, or wedding canopy, which signifies sanctity, shelter, and peace, and a vedi or altar set up to hold, most importantly, the sacred fire.

Here are some selections your celebrant may use along with these Jain-Hindu marriage rituals.

For the Ceremony: A Menu of Elements

JOINING OF THE HANDS. *The celebrant places the bride's hand in the groom's, thereby joining them for life, and says the following prayer:*

∞ Aum Arham. O Jiva, you are the one with soul. May you two become partners with the same time, mind, karma, shelter, body, action, love, desire, wishes, joy, sorrow, longevity, with the same hunger and thirst. May you have similar progress. May you enjoy the same good things. May you obtain a lasting relationship and unity by way of this joining of hands.

CIRCLING OF THE SACRED FIRE. *The following mantras, which I have abbreviated and adapted from longer versions, have a particularly Jainist feel. After explaining that the bride and groom will walk four times around the sacred fire, the celebrant might offer these words.*

∞ Please circle the fire the first time. Aum Arham. Without beginning is the world, is the soul, is time, is attachment. You have joined each other in front of God, fire, men and women, father and mother and other relatives.

Please circle the fire the second time. This love and joining together is also the fruit of your past karma. May it last as long as this world lasts.

Please circle the fire for the third time. There are karmas related to feelings of comfort and discomfort, hearing, seeing, tasting, smelling, touching. All these could be a good experience or a bad experience. May you have all good experience.

Please circle the fire for the fourth time. This is how your joining together is a natural and binding result of your karma. [From the Jain website]

CLOSING BLESSING

∞ You two have been married. Now you are equal in love, experience, and good conduct. You are two friends in happiness and misery, in virtues and faults. May you become equal in mind, speech, and action, and in all the good virtues.

■ ■ ■

What is your tree of life? A tree of life—the soul's place of discernment,
the mind's place of enlightenment, the heart's place of connection.
—Deuteronomy 6

Judaism

It is remarkable how in the face of everything—exile, slavery, pogroms, the Holocaust, political and racial prejudice—the Jewish people have not only survived but flourished, not only persevered but continued to affirm and celebrate life. Today there are about 14 million Jews in the world, including approximately 6 million living in the United States. If we consider the size of their population at any given point in history, we find the Jewish contribution has been monumental. Since it is from the seed of Abraham, and therefore Judaism, that Christianity and Islam sprang forth, one can say that Judaism is the father of the Abrahamic family of religions.

AN IMPASSIONED SEARCH FOR MEANING. Jewish history is filled with sublimity and tragedy, suffering and hope, blessing and burden. Through a history that spans over 3,300 years, we find within the Jewish psyche an impassioned search for meaning—meaning in relationship to God, in relationship to the law, and in human existence. Jacob received the name Israel, which means "the one who struggled with God," after he wrestled all night with an angel of God that took him to a higher level of spiritual awareness. Jacob's descendants were thereafter known as the Israelites.

In his book *The World's Wisdom,* Philip Novak writes, "Judaism can be viewed as the evolution of a people in the grip of two towering great ideas. The first is the idea of One God—imageless, primordially creative, and utterly transcendent—who, nevertheless, cares for the creation. God is viewed as loving and compassionate; he is good, and so is his creation. We read the first chapter of the Bible, Genesis, and see the affirmation of life's inherent goodness: 'In the beginning God created the heaven and the earth . . . and behold, it was very good.' The second is the idea of human dignity: Men and women become fully human only by responding to the moral institutions divinely etched in their hearts."

The great physicist Albert Einstein wrote, "There remains, however, something more in the Jewish tradition, so gloriously revealed in certain of the psalms; namely, a kind of drunken joy and surprise at the beauty and incomprehensible sublimity of this world, of which man can attain but a faint intimation." Indeed, the Jewish celebration of life is ebullient and hallowed. Eating and drinking, marriage, children, holidays, death—all are blessed, sanctified, and given meaning; all reflect God. Life, law, faith, tradition, and history come together in daily ritual. God's creations are good; they are to be enjoyed.

WHAT DOES IT MEAN TO BE A JEW? Here are words from a prayer for Rosh Hashanah, the Jewish New Year: "What does it mean to be a Jew? You shall be holy." To live a holy life, one must serve God, and one serves God by serving humanity—through kindness, ethical conduct, and social activism. In Judaism, it is believed that one has the moral imperative to improve things that are not right, to consider what must be done to advance the human condition.

Judaism is both a religion and a culture, so being Jewish means many things. In fact, one may be an atheist and still be culturally Jewish or have a Jewish identity. Jews are linked by history, language, lore, humor, and a homeland. Theirs is an ancestral heritage.

THE NEED FOR LAW. In Judaism, humanity's essence is considered both human and divine, but the need for restraints, for law, is understood. Consider the power of the Ten Commandments, the fundamental moral code given to Moses by God on Mount Sinai (Deuteronomy 5:6–22), later absorbed by Christianity. Here we can appreciate the Jewish influence on the ethical foundation of Western civilization.

Attending a synagogue service, one would see the Torah, a physical scroll, brought forth; it consists of the Pentateuch, the first five books of the Bible: Genesis, Exodus, Leviticus, Numbers, and Deuteronomy. The Torah contains 613 laws, all meant to guide the Jew in how to live in a fruitful, life-affirming, lawful, and holy manner. The Tanakh consists of the Torah, the Prophets, and the Writings. This is what Christians refer to as the Old Testament, which Christianity and Judaism share. In addition, Jews are guided by the Talmud, a vast collection of rabbinical teachings and lore. The Kabbalah are the mystical teachings, of which the Zohar (The Way of Splendor) is considered the most important. In ancient times these mystical teachings were kept secret. Today people from various backgrounds study them.

A CHOSEN PEOPLE. The Jewish people were chosen when they answered God's call. The call came to them through Moses at the time of the great Exodus, when God led the Israelites out of slavery under the Egyptian pharaoh. This notion of a chosen people has been puzzling or confusing to many, but it is critical to understand that most Jews do not consider themselves chosen because they were more deserving than others. Answering the call—accepting the covenant offered by God—required them to uphold the highest spiritual example as servants of God, and many Jews feel the call is still available for all people. The example is to be offered humbly: "As water flows from the high ground and settles in the low, so are the words of the Torah alive only in the humble" (from the Talmud).

With the covenant come great blessing and great burden, for the Jewish people are called to radiate light for the world by virtue of example, even through suffering. The words of Anne Frank come to mind: "If we bear always all this suffering and if there are still Jews left, when it is over, then Jews, instead of being doomed, will be held up as an example. Who knows, it might even be our religion from which the world and all peoples learn good, and for that reason only do we have to suffer now." It seems to me that to be a light unto the world is a call and a challenge for all religions. Even after enormous persecution and suffering, Jewish faith remains strong and alive—a testament to Jewish spirit, certainly, and some would say a miracle.

Marriage in the Jewish Tradition

Though in Judaism it is not a sacrament, as in Christianity or Hinduism, the act of marriage is considered a peak moment, a sacred experience, and a mitzvah—a holy obligation. It is said that when a man or woman marries, he or she is forgiven all past sins. As does the high holy day of Yom Kippur, the wedding day brings atonement, and bride and groom begin life together in a state of sanctified purity. Everyone rejoices, as each marriage represents a reenactment of the first marriage, between Adam and Eve. The bride's maid of honor and groom's best man are said to represent the first witnesses—the angels Gabriel and Michael.

Rabbis have long considered marriage to be divinely ordained. This is the concept of *b'shert*, "meant to be," a common phrase in Jewish daily life. Judaism accepts divorce as a fact of life; when a marriage dissolves, however, the Talmud says, "even the altar sheds tears."

Practical Wedding Considerations and Customs

THE CELEBRANT. You may decide to have a rabbi perform your ceremony. Although marriage between Jews and non-Jews is opposed by all major Jewish groups, most allow a rabbi to make his or her own decision about officiating at an interfaith wedding. Conservative rabbis will not perform an interfaith ceremony; sometimes, however, a rabbi who will not perform the actual ceremony will agree to give a blessing. To find a rabbi, try calling a Reformed or Reconstructionist temple in your area. If you live in a major city, you may not have much difficulty locating one who will serve you. Cantors also can marry a couple, and they are often happy to perform ceremonies (they will sing in Hebrew).

A second option: You may have dual celebrants—a rabbi and a priest, for example, or a rabbi and a minister. If one of you is Hindu or Muslim, however, it may be extremely difficult to find a rabbi who will co-officiate. If you are Greek Orthodox, Evangelical Christian, or Muslim, a member of your clergy will not officiate. When choosing dual celebrants, be sure to put them in touch with each other so that they may collaborate to ensure a smooth-running ceremony without any unwanted surprises! And, of course, an interfaith minister, Unitarian Universalist minister, or civil officiant will be happy to perform your ceremony.

THE SETTING. Historically, Jewish weddings took place out-of-doors, "under the stars." Today any appropriate site is suitable. In Judaism, the place is made sacred by intention and action. A wedding in which one partner is Jewish should not be held on a major holiday, such as Rosh Hashanah, Yom Kippur, Sukkot, or Passover. Technically, weddings should not take place between sundown on Friday and sundown on the following Saturday evening, the duration of the Sabbath, and these may be important considerations if either you or your guests are observant.

THE CHUPPAH. Jewish weddings take place under a chuppah, a canopy that consists of four poles with a cloth cover. The chuppah is steeped in history and rich in symbolism. In ancient times it was set up in the desert as a place for the couple to consummate their marriage; later it became the enclosure under which the rabbi, the couple, and their families and friends held a formal ceremony. If you have a chuppah at your wedding, you may choose to explain its significance. We have listed some poetic explanations you may want to use. At a Jewish-Hindu ceremony, I like to point out the correlation between the chuppah and the Hindu mandap, for which the spiritual meaning is very much the same.

Chuppahs can range from the plain to the elaborate, from the traditional to the creative. The cloth covering on a chuppah can be an item of personal significance—an embroidered tablecloth that belonged to a beloved grandmother, for example. Religiously the covering would be a tallith, or Jewish prayer shawl. Although many interfaith couples select a more neutral cloth, sometimes a tallith is quite appropriate. At one wedding the couple used a tallith belonging to the groom's grandfather, who was dying of cancer; we made special mention of its ownership during the service, which meant a lot to the family. One of the most interesting chuppahs I have seen, made of intricate ironwork decorated with flowers and hung with a shimmering cloth, was created by a sculptor as a gift to the bride and groom. You can have a chuppah constructed by your florist, make one yourself, or simply rent one.

A chuppah can be erected anywhere. It can be stationary or a part of the procession and handheld during the ceremony. If you plan to have the chuppah walked in and held throughout the service, I strongly suggest that the poles reach the floor to reduce strain on the arms of those supporting it! To be a chuppah bearer is considered an honor, one usually reserved for close family and friends. In an interfaith ceremony, I always suggest inviting members from both families to be chuppah bearers.

THE KETUBAH. The ketubah, the Jewish marriage contract, was originally a legal document—a revolutionary one at that, for it served to ensure a woman's rights. Today it's a spiritual covenant between the bride and groom, a reminder of their love, and a sentimental keepsake. The couple usually read and sign the ketubah immediately before the ceremony. At an interfaith wedding, it can be signed either before or after the ceremony, and you might wish to make that decision based on whether you want to see each other before the service begins. The ketubah can be signed in conjunction with the marriage license. Two witnesses and your celebrant must be present. Ketubahs can be quite beautiful; many couples frame theirs to display in their homes.

THE WEARING OF YARMULKES. The yarmulke, or kippa, serves as a personal reminder to its wearer of God's presence. Whether a Jewish groom or members of his family will wear yarmulkes at an interfaith service depends largely on his preference and family history. It is not obligatory for a non-Jewish groom or non-Jewish male guests to wear yarmulkes.

THE PROCESSIONAL AND PLACEMENT OF THE PARTICIPANTS. Typically in the Jewish tradition the groom walks in accompanied by both his parents, and the bride walks in accompanied by both parents. Though in the Christian tradition the bride's mother is formally seated by an usher or family member while the bride ends the procession escorted by her father, many Christian mothers love the idea of walking their daughters down the aisle on equal footing with their husbands!

If the chuppah is to be carried in, the bearers will walk it down the aisle first and take their places. Here is a typical procession: After the chuppah is in place, the groom's grandparents and then the bride's grandparents walk in (a widow may be escorted by an usher) and sit in the front row; the ushers, followed by the best man, followed by the groom and his parents enter; the bridesmaids, followed by the maid or matron of honor, followed by the bride and her parents enter. The bride stands to the groom's right. (In a Christian wedding, the bride stands to his left.)

Think about what will feel right for you. A non-Jewish groom may prefer to enter from the side with his best man and the celebrant and wait up front while his parents are seated. In any case, the arrival of the bride is always the grand finale. Christian custom has all guests stand as she walks down the aisle; in Jewish custom, all remain seated. Whether everyone stands should be the bride's decision. She must decide in which scenario she will be most comfortable, because all eyes will be on her. You may wish to inform your celebrant whether guests should stand or remain seated, as he will be the one to tell them to rise.

THE YICHUD. Traditionally, the just-married bride and groom walk from the ceremony to a private room, where they spend a short time alone before greeting their guests. This is the yichud—the union or bonding period—and it's a custom that many interfaith couples (Jewish or not) find appealing. It is an opportunity to take twenty minutes or so to gather yourselves and simply bask in each other's presence. This is a moment to allow yourselves to feel the power of what has just transpired. Arrange for champagne, if you wish, and some scrumptious edibles—this may be the only opportunity you'll have to relax and eat!—and station your best man and maid or matron of honor at the door to ensure your privacy.

For the Ceremony: A Menu of Elements

OPENING WORDS. *You may want your celebrant to include one of the following in her opening remarks.*

∽ An old Jewish legend states: Two souls are created in heaven, and an angel cries out: "This man is made for this woman." Should these two souls, these two people meet on earth and recognize each other for who they truly are, they will fall in love and become as one, working together in unison. Then no hardship can alter the strength of their enduring love. Everything they do shall succeed.

∽ God creates new worlds constantly. In what way? By causing new marriages to take place. [From the Kabbalah, Zohar 1.89a]

∽ From every human being there rises a light that reaches straight to heaven. When two souls who are destined for each other find one another, their streams of light flow together and a single brighter light goes forth from their united being. [From the Ba'al Shem Tov, founder of Hasidism, the eighteenth-century mystical revival movement. This quotation is often used in a Christian-Jewish ceremony with the lighting of the unity candle. For a humanist ceremony, change "heaven" to "the heavens."]

∽ He who loves his wife as himself; who honors her more than himself; who rears his children in the right path, and who marries them off at the proper time of their life, concerning him it is written: And you will know that your home is at peace. [From the Talmud. This quotation can be adapted to read, He who loves his wife as himself, she who loves her husband as herself, who rear their children . . .]

∽ Whenever two people begin to write their lives' poem on a single leaf of hammered paper, the angels sing. [From James R. Scher]

INVOCATION. *After the opening words, your celebrant may offer an invocation or blessing. Following are some suggestions, including the Hebrew versions.*

Incorporating Hebrew passages in your ceremony is a personal decision, and it can be a touchy matter. Jewish families I've worked with have had varying feelings on the subject. For many the use of Hebrew links them to their heritage and their ancestors; others feel it is not integral to their lives. Its use would be inappropriate in a Jewish-Muslim wedding or in a Jewish-Christian wedding if the

Christian side is highly conservative. Of course, there are always exceptions, and this is a matter to discuss between yourselves and with your celebrant.

It may feel right to include some Hebrew passages if they are balanced elsewhere during the ceremony with verses or blessings in the language of the non-Jewish spouse—Sanskrit, for example, or Greek, Chinese, Farsi, or Arabic. If you decide to use Hebrew and your celebrant does not speak it, it's most appropriate and wonderfully inclusive to invite a family member or friend to recite those portions.

   Mi Adir el hakol,
Mi Baruch el hakol
Mi Gadol el hakol
Hey' varesh h'atan v'hakallah.

Splendor is upon everything
Blessing is upon everything
Who is full of this abundance
Bless this groom and bride. [From *The New Jewish Wedding* by Anita
   Diamant]
   Blessed be you who have come here in dedication to all that is loving, good and sacred.
   May the source of life sustain you in life.
May all that is noble and true in the universe
inspire your lives together and bring peace to all humankind. [From
   Celebrating Interfaith Marriages by Rabbi Devon Lerner]
   B'roochim Habaim B'shem Adonai
May you who come in the name of God be forever blessed.

EXPLANATION OF THE CHUPPAH. *You may wish to have your celebrant explain the meaning of the chuppah with one of the following passages:*

   Today we bless this union under a wedding canopy, called a chuppah in the Jewish tradition. It represents shelter, sanctity, and peace. The four poles correspond to the four directions, as the couple's love spans to the four corners of the earth. The chuppah is the house of promises. It is the home of hope. [These last two lines are from Debra Cash's poem "The Succah and the Chuppah."]

   The bride and groom stand before us under a wedding canopy, called a chuppah, in the Jewish tradition of shelter, home, and peace. Your lives are part of their home, a home of hope, a safe haven, symbolized by the chuppah. Here, in part, are the words of the poet Marge Piercy. [The poem itself may be read by an honored guest or family member, in which case your celebrant may announce who will do the reading.]

The chuppah stands on four poles.
The home has its four corners.
The chuppah stands on four poles.
The marriage stands on four legs.
Four points loose the winds
that blow on the walls of the house,
the south wind that brings the warm rain,
the east wind that brings the cold rain,
the north wind that brings the cold sun
and the snow, the long west wind
bringing the weather off the far plains. . . .
O my love O my love we dance
under the chuppah standing over us
like an animal on its four legs,
like a table on which we set our love
as a feast, like a tent
under which we work
not safe but no longer solitary
in the searing heat of our time.

∾ Surrounded by loved ones whose joy and prayers are with you, you stand at this chuppah, a symbol of your new home. Its four sides are open, symbolizing the importance of community and of participation in each other's lives. Friends and family fill the home. May your home be a shelter against the storms, a haven for peace, a stronghold of faith and love. [From *Celebrating Interfaith Marriages* by Rabbi Devon Lerner]

READING. *The following Bible reading would be appropriate.*

∾ My Beloved lifts up his voice, he says to me:

Come then, my Love, my Lovely, come. My dove, hiding in the clefts of the rock, in the coverts of the cliff, show me your face, let me hear your voice; for your voice is sweet and your face is beautiful.

My Beloved is mine and I am his. He said to me: Set me like a seal on your heart, like a seal on your arm. For love is infinitely strong. . . . A flame of the Lord himself. Love no flood can quench, no torrents drown. [Adapted from the Song of Songs]

BLESSING OVER THE WINE. *The kiddush cup—kiddush means "sanctification"—will be held up by your celebrant, who explains its meaning and offers a blessing, then hands it to the bride and groom, who each in turn drink from it. Wine and sanctification are associated with all Jewish celebrations; where there is wine, there is blessing and great joy. Many brides and grooms purchase a special cup to be kept for sentimental reasons; others may use a family heirloom.*

The blessing over the wine is usually done as the last of the seven Jewish wedding blessings. Alternatively, in an interfaith service, you may perform this ritual on its own. Following are suggested explanations and blessings. (You may need to adjust the sequence of events in your ceremony to create the optimum flow and rhythm.)

∞ This cup of wine is symbolic of the cup of life. As you share the one cup of wine, you undertake to share all that the future may bring. All the sweetness life's cup may hold for you should be sweeter because you drink it together; whatever drops of bitterness it may contain should be less bitter because you share them. [From *Celebrating Interfaith Marriages* by Rabbi Devon Lerner]

∞ In Judaism, wine is a symbol of the joy and richness of life. Of the sweetness of love. On this joyous occasion, we make a toast together— *l'khayim*—to life and to love! May you find life's joys heightened and its bitterness sweetened. May there always be peace in your home and confidence in your hearts. And as you share wine together from this cup, so may you share joy and fulfillment from the cup of life. [Adapted from the Central Conference of American Rabbis, 1988; provided by Rabbi Joel Braude]

∞ Baruch ata Adonai, Eloheynu Melech Ha-olam, borey p'ree ha-gaffen.

We praise God, Creator of the fruit of the vine.

∞ Holy One of the Blessing, your presence fills creation, forming the fruit of the vine.

CIRCLING. *Circling, in which the bride walks around the groom three or seven times, is not a common feature in most modern interfaith ceremonies, but if yours is a Jewish-Hindu or Jewish–Greek Orthodox union, you may wish to include it. Correlation can be made with the Hindu tradition of circling of the sacred fire in the seven steps or with the Greek Orthodox tradition of circling the altar three times. In addition to describing the Hindu or Greek Orthodox significance, your celebrant can offer the following explanation:*

∞ It is an old Jewish ritual for the bride to circle the groom three or seven times; thus, according to the Kabbalists, Jewish mystics, were the lovers helped to enter the spheres of each other's souls. Today, [bride] and [groom] will circle each other three times, as we listen to these words from Hosea:

I will betroth you to me forever;

I will betroth you to me in righteousness and in justice, in steadfast love, and in mercy.

I will betroth you to me in faithfulness.

EXCHANGE OF RINGS. *The exchange of rings is a significant element of the Jewish ceremony, for in Jewish law a verbal declaration of marriage is not legally* *binding until a ring, or something of nominal value, is given to the bride. A wonderfully romantic Jewish tradition that many interfaith couples have incorporated has the bride and groom put their rings on their index fingers. The celebrant can explain with the words here.*

Chapter 7 provides a selection of ring vows. Here are two simple ones often used in Jewish ceremonies. (The couple repeat the vows after the celebrant.)

∞ It is an old Jewish custom first to place the ring on the index finger, for it is believed that there lies an artery that leads directly to the heart. [Bride] and [groom] hereby join their hearts. The ring is then moved to the ring finger signifying acceptance.

∞ I am my beloved's and my beloved is mine.

∞ I will betroth you to me forever.

I will betroth you to me in righteousness and in justice, in steadfast love and in mercy.

I will betroth you to me in faithfulness. [From Hosea]

THE SEVEN BLESSINGS. *In a Jewish ceremony, the bride and groom are bestowed with seven wedding blessings—a way of wishing the couple well, expressing thoughts that they themselves consider significant, and praising God. If you include the seven blessings, your celebrant might offer a brief explanation to your guests, such as one of the two versions presented here.*

Following the explanation, the seven can be read by the celebrant, or by family members or friends, alternating lines. The three versions here are samples of, first, a humanist and personal blessing; second, a spiritual or religious blessing; and, third, a contemporary blessing. You may want to write your own!

∞ In Jewish tradition, the bride and groom receive seven wedding blessings. Seven is considered a mystical number. The Kabbalists, the Jewish mystics, believed there are seven spheres of the soul and seven heavens. [Bride] and [groom], as we recite these blessings, we pray that you will enter into each other's souls.

∞ It is customary in Jewish tradition that the bride and groom are bestowed with seven blessings. These blessings represent [bride's] and [groom's] hopes for the future.

∞ May your marriage enrich your lives.

May you work together to build a relationship of substance and quality.

May the honesty of your communication build a foundation of understanding, connection, and trust.

May you respect each other's individual personality and philosophy, and give each other room to grow and fulfill each other's dreams.

May your sense of humor and playful spirit continue to enliven your relationship.

May you understand that neither of you is perfect: you are both subject to human frailties; and may your love strengthen when you fall short of each other's expectations.

May you be "best friends," better together than either of you are apart. [From *Celebrating Interfaith Marriages* by Rabbi Devon Lerner; blessings created and provided courtesy of Ron Shaich and Nancy Antonoacci, married 1998]

    ~ Blessed be God whose name is Peace. May this marriage experience the peace of complete sharing and tranquillity.

Blessed be God whose name is Unity. May this marriage find its sacredness in the commitment of One to the Other.

Blessed be God whose name is Justice. May this marriage seek the ultimate right and respect of the right of compromise.

Blessed be God whose name is Wisdom. May this marriage compose a new chapter in sharing each other's tradition, husband and wife learning from each other.

Blessed be God whose name is Unique. May this marriage be special in its dreams to be fulfilled with love.

Blessed is the Creator of Celebration. May this marriage be celebrated by this gathering and throughout the world.

We praise God, Creator of the fruit of the vine. [Adapted from *Jewish Life Cycle Events: A Treasury for Rabbis,* the Central Conference of American Rabbis, provided by Rabbi Joel Braude]

    ~ May you be blessed with love. May understanding bring a deep and abiding peace into your lives, fostering a love that is not only passionate but serene. May this love between you be strong and enduring.

May you be blessed with wisdom. May you continually learn from one another and from the world. Together, may you grow, deepening your knowledge and understanding of each other and of your journey through life.

May you be blessed with community. May you always be blessed with the awareness that you are an essential part of a circle of family and friends. May there always be within this group a sense of mutual love, trust, support and respect.

May you be blessed with art and beauty. May your creative aspirations and experiences find expression and bring you joy and fulfillment.

May you be blessed with health. May life bestow upon you wholeness of mind, body, and spirit. May you live long that you may share many happy years together.

May you be blessed with the experience of nature. May nature in her magnificence continue to inspire you and bring you a sense of transcendence. May the elements of earth, air, fire, and water sustain you and heal you.

May you be blessed with the fruit of the earth. This wine of which you will partake was produced by the earth and perfected by time. So may your bond here represented by this gift of the earth be likewise perfected by the time of your years tgether. [Created and provided courtesy of Brian Pekarsky and Chriselle Tidrick, from their wedding ceremony]

CLOSING BLESSING. *Here are two suggestions.*

∽ [Bride] and [groom], as you go into the world as husband and wife, we call upon four angels to assist you upon the journey of your life together. To your right shall walk the angel Gabriel, who will give you strength. To your left is Michael, who shall protect you. Behind you is Raphael, who shall heal you. And directly in front of you is Uriel, whose name means "the Light of God". He will guide your way. [Provided by Rabbi Joseph Gelberman, "The Blessing of the Four Archangels"; this would be appropriate for a Jewish-Christian ceremony.]

∽ May God bless and keep you.

May God's countenance shine upon you and be gracious unto you.

May God's presence be with you and grant you peace. *[This may be used as either an invocation or a closing blessing.]*

THE BREAKING OF THE GLASS. *The breaking of the glass is a joyous ritual and perhaps the best known element of the Jewish wedding. It is a tradition that was originally nonreligious and was later given poetic and religious interpretation. The glass, which can be a long-stemmed wineglass that is easily broken, is wrapped in a white cloth. The celebrant speaks of its significance and then places it on the floor. The groom swiftly (and often fiercely!) steps on it. Upon hearing the distinct crushing sound, everyone in the congregation shouts "Mazel tov!"—"congratulations" and "good luck!" The ceremony thus ends with an explosion of good wishes.*

The interpretations for the breaking of the glass accumulated over the years are numerous. The following explanations work well for interfaith unions.

∽ The traditional breaking of the glass is a joyous ritual. It indicates that marriage is a transforming and irrevocable experience, one that leaves the couple forever changed. [Bride] and [groom], this glass is broken with our implied prayer: "[Bride] and [groom], may your bond of love be as difficult to break as it would be to put together the pieces of this glass." When it is broken, we invite you all to shout, "Mazel tov," which means congratulations and good luck, in your very loudest and happiest voices! [Adapted from

Celebrating Interfaith Marriages by Rabbi Devon Lerner and *The New Jewish Wedding* by Anita Diamant]

∞ The breaking of the glass is a reminder that sweetness coexists with sorrow. Today, we celebrate the tremendous joy of this marriage. At the same time we remember the sorrows that exist in the world. We break this glass in the prayer and hope that through love this marriage will help break down the barriers between people of different religions and cultures. We break this glass for peace. [Adapted from *Interfaith Wedding Ceremonies* by Joan Hawxhurst]

■ ■ ■

Humankind has not woven the web of life. We are but one thread within it.
Whatever we do to the web we do to ourselves.
All things are bound together. All things connect.
—Chief Seattle

Native American Spirituality

Native American spirituality is rooted in a profound sense of the interconnectedness of all living things—animals and birds, the two-legged and four-legged ones, the winged ones; trees and other plants; men and women. The sense of interconnectedness applies also to the life-giving elements of air, water, and soil. Here lies the belief in the existence of the Great Spirit, the formless and sacred force that permeates the universe. All life is considered sacred. All are to live in harmony. Giving thanks to the Great Spirit for its/his/her gifts is essential. Prayer, ritual, fasting, and meditation are important to the keeping of a sacred life. As human beings, we are considered responsible for ensuring the lasting welfare of all forms of living things.

Given these basic tenets, along with deep respect for the earth, it is easy to see why many in our increasingly ecologically minded society are drawn to Native American spirituality and thinking. Here body and spirit are connected, being one with all life. It is said that Native Americans love the earth as a newborn baby loves the sound of his mother's heartbeat.

About 2 million Native Americans live in North America; perhaps half today also identify themselves at least nominally as Christian. Among the tribes and nations, traditions vary according to language, history, and environment. Native Americans continue to honor the sacred rites that have influenced and indeed benefited so many non–Native Americans. Many feel our indigenous population can teach us the balance that our Western society so badly needs.

Native American Elements Appropriate
for an Interfaith Ceremony

THE SETTING. You may hold your wedding outdoors, facing east if possible. One traditional thought, which your celebrant can mention at the opening of the ceremony, states that the sun is a manifestation of the Great Spirit, the sacred source of all life. Facing east, where the sun rises, signals hope for the union about to take place.

On a table or altar, you may place sage, sweet grass, cedar, corn, feathers, a jug of water, a fire—all have symbolic meaning, such as purification, in Native American tradition. You may also place there tied bundles or "sticks" of sacred herbs, to be used in the smudging ritual described in the next section.

DRESS. In the custom of certain tribes and nations, the bride and groom include in their dress or in the setting the following four colors, representing the four directions: black for the north, blue for the south, white for the east, and yellow for the west.

MUSIC. Drums, flutes, and rattles are often used during ceremonial events. You might wish to have live drumming or playing of the cedar flute during your procession. Drums in particular are considered sacred in many tribes and nations. Black Elk, a Sioux holy man born in the midnineteenth century, explained the importance of the drum: "It is because the round form of the drum represents the whole universe, and its steady strong beat is the pulse, the heart, throbbing at the center of the universe."

For the Ceremony: A Menu of Elements

THE WASHING OF THE HANDS. *You may choose to begin your ceremony with a symbolic act of purification, the traditional washing of hands. Your celebrant can offer water, which you in turn pour over each other's hands in silent prayer.*

SMUDGING. *Smudging, or "sweeping the smoke," is a simple but powerful Native American purification ritual, meant to clear away negative energies. Sage, considered the strongest cleansing herb, is the traditional choice, though cedar or sweet grass may also be used. Bundles of these herbs are bound together with cotton thread; smudge sticks can also be purchased. The smudge stick can be kept on the altar inside a shell or ceramic pot.*

At the smudging (which can take place toward the beginning of the ceremony, perhaps after the opening words), the herbs are lit with matches and burned until they give off clouds of smoke. Prayers may be offered silently or aloud. Then, either the celebrant or a designated person of honor "bathes" the couple in the purifying smoke. The celebrant first offers the stick to the four corners or directions; then he waves the stick about the bride and groom, starting from the lower bodies and working up to the heads. Sacred intent is paramount in this ancient ritual. Your celebrant might offer the following explanation:

∽ We shall open this ceremony with the Native American tradition of smudging. This is an act of purification, of cleansing. Sage is considered a sacred plant. It is. offered now to the four corners of the earth. All thoughts, all energies are purified and transformed—from the negative to the positive, from darkness to light, from fear to love, and from disharmony to peace.

READINGS, BLESSINGS, AND PRAYERS. *These lovely passages are extremely popular with many couples of all backgrounds. You may wish to include one or more in your ceremony.*

∽ Now you will feel no rain
For each of you will be shelter to the other.
Now you will feel no cold,
For each of you will be warmth to the other.
Now there is no more loneliness,
Now you are two bodies,
But there is only one life before you.
Go now to your dwelling place
To enter into the days of your life together
And may your days be good and long upon the earth. *[An Apache
    wedding prayer. This works best as a closing blessing.]*
∽ May you have the strength of eagle's wings,
and the faith and courage to fly to new heights;
and the wisdom of the universe to carry you there. *[A Native American
    blessing. This would be a lovely conclusion to the celebrant's address.]*
∽ May you walk in beauty.
Beauty before you,
Beauty behind you,
Beauty above and below you.
It is finished in beauty.
It is finished in beauty. *[Adapted from a Navajo song. This works well as a
    blessing after the vows.]*
∽ My feet shall run because of you.
My feet dance because of you.
My heart shall beat because of you.
My eyes see because of you.
My mind thinks because of you.
And I shall love because of you. *[An Eskimo blessing. One groom
    incorporated this passage into his vows.]*

❰❱ God in heaven above, please protect [bride] and [groom] as they pledge their hearts and lives together. We honor all you created. We honor mother-earth, and ask for this marriage to be abundant and grow stronger through the seasons. We honor fire, and ask that this union be warm and glowing with love in their hearts. We honor wind, and ask that they will sail through life safe and calm as in our father's arms. We honor water, to clean and soothe their relationship that it may never thirst for love. With all the forces of the universe you created, we pray for harmony and true happiness as they forever grow young together. [A Cherokee prayer, adapted]

■ ■ ■

We human beings, not only human beings but everything existing in this
world, are one of the cells which form this great universe.
—Hitoshi Iwasaki, a Shinto priest

Shinto

Although Shinto, the indigenous faith of the Japanese people, is an ancient system of belief, its origin cannot be traced to any one point in time or founding father. Before the fifth century, its myths and rituals were transmitted only orally; it has no sacred scripture. Over the centuries Japan has adopted religions and beliefs from other countries such as Buddhism, Christianity, and Confucianism, and many Japanese combine practices from several. Yet Shinto—the word means "the way of the gods"—remains Japan's unique path. More than a religion, it is an amalgam of attitudes and ideas that have become integral to the Japanese sensibility.

The kami way. Kami is spirit, divine essence, and that which is noble and sacred. It is within us, and it transcends us. It is present in all beautiful and powerful places—in the sun, mountains, trees, flowers, rocks, rivers, animals, wind, and rain. Kami resides in the spirits of our ancestors; it is displayed in creativity and growth; today it includes the concepts of justice, order, and blessing. A central aspect of Shinto is harmony with the spirits, and Japan is home to some eighty thousand shrines, visited by 80 million Japanese each year.

In Japan, Shinto remains the wellspring for many seasonal rites, thanksgiving rituals, blessings, and rites of passage. Many Japanese homes also have a kami shelf, a private shrine that may be in place alongside the family Buddhist altar. Yet the kami (the word is both singular and plural) are not necessarily depicted as forms; often the representation may be a mirror, reflecting the brightness and purity that is the natural order of the universe. Indeed, some Shinto scholars believe that a specific image of a deity will actually interfere with a worshiper's true communion.

THE WORLD'S UNSPEAKABLE BEAUTY. Another core aspect of Shinto is affinity with nature, absolute love of the exquisite beauty that permeates Japan's landscape. In his book *The Way of The Kami,* the Reverend Yukitaka Yamamoto writes, "To be fully alive is to have an aesthetic perception of life because a major part of the world's goodness lies in its often unspeakable beauty." Even today, in this highly industrialized country, aesthetic beauty is revered. "In traditional rock gardening, flower arranging, the tea ceremony, and poetry, Japanese artists continue to honor the simple and natural," write Mary Pat Fisher and Robert Luyster in *Living Religions.* "If a rock is placed just right in a garden, it seems alive, radiating its natural essence. In a tea ceremony, great attention is paid to each natural delight, from the purity of water poured from a wooden ladle to the genuineness of the clay vessels."

We human beings, ourselves kami or potential kami, are by nature innocent and pure. In Shinto, there is no concept of sin, but through evil or unkind behaviors we sully ourselves. Cleansing rituals and blessings, such as the New Year's purification ritual and celebration, are required to restore our purity.

Practical Wedding Considerations and Customs

In Japan today many couples have two wedding ceremonies, a Western-style one and a Shinto ceremony, the heart of which is the elegant sake ceremony, the san-san-kudo. Sometimes couples elect to perform the sake ceremony at the reception instead of during the wedding service. The bride then may wear a white, Western-style gown for the service and change into a traditional kimono for the reception.

If you are a Japanese-American couple, or an interfaith couple including one of Japanese heritage, you may prefer to honor Japanese tradition, including the san-san-kudo, within the format of a Western-style ceremony. Here is a Japanese song (adapted from *Into the Garden: A Wedding Anthology*) that couples sometimes print on their programs:

The bride and groom
Sip about one dewdrop
Of the butterfly wine.

THE SETTING. To reflect the Japanese Shinto sensibility and incorporate the sake ceremony, you will want to arrange an altar that is simple and pleasing to the eye. On the altar should be a sanpo, a small platform or base, to hold three stacked cups—large, medium, and small—and a flask of sake. You may also place on the altar tamagushi, sacred leaves usually tied to a paper stem that are said to connect humans to the kami and that will be used as offerings toward the end of the ceremony, and a haraigushi, a "purification wand" made with strips of paper. Many couples like the ritual of presenting orchids or other flowers to their parents at the part of the service honoring family. These symbolic gifts can also be waiting on the altar.

Suspended above the altar, you may want to mount a shimenawa—the traditional, very beautiful thick woven rope from which hang folded flax pendants. Shimenawa hang at the entrances to many Japanese shrines and smaller versions above kami shelves in private homes; symbolically, they indicate sacred places where kami are believed to dwell. On the pendants, horizontal braided straw represents clouds; diagonal flowing strips signify rain; and stacked zigzag rectangles of folded paper stand for thunder. As the bride and groom stand below the shimenawa, they are said to be purified and blessed. The shimenawa and the other items mentioned can be purchased at Japanese stores.

THE PROCESSION. You may be interested in following this traditional Shinto procession: A young girl, referred to as miko, heads the wedding party; after her, the bride and groom enter, the groom to the bride's right; the best man and matron of honor (usually a married couple) come next, followed by the groom's parents, the bride's parents, the groom's relatives, and the bride's relatives. At the last, the celebrant enters. Traditionally, all stand and bow as a Shinto priest makes his way down the aisle. When I have conducted Japanese ceremonies, it is I who bow to all. And they usually bow in return!

For the Ceremony: A Menu of Elements

PURIFICATION RITUAL. *The celebrant symbolically purifies the energy around the couple by waving the haraigushi, the purification wand.*

PRAYER: *After the opening words, you may wish to have your celebrant offer the following Japanese ritual prayer.*

 We respectfully pray:

O Supreme Ruler of Heaven,

O sun and moon and stars,

O King of the East on the left,

And Queen of the West on the right,

O five rulers of the five directions,

O four seasons and four weathers:

We present to you a man and woman of happiness

And pray you remove all disasters.

Grant them abundance.

Grant them peace. [Adapted from *Norito* by Donald L. Philippi]

HONORING OF FAMILY. *Honoring of ancestors is central to the Shinto and Japanese culture, and most appropriate at your ceremony. After the celebrant has acknowledged these individuals, she may conclude with the words "On this, your children's wedding day, we thank you. We honor you" as she bows reverently to each parent. The quotation from Native American writer Linda Hogan (page 88) works very well here.*

The celebrant then can give orchids to the bride and groom to present to their parents.

SAN-SAN-KUDO, THE SAKE CEREMONY. *The san-san-kudo often takes place after the celebrant's address to the bride and groom. The miko steps forward to pour sake into each of the cups. You may choose to have a family member perform the ritual or do it yourselves. Receiving the small cup from the miko, the groom touches his lips to it twice; on the third touch he sips. The bride then does the same with the same cup. The middle cup follows this form, but the bride begins. Finally, the groom begins the last round with the large cup. In a traditional ceremony, the family then take part, with the bride and groom offering the cups to the groom's father, groom's mother, bride's father, bride's mother, best man, matron of honor, and other relatives. In a small ceremony, including the family in this manner is feasible. In a larger ceremony, you will have to limit the participants.*

The celebrant can introduce the ritual with the following words.

∽ You are about to witness a sake ceremony, or san-san-kudo. This is the heart of the Japanese marriage ceremony. Literally translated it means "three, three, nine times." The bride and groom will take turns sipping three cups of sake in rounds of three for a total of nine. This is a powerful gesture, for by sipping from the cups, the bride and groom are in essence taking their marriage vows. By drinking from the small cup, they give thanks to their ancestors for nurturing them, protecting them, and bringing them together. By drinking from the medium-size cup, they promise they will live and work together for the rest of their lives. By drinking from the large cup, they pray that their home will be a happy place filled with children. Each gesture is done with reverence and devotion. The san-san-kudo is carried out in silence. The silence is sacred.

RITUAL OFFERINGS. *The celebrant hands the sacred leaves to the bride and groom, who bow to receive them and then place them on the altar. The ritual may be carried out in silence, or the celebrant can recite the following norito, which I have edited and adapted. At the conclusion of the ritual, the celebrant may clap twice; then the couple and the celebrant bow to one another.*

∽ Receive tranquilly, we pray, these noble offerings as offerings of peace, as offerings of plenty. Bless the home of the bride and groom as eternal and unmoving, prosper it as an abundant reign, and grant that their spirits may abide tranquilly in their abode. [Adapted from *Norito* by Donald L. Philippi]

PRONOUNCEMENT. *The following pronouncement may be appropriate. In a traditional Shinto ceremony, the bride and groom typically do not share the kiss after the pronouncement, but you may wish to include this delightful ritual.*

∽ [Bride] and [groom], you have exchanged sacred vows. You have shared in the ancient san-san-kudo, the sake ceremony. Therefore, by the power of your love and commitment to each other, in the presence of all your loved ones, and in the presence of your ancestors, I now pronounce you husband and wife.

CLOSING BLESSING. *Either of these blessings (the first is a Japanese norito, the second is an Apache prayer) would work well.*

∽ Bless them as unmoving and eternal.

May their lives flourish like luxuriant trees.

May they, bride and groom, together with heaven and earth, with the sun and the moon, continue to give out light and radiance.

Thus do we reverently pray. [Adapted from *Norito* by Donald L. Philippi]

∽ May the sun bring you energy by day,

May the moon softly restore you by night.

May the rain wash away your worries

And the breeze blow new strength into your being,

And all the days of your life may you walk gently through the world and know its beauty.

■   ■   ■

There is neither Hindu nor Mussulman [Muslim] so whose path shall I follow?
I shall follow God's path. God is neither Hindu nor Mussulman.
—Guru Nanak

Sikhism

These words from Guru Nanak, the founder of Sikhism, point to the powerful truth at the center of the Sikh's belief: There is one God, who is omnipotent and infinite; he is the only truth and ultimately beyond our understanding but felt in his creation if one seeks him. Call him what you will, the Sikh says; God may be worshiped under many names, for God is beyond names and forms, beyond time and space. Sikhs are literally "seekers or students of the truth." Here is the mool mantra, the sacred mantra that prefaces every Sikh prayer:

There is One Supreme Being
Truth Eternal is the Name,
Creator of all,
Fearless
Without rancor,
Timeless Form
Beyond the realm of incarnation,
Self-existent,
Revealed through Divine Grace.

Born around 1469 in the Punjab in Northern India, an area that was half Muslim and half Hindu, Guru Nanak was thirty-six when his life was transformed and his mission began. After a late-night immersion in a river, from which he did not emerge for three days, he was charged by God to redeem the world by teaching people to pray, to give charitably, and to live clean lives. Nanak thereafter traveled throughout India, the Himalayas, Afghanistan, Sri Lanka, and Arabia, spreading the message. A succession of gurus, or teachers, followed Nanak in the years after his death, the last being Guru Gobind Singh, who transferred authority from a human guru to the sacred scriptures, to be known as Sri Guru Granth Sahib. Considered the living presence of the Guru, the holy book is central to Sikh worship services and ceremonies.

Significantly, Sikhs believe in the equality of all peoples and reject discrimination on the basis of gender, caste, creed, race, or country. Heaven and hell, it is said, are states of mind. An individual's ultimate goal should be mystical union with the divine, which calls for subjugation of the ego. Today there are almost 23 million Sikhs in the world, with about 514,000 living in North America. Men and women both cover their heads, men with turbans and women with veils, baring their heads only to God.

Marriage in the Sikh Tradition

Marriage in Sikhism is regarded as a sacred bond, a holy union whereby two souls are united as one spirit within two bodies. This is a distinctive and quite lovely perspective, which is revealed throughout the ceremony: Marriage isn't a social contract but a joining that fuses a man's and a woman's souls, analogous to each individual's ultimate goal, which is union with God. God is the only husband, says Sikhism; the rest of us are his brides.

Practical Wedding Considerations and Customs

THE CELEBRANT AND THE SETTING. In the Sikh tradition, a marriage ceremony usually takes place in the morning, perhaps at the bride's home or at the gurdwara, the Sikh temple or place of worship. A Western-style service, even if heavily imbued with Sikh readings and customs, may be held in any appropriate venue. The celebrant may be a Sikh priest. Actually, any respected and learned Sikh man or woman, agreed upon by both families, may conduct the ceremony.

Traditionally, men and women guests wear head coverings, remove their shoes at the door of the place of worship, and take their seats on the floor. Not all these customs need be followed within Western interfaith ceremonies. It is courteous, however, for women to dress in dark, vibrant colors, such as red or purple, or at least to avoid wearing white, which is considered unlucky.

THE ALTAR. The central elements of a Sikh wedding include four readings, the lavans, and the circling of the bride and groom around the Guru Granth Sahib, the Sikh Holy Book. If you do wish to incorporate these practices—and if your Sikh family or relatives are deeply religious, they will expect to witness them, for only through these rites is the couple considered married—you will want to arrange to have the Holy Book set up on your table or altar in a central location.

Flower petals are showered on the couple as a final blessing from the guests. If you like, provide bowls of petals at the ends of the rows of seating, or they may be handed out in small bags as guests arrive. At the beginning of the service, the bride and groom may exchange flower garlands, and these should also be in place at the altar or table.

TYING OF THE SCARF. The bride's father brings with him (or it may be kept near the altar) a long pink or saffron scarf, which will be used to join bride and groom.

THE PROCESSION. The groom enters first, perhaps escorted by his parents or other relatives. Then, in royal fashion, the bride may walk in (her father may escort her), followed by a large contingent of female members of her family. She takes her place to the groom's left.

For the Ceremony: A Menu of Elements

INVOCATION. *The celebrant's invocation might include this quotation from Guru Amar Das, the central truth about the meaning of marriage. At this point the bride and groom may place garlands around each other's necks.*

∽ In the words of the Sikh Guru Amar Das: They are not said to be husband and wife who merely sit together. Rather, they alone are called husband and wife who have one soul in two bodies.

CELEBRANT'S ADDRESS. *According to Sikh tradition, the celebrant should explain to the couple the notion of a single soul in two bodies, which is to be achieved through love. Also, he may talk about the meaning of their union, what it signifies concerning their spiritual journey. He can speak to the bride and groom about the need for fidelity and loyalty, to each other and to their families, through sorrow and joy.*

TYING OF THE SCARF. *The bride's father comes forward, places one end of the scarf in the groom's right hand, passes it over his shoulder, and places the other end in the bride's hand. The celebrant may explain this ritual with the following words:*

∽ [Bride's] father will now join [bride] and [groom] with a scarf in the Sikh tradition. The scarf symbolizes the strength of their union, the uniting of two into one. Thus joined, [bride] and [groom] will take their vows.

THE CIRCLING OF THE GURU GRANTH SAHIB. *The circling of the Guru Granth Sahib corresponds to sacred vows in the Sikh religion. The bride and groom (he leads) circle the Holy Book four times clockwise; this circling is said to correspond to the four stages of spiritual development. You may wish to have your celebrant offer an explanation of the ritual. A respected member of the Sikh side of the families can read the holy verses. The verses may be sung or chanted, but typically they're read. Here is a suggested address for the celebrant, followed by a translation of the lavans.*

∽ The Guru Granth Sahib is the Holy Book for all Sikhs, considered a living sacred presence. In honor of [bride's or groom's] heritage, four verses of the levans, the marriage hymns, will be read by [state the relation of the reader to the bride or groom]. He is called the pathi, the man who reads the Holy Book.

After the reading of each verse, [bride] and [groom] will circle the Granth. The four verses reflect stages of spiritual development; they are considered the basis of a man's and woman's marriage. The first verse emphasizes the couple's duty to family and community. The second verse emphasizes the need to purify the mind through the abandoning of ego. The third verse refers to detachment from the mundane objects and interests of the world, and the fourth refers to the final stage of harmony and eternal love—human love that blends with the love of God. The teachings of Guru Nanak are recited. With our utmost reverence, let us now witness this ancient ritual.

[The designated person comes to the altar and reads the lavans, here adapted from the Sikh website.]

∞ Here is the first lavan. In the first round of the marriage ceremony, the Lord sets out His instructions for performing the daily duties of married life. By uttering the Gurbani—which means Guru, the Lord's Name, Divine Light, or the Word—embrace the righteous conduct of Dharma, or right living, and renounce sinful actions. Embrace the righteous conduct of Dharma, contemplate the Lord's Name. Worship and adore the Guru, the Perfect True Guru, and all your sins and misdeeds will be dispelled. By great good fortune, celestial bliss is attained, and the Lord seems sweet to the mind.

Servant Nanak proclaims that, by this first round, the marriage ceremony has begun.

In the second round of the marriage ceremony, the Lord leads you to meet the True Guru, the Primal Being. With the fear of God, the mind becomes fearless, and egotism is eradicated. In the fear of God, the Immaculate Lord, sing the glorious praises of the Lord, and behold the Lord's presence before you. The Lord, the Supreme Soul, is the Master of the Universe, pervading and permeating everywhere, fully filling all spaces. Deep within, and outside as well, there is only the One Lord. Meeting together, the humble servants of the Lord sing the songs of joy.

Servant Nanak proclaims that, in this, the second round of the marriage ceremony, the unstruck sound current of the Shabad resounds.

The third lavan. In the third round of the marriage ceremony, like the mind of a Bairaagee, a detached one, my mind is filled with the pleasure of Divine Love. Meeting with the humble saints of the Lord, I have found the Lord, by great good fortune. Singing the glorious praises of the Lord, and uttering the Divine Gurbani, I have found the Immaculate Lord. By great good fortune, I have found the humble saints, and I speak the Unspoken Speech of the Lord. The Name of the Lord vibrates and resounds within my heart; and by the destiny inscribed upon my forehead, I meditate on the Lord.

Servant Nanak proclaims that to attain the Lord, in this, the third round of the marriage ceremony, the mind is filled with the Bairaag.

And the fourth lavan. In the fourth round of the marriage ceremony, my mind has become peaceful; I have found the Lord. As Gurmukh, I have met Him, with intuitive ease; the Lord seems so sweet to my mind and body. The Lord seems so sweet; I am pleasant to my God; night and day, I lovingly focus my consciousness on the Lord. I have obtained my Lord, the fruit of my mind's desires; the Lord's Name resounds and resonates. The Lord, my Master, blends with His bride, and her heart blossoms forth.

Servant Nanak proclaims that in this, the fourth round of the marriage ceremony, the soul-bride has attained the Eternal Lord.

CLOSING BLESSING. *Before the closing blessing, it is in keeping with the traditional Sikh wedding ceremony for the celebrant to address the gathered family and guests regarding their roles in supporting the newly married couple. Of course, I like to consider this a "standard feature" of interfaith ceremonies. Universal blessings (see Chapter 7) are appropriate; the following sacred words may be included as well.*

༄ From the Guru Granth Sahib: Thou O God art my Father and Thou my Mother. Thou art the Giver of Peace to my soul and very life.

By great fortune, celestial bliss is attained and God seems sweet to the mind.

SPRINKLING OF FLOWER PETALS. *You may wish to incorporate the explanation of the symbolism of this ritual from the Hindu ceremony (see page 168). Or you may use this wording:*

༄ In the Sikh tradition, it is customary for the bride and groom to be sprinkled with the beauty and fragrance of flower petals. We now invite you, their beloved family and friends, to participate in this lovely tradition.

■   ■   ■

Sufism is the heart standing with God, with nothing in between.
—Abu Sa'id Abel-Khayr

Sufism

Sufism—*tasawouf* in Arabic—is the inward, mystical sect of Islam. To Sufis there is nothing but God. Nothing is real except the Real (God). Sufis yearn to have a direct encounter with God, and to reach oneness with God. Through prayer, contemplation, singing, dancing, whirling, and study, the Sufi hopes to achieve this end. Like a moth drawn to the flame, the Sufi wishes to be "burned" in ecstatic union with God.

We can intimate the mystical nature of Sufism through its poetry. The great Persian poets—the most famous being Jalal al-Din Rumi—have written of the ecstasy of union with God. Sufi poetry is exquisite love poetry, in which God is the Beloved. To be one with the Beloved is to be intoxicated in the supreme state where nothing exists beside God, beside love.

To experience closeness with God upon this earth, Sufis say, we must peel away 22,000 veils—the veils of ego, self-consciousness, craving, arrogance, illusion, expectation, and so on. Only then are we able to view the world with "the eye of the heart." Only then do we find out who we really are. In the words of Rumi, "The Beloved is all, the lover just a veil." And, "What makes the Sufi? Purity of heart." As they strive for the pure essence of self that leads to the experience of God, Sufis often engage in continual repetition of the powerful phrase "al ilaha illa 'llah" (There is no god but God). This is known as *dhikr* or "remembrance." To chant God's name over and over is to purify the self.

At the same time, Sufis are not called to withdraw from the world. Rather, the goal is to bring the substance of the ecstatic experience back into daily life, while one's feet are still firmly planted on the ground.

In the Sufi mystical experience, by whatever name and by whatever messenger, there remains only One God, One Truth, One Love. Hazrat Inayat Khan, the man who introduced Sufism to Europe (his son, Pir, brought it later to America), wrote, "When we are face to face with truth, the point of view of Krishna, Buddha, Christ or any other Prophet is the same. When we look at life from the top of the mountain, there is no limitation; there is the same immensity." And the words of the Persian poet Hafiz: "I am in love with every church and mosque and temple and any kind of shrine, because I know it is there that people say the different names of the One God."

Sufis date back to the time of Muhammad. Around him in his mosque in Medina gathered a group of intellectuals who had detached themselves from worldly concerns. These individuals came together almost daily on the mosque platform or suffe to pray, meditate upon Allah, and discuss the paths to inner knowledge, the truths of revelation, and the meanings of the verses of the Koran. Sufis embrace these four mystical verses from the Holy Book:

Whereso'er ye turn, there is the Face of God.
There is no refuge from God but in Him.
It is not their eyes that are blind, but their hearts.
Verily we are God's and unto Him we shall return.

There is also this: The attainment of knowledge that comes from the mystical union with our creator is the very purpose of our existence. In this, Sufis point to the passage in the Hadith in which Allah, speaking to Muhammad, says, "I was a hidden treasure and I loved that I be known, so I created the world." Thus it is through us that God is known—a concept that I find most illuminating.

The roots of Sufism lie unquestionably in Islam, although some today believe the sect is outside the sphere of that religion. According to Professor Alan Godlas, of the University of Georgia, Sufism in the West falls into four general categories: Islamic Sufi orders, Quasi-Islamic Sufi orders, Non-Islamic Sufi Orders, and organizations or schools related to Sufism or Sufi orders.

Practical Wedding Considerations and Customs

Many Sufi orders follow the same guidelines for marriage as in Islam. Some orders allow the incorporation of traditions from other religions within a universal context. Culture, of course, plays a significant role in the ceremony as well.

For the Ceremony: A Menu of Elements

READINGS. *As I indicated, in poetry and verse is the nature of Sufism revealed, and Sufi poetry is famous the world over. The passages listed here are often included by both Sufis and non-Sufis in their wedding ceremonies. You may find one or more of these selections a beautiful addition to your service.*

∞ May these vows and this marriage be blessed.

May it be sweet milk, this marriage, like wine and halvah.

May this marriage be full of laughter, our every day a day in paradise.

May this marriage be a sign of compassion, a seal of happiness here and hereafter.

May this marriage have a fair face and a good name, an omen as welcome as the moon in a clear blue sky.

I am out of words to describe how spirit mingles in this marriage. ["This Marriage," by Jalal al-Din Rumi, translation by Kabir Helminski]

∞ Come along! Today is a festival!

Clap your hands and say, "This is a day of happiness!"

Who in the world is like this bridal pair?

The earth and the sky are full of sugar. Sugar cane is sprouting all around!

We can hear the roar of the pearly ocean. The whole world is full of waves!

The voices of Love are approaching from all sides. We are on our way to heaven!

Once upon a time we played with angels. Let's all go back up there again.

Heaven is our home! Yes, we are even higher up than heaven, higher than the angels.

My dear, it's true that spiritual beauty is wonderful. But your loveliness in this world is even more so! [By Jalal al-Din Rumi, in *Wedding Readings*]

∞ Out beyond ideas of right and wrong, there is a field. I'll meet you there. When the soul lies down in that grass, the world is too full to talk about. Ideas, language, even the phrase "each other" doesn't make any sense. [By Jalal al-Din Rumi]

∞ The moon has become a dancer
at this festival of love.

This dance of light,
This sacred blessing,
This divine love,
beckons us
to a world beyond
only lovers can see
with their eyes of fiery passion.
   They are the chosen ones
who have surrendered.
Once they were particles of light
now they are the radiant sun.
They have left behind
the world of deceitful games.
They are the privileged lovers
who create a new world
with their eyes of fiery passion. ["The Privileged Lovers," by Jalal al-Din
   Rumi]

∞ Your hope in my heart is the rarest treasure.
Your name on my tongue is the sweetest word.
My choicest hours are the hours I spend with You. [By the Islamic Sufi
   Saint Rabi'a]

∞ [Here are some Rumi quotations; I have often used one or more of
these in wedding ceremonies.]

- The tender words you have said to one another are stored in the secret
  heart of Heaven. One day like rain they will fall and spread, and your
  mystery will grow green over the world.
- The minute I heard my first love story I started looking for you, not
  knowing how blind that was. Lovers don't finally meet somewhere.
  They're in each other [or in each other's souls] all along.
- Apart from Love, everything passes away. The way to Heaven is in your
  heart. Open and lift the wings of Love! When Love's wings are strong, you
  need no ladder.

  ∞ [Two quotations from the Persian poet Hafiz]

- How should two people treat each other if they both know God? Like
  a musician touching his violin with utmost care to caress the final note.
- Enjoy the one you love, drink deep and embrace; seek not with her to
  please your world, just give love and be kind.

  BLESSING

  ∞ May the blessing of God rest upon you,
  May God's peace abide in you,

May God's presence illuminate your hearts
Now and forevermore.

■　■　■

Do nondoing, strive for nonstriving.
—Tao Te Ching

Taoism

The roots of Taoism (pronounced "Dowism") stretch far back in Chinese history, the earliest writings perhaps originating in the eighteenth century B.C.E. In recent times, many in the West have become familiar with the I-Ching, the Book of Changes, considered an ancestral Taoist text. It is an assemblage of wisdom and divination said to point the way to proper action and believed to date from 1150 B.C.E. Here we find the idea of One Ultimate Reality, containing within it a constant interplay of yin, the feminine aspect, which is receptive, and yang, the male aspect, which is assertive. This interplay is in all of nature, including ourselves. But it is in the figure of Lao Tzu—"the Old Fellow" or "the Grand Old Man"—and a very short book he wrote that the widespread appeal of Taoism's subliminal message can be found.

Perhaps he was an actual man, perhaps he wasn't; scholars are not sure. The story says that Lao Tzu, a sage born in China around 604 B.C.E., tired of the state of affairs of the world around him and headed off on a water buffalo toward Tibet to pass the remainder of his life in seclusion. Along the way a gatekeeper who recognized him begged him to record his teachings for future generations. Lao Tzu left and returned three days later with a slim document—no more than five thousand Chinese characters. This was the Tao Te Ching (The Way and Its Power), which would eventually be translated into more languages than any other book except the Bible. It can be read in minutes, but many spend decades studying it.

Lao Tzu's teachings became the sacred text of the Tao church or Tao Chiao that developed in China about two centuries into the Christian era and that lives today primarily in Taiwan and Hong Kong. Most adherents, however, are drawn to Taoism for its philosophical message of simplicity, ease and, in the deepest sense, the joy of life.

The Tao Te Ching tells us that the eternal Tao—the Way, the Path, or the natural course of things—cannot be named, yet it is within all and accessible to all. Both transcendent and immanent, it existed before the cosmos; at the same time, it is the nature of the cosmos and the nature of human beings. To unblock the flow of the Tao's power (te) within, one is instructed to practice doing without doing ("Do nondoing, strive for nonstriving"). This is wei wu wei, or creative letting go. First, we must "be"—resist conscious effort and stop trying so hard. In doing so, we unblock a natural, unlimited source of energy available to us all—then creative right action will follow.

When I read the Tao Te Ching, I immediately feel myself begin to let go into the natural order and into the cosmos itself. With this letting go comes not only ease but a sense of delight in participation in the flow of life. In his book *The World's Religions,* Huston Smith writes that "life lived above tension" defines the concept of wei wu wei: "One simply lets the Tao flow in and flow out again until all life becomes a dance in which there is neither feverishness nor imbalance."

This state can be encouraged through physical regimens, as by practicing the movements of tai chi chuan, and through meditation, in which one focuses on calming the mind, controlling breathing, and letting go of distracting emotions, both pleasant and unpleasant. The more successful one is, the easier life becomes; for even in the midst of busyness, speech and actions proceed naturally and for the greatest good.

Taoism appeals intuitively rather than intellectually, and it's hardly surprising that so many Westerners have been captivated by its message. Reading the essential writings—first, the Tao Te Ching and, second, the teachings of Chuang Tzu, another Taoist master (many translations are available)—affords the best introduction to this tradition. The following passages from the Tao Te Ching, excerpted from *The World's Wisdom* by Philip Novak, give some of Taoism's flavor and illuminate the concept of wei wu wei. We can hear in these words echoes of Zen Buddhism, which indeed was enormously influenced by Taoist philosophy.

> *The Tao is called the Great Mother:*
> *Empty yet inexhaustible,*
> *It gives birth to infinite worlds.*
> *It is always present within you.*
> *You can use it any way you want. . . .*
> *He who stands on tiptoe doesn't stand firm.*
> *He who rushes ahead doesn't go far.*
> *He who tries to shine dims his own light.*
> *He who defines himself can't know who he really is.*
> *He who has power over others can't empower himself.*
> *He who clings to his work will create nothing that endures.*
> *If you want to accord with the Tao, just do your job, then let go. . . .*
> *Free from desire, you realize the mystery. Caught in desire, you see only the manifestations.*

I have just three things to teach: simplicity, patience, compassion. . . .
These are your greatest treasures. Simple in actions and in thoughts, you will
return to the source of being. Patient with both friends and enemies, you
accord with the way things are. Compassionate toward yourself, you
reconcile all beings in the world.

For the Ceremony: A Menu of Elements

READINGS. *If you wish your ceremony to incorporate elements of Taoist thought, it's appropriate and may feel right to quote passages from the Tao Te Ching, from the I Ching, and from the writings of Chuang Tzu. Consider having your celebrant or a family member read one or more of the following at points in the service. All would work well in the context of an interfaith or intercultural wedding.*

∽ Fame or integrity: which is more important? Money or happiness: which is more valuable? Success or failure: which is more destructive?

If you look to others for fulfillment, you will never truly be fulfilled. If your happiness depends on money, you will never be happy with yourself.

Be content with what you have; rejoice in the way things are. When you realize there is nothing lacking, the whole world belongs to you. [From the Tao Te Ching]

∽ Good construction does not fall down, a good embrace does not let go; their heirs honor them unceasingly.

Cultivate it in yourselves, and that virtue is real; cultivate it in the home, and that virtue is abundant; cultivate it in the locality, and that virtue lasts; cultivate it in the nation, and that virtue is universal.

So observe yourselves by yourselves. Observe the home by the home. Observe the nation by the nation. How do I know the world is as it is? By this. [Adapted from *The Essential Tao* by Thomas Cleary]

∽ The Way produces one; one produces two, two produce three, three produce all beings. . . . [From *The Essential Tao*]

The following passage is adapted from "Simple but Sublime Marriage Ceremony," from Workbook for Spiritual Development of All People *by Hua-Ching Ni, a Taoist master. This reading fits perfectly in the portion of the ceremony right before and immediately after the blessing and exchange of rings, as I have indicated, including a popular and beloved quotation from the I Ching.*

∽ Tao is one.

It is the perfect harmony of the universe.

Tao divides itself into Heaven and Earth, or yin and yang. It manifests in men and women as subtle yin/yang energies. Men and women complement each other, and each contains an integral part of the other.

As students of the Integral Truth, a man and a woman build their earthly relationship on the refinement of their subtle energies. They cultivate together to reach a state of perfect harmony. Their relationship remains untouched by the constant changes of earthly life.

They unite their virtue in Tao and their union is everlasting. Their lovers' hearts transform to be rainbows, that join each other in perfect harmony.

[At this point, the celebrant can proceed with the following exchange of rings.]

Wholeness is the state where nothing is missing and everything is possible. Let these rings therefore represent wholeness. Let them remind you of a coming around of an eternal cycle—from want to plenty, from despair to joy, from failure to possibility, from loneliness to love. The I Ching states most beautifully: When two people are at one in their innermost hearts, they shatter the strength of iron or even of bronze. And when two people understand each other in their innermost hearts, their words are sweet and strong like the fragrance of orchids.

[After the exchange of rings, the celebrant may place his hand over the couple's joined hands; he then softly intones the following words:]

[Bride] and [groom], in accepting each other as husband and wife, you wholeheartedly join together to become one.

[The celebrant can then finish with the remaining words of the Taoist marriage ceremony and the ringing of small bells.]

This beautiful marriage shall be fulfilled by the witness of your family and friends.

I pronounce you husband and wife, and sanctify your marriage to become a perfect union in Tao. We offer three bells in celebration of this marriage.

■ ■ ■

Humata, Hukta, Huverashta [good thoughts, good words, good deeds].

Zoroastrianism

Humata, Hukta, Huverashta represents the cornerstone of the Zoroastrian religion; or, as it is expressed in an English translation of the texts (Yasna 28:11): "To think a good thought, to speak a good word, to do a good deed is the best. Everlasting happiness to him who is righteous."

A system of belief dating back thousands of years and once the dominant faith of the great Persian Empire, Zoroastrianism is considered by many to be the first monotheistic religion. It teaches of one Creator God, of the existence of heaven and hell, of good and evil forces, and of an afterlife—the apocalyptic ending of the world and the resurrection of the dead, when the righteous walk into the realm of light. Many believe that it may have influenced Judaism, and therefore Christianity and Islam as well.

With the expansion of Islam, great numbers of Zoroastrians fled Persia and settled in western India around the eighth century C.E. Their descendants, the Parsees or Parsis (meaning Persians), kept the faith alive; today many still live around Bombay. In Iran the faith is called Mazdayasna, "the worship of Ahura Mazda." Estimates of the number of present-day Zoroastrians range from 130,000 to about 2.5 million worldwide.

ZARATHUSHTRA. Though Zoroastrian roots stretch back many centuries before the Common Era, the genesis of the religion lies in the figure of Zarathushtra (or, in Greek, Zoroaster), the mystic, teacher, and prophet generally thought to have been born between 1100 and 500 B.C.E.

Around the age of thirty, after years in spiritual study and retreat, Zarathushtra received a divine revelation. Emerging from a river, symbolically purified, he was led by a great light to Ahura Mazda, whom he came to understand as Supreme Lord, the Creator from which all good things flow. Ahura Mazda was surrounded by six attendants—the Amesha Spenta (the Bountiful Immortals), who are essentially archangels and chief of the Yazata (angels). In opposition to this combined force of good were the spirits of evil and violence, headed by Angra Mainyu—and therein lay the challenge for human beings. To choose good over evil was the road to Asha, or the path of righteousness. Asha requires conscious choice; this is the determination to think a good thought or cultivate Vohu Man, a good mind ("May the evil mind be vanquished!"), to speak a good word, and to do a good deed.

MORAL PURITY. In Zoroastrianism, moral purity is key. Right action or the effort to maintain moral purity in the here and now is the best way to worship God and to strive for the ideal of becoming more godlike. Zoroastrians believe it is up to humankind to bring about "a kingdom of truth and good thinking" on the earth. Hell is not considered eternal; goodwill, it is believed, will eventually prevail. The more successfully people pursue the righteous path, the more the universe as a whole will be transformed toward goodness, until evil is obliterated. Then all creation will attain the rewards of perfection and immortality, and all the world will be resurrected.

These teachings, along with specific rituals and practices, are put forth in ancient texts called the Avesta (holy texts) and the Pahlavi texts, written largely in an old form of Iranian. Much of this writing was altered over the centuries, but the oldest section, a series of five hymns called the Gathas, is believed to be the words of Zarathushtra himself.

Practical Wedding Considerations and Customs

Marriage in Zoroastrianism is a sacrament, part of the soul's unfolding in the spiritual path, and greatly to be desired. Marriage promotes happiness, and a married person, it is believed, can better endure the hardships of everyday life. Zoroastrians are expected to marry members of the faith; although inter-marriage does occur, it is officially forbidden.

Zoroastrian weddings are celebrated with pomp and gaiety, and include several days of elaborate prewedding rituals. The actual ceremony usually takes place just after sunset, when day dissolves into night, as it is believed the bride and groom will merge into each other. The wedding should be per-formed in the presence of at least five witnesses.

The traditional color for a Zoroastrian bride's dress is white or very pale pink. The groom bears an elongated mark of red powder on his forehead, while the bride bears a round mark of red powder. The hall or grounds where the wedding takes place are usually lavishly decorated with flowers and chalk designs. At the dais (also decorated) where the ceremony is conducted, there are chairs, facing east, for the bride and groom. One or two tables should be in place to hold the ses, a collection of symbolically auspicious items arranged on a silver tray.

THE PROCESSION. As the groom waits up front, the bride enters, escorted by her father; they are followed by two married women, who carry the ses, and by other close female relatives.

For the Ceremony: A Menu of Elements

HANDFASTING; THROWING OF RICE. *In these opening rituals, the celebrant loosely binds the couple's right hands, encircling them seven times with a cord. Seven is a significant number in many religions; the celebrant may offer this brief explanation along with the following Zoroastrian prayer, which I have adapted.*

∞ [Bride] and [groom], your hands are bound seven times, a mystical number in the Zoroastrian faith and in [the partner's religion]. In binding your hands, we make a wish, a lifelong prayer, that your union may never be broken.

"The two will this day become one. Let them love each other faithfully, wholly, and unceasingly. Let each dedicate his or her dear self with the deep-est love. Let them jointly share the ups and downs of life and with one mind seek their relief. Let each one rely upon the other as upon one's own self. Let each give his or her heart to the other. Let the husband be all the world to the wife, and let the wife be all the world to the husband. Let each one reign in the other's heart. Let there be complete harmony between their souls. Let each one's place be by the side of the other. Long after they live and after the longest of life allotted to humankind, may they both go hand in hand to the highest heaven."

The celebrant next places in the bride's and groom's left hands a few grains of rice. She also puts some frankincense in the fire, and explains:

∽ The bride and groom will now throw rice one over the other in demonstration of their love and devotion. It is said that the one who throws the rice first will be foremost in loving and respecting the other!

OPENING WORDS. *If you wish, you may include in your program a brief explanation of the symbolism of the elements on the altar, or your celebrant may offer the following description:*

∽ In honor of Zoroastrian tradition, the bride and groom have arranged a ses. The symbolic items of the ses include the oil lamp and burning incense (frankincense and sandalwood), which are considered sacred, because fire is a symbol of the divine. The rice represents abundance; rose petals are for love; rose water is for purification. There is also ghee—purified butter—for gentility; gur—molasses—for sweetness; coconut, for resourcefulness; and dates for fertility. The two burning candles represent the light of the souls of our bride and groom.

INVOCATION.

∽ O Lord of life and wisdom, I will forever uphold Thy Divine Law and Thy Good Mind. Teach me Thyself, through Thy spoken Word which springs from the Spirit, and with Thy very own mouth, whence life first came into being. [Gatha Ahunavaiti, Yasna 28:11]

READING. *Passages from Kahlil Gibran (see page 116) or Rumi (pages 120, 202) would be appropriate.*

CELEBRANT'S ADDRESS TO THE COUPLE. *In his address to the bride and groom, the celebrant may wish to include the following message, which is essentially a Zoroastrian prayer or blessing that I have adapted.*

∽ I say these words to you, marrying brides and grooms, and hope you bear them in your minds carefully: Always live according to the principles of good mind and love; try to strive one with the other in truth and righteousness, so that you may reap the reward of joy and happiness. The reward of fellowship shall be yours as long as you remain united in weal and woe, with love and fidelity in matrimony.

DECLARATION OF INTENT AND VOWS. *The declaration of intent is crucial in the Zoroastrian ceremony, and traditionally the celebrant asks the couple three* *times if they consent to the marriage. In a modern adaptation, the celebrant should ask for their consent at least once, perhaps preceding the request with an appeal to the families.*

∞ [To the families] Have the families with righteous mind, and truthful thoughts, words, and action, and for the increase of righteousness, agreed to give, forever, these children in marriage?

[They reply: We have agreed.]

[To the couple] Do you agree to enter into this contract of marriage till the end of your life with righteous mind?

[They reply: We do.]

Closing blessing.

∞ May the Almighty bless you with health, strength, joy, wise offspring, a long life, and the Kingdom of Heaven.

Chapter Nine

Wedding Customs from Around the World

The following cultural customs and rituals may be incorporated into your wedding ceremony. They are presented here in a universal context appropriate for intercultural and interfaith unions; we have included words the celebrant or another participant might use.

Many cultural traditions overlap religious traditions, so please do read through the section or sections of Chapter 8 that describe the practices and the marriage ceremony of your religious heritage. If you are Japanese, for example, refer to the Shinto marriage ceremony. If you are Chinese, read the descriptions of Confucianism and Taoism. Even if you wish to honor your heritage culturally but not religiously, you may find in Chapter 8 a reading, prayer, or blessing that appeals to you and can be easily incorporated in your ceremony.

Afghani
(See also the section on Islam in Chapter 8.)

THE PROCESSION. An Afghani bride enters like a queen, with an entourage of women, all dressed regally; sometimes a number of small children follow as well.

THE SHARING OF SWEET WATER. A ceremonial container containing sugar water covered by a handkerchief is placed before the celebrant, to be uncovered when the couple declare their intention to marry. Here is how the ritual may proceed:

Celebrant (to the assembled company): Today we celebrate an Afghani tradition. Within this vessel is sugar water, signifying that our bride and groom should forever remain sweet to each other.

(To the couple): [Bride] and [groom], have you come here freely and without reservation to give yourselves to each other in marriage?

[They reply: Yes.]

Do you promise to remain kind, loving, and understanding through all that life may bring?

[They reply: We do.]

The ceremony can then continue with the exchange of vows and rings—the ring exchange echoing the mehr, the Muslim tradition of a sum pledged for the bride. The celebrant then removes the handkerchief from the sugar water and recites a prayer, which might be from the Koran, a reading from the Hadith, or a nonreligious marriage blessing from Rumi. These selections can be found in Chapters 7 and 8. In a religious ceremony, the Koran is held over the heads of the bride and groom after they say their vows.

Celebrant: [Bride] and [groom], you have pledged yourselves to each other through solemn and sacred vows. Remember that it is only in your togetherness that life will remain sweet. [The celebrant then offers the bride and groom the sugar water for each to take a sip. This is a contemporary adaptation of the traditional ritual, in which only the man drinks the sugar water.]

SHOWERING OF SWEETS AND COINS. At the end of the ceremony, the couple may be showered by family members with candy and coins.

Celebrant: It is an Afghani tradition to shower the bride and groom with sweets and coins, to wish them sweetness, prosperity, and abundance in marriage and in life. We now invite the parents of the bride and groom forward to bless their children through this ritual.

African-American

More and more African-Americans are choosing to honor and celebrate their African heritage in their marriage ceremonies. African-American spirituality is rich and multifaceted; its traditions, music, and literature are beautiful to hear and behold. It is of the soul and feeds the soul, and its influences range from ethnic to religious. Ethnic traditions come from Africa, the Caribbean, and the southern United States, while religious traditions of influence include Christianity and Islam, as well as Yoruba and other indigenous African religions. If you wish to honor your African heritage in a Christian ceremony in a church, check with the pastor regarding any possible restrictions concerning music, dress code, ritual, and so on.

DRESS. Native African dress is varied and can be quite regal. An African-American bride or groom may choose to wear full traditional regalia or simply accents, such as an Afrocentric cummerbund or a gele (the bride's head wrap), based on regional variations. The use of kente cloth—as part of the bride's or groom's dress, as ornamentation for the altar, or for the handfasting ritual—is popular with many African-American couples. Kente cloth, developed in Ghana over three thousand years ago, is brightly colored fabric of cotton, silk, or rayon, handwoven and elaborately designed. Cowrie shells, symbolizing fertility, are also a favorite wedding ornament.

MUSIC. In an African-American ceremony, music—live or on CD—may be gospel, traditional African drumming, jazz, the blues, contemporary, or classical music. On the island of Anjouan off the East African coast, drummers in double file lead the groom in the procession, a custom that might be a striking addition to a Western ceremony.

THE SETTING. You may wish to create an African-inspired altar, which works particularly well in an outdoor setting. Or simply drape kente cloth over the existing altar. Your altar should hold the elements required for whatever rituals you choose. One couple used colorful candles with African designs for the Christian lighting of the unity candle. Another chose bowls with African-inspired motifs for the spice-tasting ritual. Still another bride and groom wanted to state their vows while kneeling on pillows made from African fabric.

CEREMONIAL WASHING OF THE HANDS. In Africa there are many variations on the ritual of washing the hands. In one region water is poured from a gourd over the bride's hands. You may want to begin your ceremony with a ceremonial washing of the hands by having your celebrant pour a bit of water over the hands of both bride and groom.

THE PARTAKING OF SPICES. The partaking of spices is a delightful African tradition, rich in symbolism. Four or more herbs or spices in bowls are set on the altar. Each spice represents an element of life: lemon juice for sorrow, vinegar for bitterness, cayenne pepper for passion, honey for sweetness. Some couples also include finely chopped kola nuts for strength, palm oil for peace and serenity, and water for purification and blessing. I very much like the idea of the bride and groom feeding the spices to each other. After the celebrant states the significance of each spice, the bride and groom take turns feeding it to each other, ending with a taste of the sweet honey. You may feed each other with small spoons, or do as many of my couples have done: Use your fingers! To watch the faces of the couple as they feed each other cayenne pepper is especially interesting. Have a glass of water on hand! I tell my couples to have fun with this ritual—and they do. Your celebrant can offer the following explanation:

Celebrant: The bride and groom will now take part in an African wedding tradition whereby they will taste various herbs and spices.

[Bride] and [groom], in marriage you commit to endure all aspects of life together. Whether life be bitter as represented by this vinegar . . . or full of sadness, sour like lemon juice . . . or passionate, full of emotion, intense, like hot cayenne pepper . . . or whether peaceful, calm, and smooth like palm oil . . . we pray for you strength, as represented by these kola nuts. Finally, remember this: Should your love endure all the elements that life brings, only then will your life be truly honey sweet. [Adapted from *Going to the Chapel* by the editors of *Signature Bride* magazine; passage provided by Rev. Valentine]

In a Jewish–African-American interfaith ceremony, the partaking of herbs and spices works very well under the chuppah. In place of cayenne pepper you can substitute horseradish, reminiscent of the tasting of bitter herbs (including horseradish) at the Passover seder. Here are words the celebrant might use:

Celebrant: The bride and groom will now honor an African wedding tradition whereby they will partake of herbs and spices representing the four elements of life. Four is a significant number in the Jewish tradition, as the four poles of the chuppah represent the four directions of the earth.

[Bride] and [groom], as a couple you commit to endure all that life may bring. Remember this: Life may become bitter as vinegar . . . or full of sorrow, sour like lemon juice . . . or emotional and intense like horseradish. However, if you remain united through all these elements, then will your life together truly be sweet as honey.

THE POURING OF LIBATION. Many couples are now choosing to include a pouring of libation in their ceremonies. The celebrant pours an alcoholic beverage (typically gin, rum, or brandy) on the ground. This works well outdoors; at an indoor ceremony the celebrant may simply pour the libation in a bowl or vessel and later pour it into the ground. The celebrant explains the ritual and offers a libation prayer.

Celebrant: Today we call upon our couple's ancestors and all assembled guests in witnessing and blessing this sacred union with the African tradition of the pouring of libations.

All praise to God Almighty,

Praise to our African ancestors and roots.

God gave his power for the roots of the trees to spread its branches wide.

If a man does not know his roots, then he does not know his God.

Let the spirit of God and our ancestors bring us closer in unity. [From *Going to the Chapel* by the editors of *Signature Bride* magazine; may be adapted to "Praise to our African and [other heritage] roots"]

The following African wedding benediction is also appropriate.
Celebrant: Libations! Libations! [or: *Blessings! Blessings!*]
To the wandering spirits below!
To the spirits of the mountains,
To the spirits of the East,
To the spirits of the West,
To the spirits of the North,
To the spirits of the South,
To the bride and groom, together, libation! [or: *blessing!*]
May the spirits on high, as well as the spirits below, fill you with grace.
    [Adapted from *Wedding Readings* by Eleanor Munro]

You may also choose to drink from the libation and later pour the remainder on the ground. This variation works particularly well in an interfaith ceremony where one of the partners is Jewish, as the pouring of libation can be joined with the Jewish blessing over the wine. Please note, however, that alcohol is forbidden in Islam as well as in some other traditions. The couple may share the libation silently or may wish to say alternately the following lines (from "Devoted to You," by Annette Jones White) just before drinking:
    I'm glad we drink from the same cup
    Whether honey or whether brine . . .
    I'll gladly share your joy and pain
    Through all of our earthbound years.

TYING THE KNOT. The couple are literally and symbolically bound together at the wrists during the ceremony. In Kenya a leather band is used; other regions use braided grass. If you wish to honor your African roots with this ritual, I suggest you have your celebrant bind your hands with a sash of kente cloth.

KWANZAA. If your marriage will take place at the time of Kwanzaa, in December, you may choose to incorporate celebration of the holiday in your ceremony. After they state their intention to marry, the celebrant directs the bride and groom to begin at opposite ends of a table, each lighting three candles and meeting in the middle to light the seventh jointly. Couples sometimes choose to incorporate the Kwanzaa principles into their wedding vows.

Celebrant: In honor of Kwanzaa, [bride] and [groom] will light seven candles, representing the seven tenets of Kwanzaa: umoja—unity; kujichagulia—self-determination; ujima—collective responsibility; ujamaa—cooperative economics; nia—purpose; kuumba—creativity; and imani—faith.

[Bride] and [groom], as you light these candles you affirm always to keep the light of these principles within your hearts and within your lives. [Adapted from uticaOD.com Holiday Guide]

THE JUMPING OF THE BROOM. The jumping of the broom is a popular tradition with roots in Mother Africa. African-American slaves were not allowed to marry; consequently, they developed a simple ritual in which the elder of the family placed a broom across the threshold. When the couple jumped over the broom, it signified the beginning of their making a home together and sealed the union in the eyes of the community.

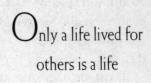

Only a life lived for others is a life worthwhile.

—*Albert Einstein*

The broom can be handmade of bound twigs and adorned with bells, cowrie shells, and ribbons, or it may be a standard broom that is decorated. Some brooms are so beautiful that they are displayed in the couples' homes as keepsakes. During the ceremony the broom may be placed either in front of or behind the altar, or it can be held by an elder.

At the end of the ceremony, the celebrant explains the ritual. Three versions of the explanation follow:

Celebrant: We end this ceremony with the African-American tradition of jumping of the broom. Slaves in this country were not permitted to marry, so they jumped a broom as a way of ceremonially uniting. This marks the beginning of making a home together. It symbolizes the sweeping away of the old and the welcoming of the new. It is also a call of support for the marriage from the entire community. It represents great joy and at the same time serves as a reminder of the past and the pain of slavery.

(This version honors the grandmothers) *Celebrant: The bride and groom will now jump the broom, a tradition with roots in Africa. It symbolizes the beginning of making a home together. It seals the union in the eyes of our community. It is traditional that the elders of the family conduct the ritual. We therefore call up [grandmother] and [grandmother].*

The celebrant then hands the broom to the elder of one family, who makes sweeping gestures to eliminate any negative energies. In this way the bride and groom begin their new life with a clean sweep! That individual then hands the broom to the other elder, who places it on the ground. The bride and groom jump, then kiss. Immediately the music begins, and the couple recess down the aisle to the cheers of family and friends!

(This is a good choice for intercultural and interfaith unions) *Celebrant: Our couple will now jump the broom, a ritual with roots in Mother Africa. As the bride and groom jump the broom, they physically and spiritually cross the threshold into the land of matrimony. Traditionally, jumping the broom was also a means of sweeping away any evil that may come into their paths. Therefore, in honoring this ritual, [bride] and [groom] issue a hope and a prayer of sweeping away any hatred or prejudice between people of different colors, beliefs, or traditions.*

THE CUTTING OF THE CORD. An elder representative from each family holds a ribbon for the couple to cut before they recess, symbolizing that the bride and groom belong no longer to their parents' homes but to their own.

READINGS AND QUOTATIONS. Many couples choose to include religious passages from either the Bible or the Koran, as well as a reading from the wealth of literature by African and African-American writers and poets. Here are several selections (adapted from *African-American Wedding Readings,* edited by Tamara Nikuradse) you may find appropriate for your wedding, either for your celebrant to incorporate in the opening words or the address to the couple, or to be read by your celebrant or an honored guest at some other point during the ceremony.

Selection 1 (from "My Vision," by Craig Butler)

I envision a man and a woman committed to empowering and uplifting our people.

I envision a man and a woman overcoming all obstacles placed before them collectively and individually by the support they provide to one another.

I envision a man and a woman living happily as friends, partners, and soul mates, loving each other unselfishly and unconditionally.

I envision a man and a woman living with mutual respect and patience, loyalty and honesty.

I envision a man and a woman joined spiritually, metaphysically, and emotionally, attaining inner peace and true happiness.

I envision the elders rejoicing in song and dance as they witness a man and a woman pass in righteousness, providing their souls with safe passage . . . with the love and strength of two warriors to endure the ages.

I envision a man and woman smile as they listen to the melodious voices of their children playing and growing with pride as the continuation of their . . . family created through the love and faith that God provided them.

I envision a man and a woman on bended knee facing the eastern light in meditation and prayer, asking for God's help in keeping their commitments to each other, their families, and their community on the righteous path to everlasting life.

Selection 2 (from "At an Age-Mate's Wedding," by Micere M. G. Mugo)

Come friends, come all, come join hands, come and witness!

Selection 3 (by Maya Angelou)

If you find it in your heart to care for somebody else, you will have succeeded.

Selection 4 ("Light a Holy Fire," a Masai prayer. When lighting the unity candle in the Christian tradition, you may wish to include this powerful prayer from the Masai in Tanzania, along with the traditional Christian quotation "What God has joined together, let no one tear asunder.")

> Receive this holy fire.
> Make your lives like this fire.
> A holy fire that is seen.
> A life of God that is seen.
> A life that darkness does not overcome.
> May this light of God in you grow.
> Light a fire that is worthy of your heads.
> Light a fire that is worthy of your children.
> Light a fire that is worthy of your fathers.
> Light a fire that is worthy of your mothers.
> Light a fire that is worthy of God.

Selection 5 (from "Many and More," by Maya Angelou)

> There are many and more
> who would kiss my hand,
> taste my lips,
> to my loneliness lend
> Their bodies' warmth.

I have want of a friend.

There are few, some few,
who would give their names
and fortunes rich
or send first sons
to my ailing bed.

I have need of a friend.

There is one and only one
who will give the air
from his failing lungs
for my body's mend.

And that one is my love.

Selection 6 (an interracial couple may wish to conclude their ceremony with this reading from Langston Hughes, "I Dream a World")

I dream a world where man
No other man will scorn,
Where love will bless the earth
And peace its paths adorn.
I dream a world where all
Will know sweet freedom's way,
Where greed no longer saps the soul
Nor avarice blights our day.
A world I dream where black or white,
Whatever race you be,
Will share the bounties of the earth
And every man is free,
Where wretchedness will hang its head
And joy, like a pearl,
Attends the needs of all mankind—
Of such I dream, my world!

Selection 7 (by Chester Himes)

Make time for one another.
Treat one another with respect.
It's the little things that count.
Learn to trust.

Be willing to share.
Agree to disagree.
Be willing to give in.
Communicate with one another.
Be affectionate.
Share spiritual growth.
Be kind and considerate to one another.
Be easy going.
Be flexible about growth and change.
Don't cross the line.
Don't let the sun go down on your wrath.

Selection 8 (from The Wisdom of the Elders, *by Robert Fleming)*

The healing powers of love are legendary. When we feel we are deeply loved by those around us, we are transformed by that love. We are emboldened by that love to make deep, significant changes in our lives. We become more than just flesh and bone. Our internal wounds no longer bleed or fester. With love, healthy new tissue is formed and old emotional scars vanish.

Arabic or Middle Eastern
(See also the sections on Islam and Sufism in Chapter 8 and the section in this chapter for your particular country.)

HENNA DESIGNS. The bride's hands and feet are decorated with intricate lace- and florallike patterns, painted using a henna dye.

WHITE CLOTH RITUAL. There are two variations. As they are about to say their vows, the bride and groom join right hands and a white cloth is placed over their hands. Or a larger white cloth is held over the couple's heads by family members.

THE WEDDING WAIL. In some countries the women at the ceremony greet the couple with a traditional and distinctive wedding wail, done using rapid tongue movements.

Armenian
(See also the Orthodox ritual in the section on Christianity in Chapter 8.)

RIBBON CROWNS. Crowns of gold or silver and/or red and white ribbons are placed on the heads of the bride and groom, gracing them with sanctity, wisdom, and integrity. The crowning is done in the middle of the ceremony, perhaps just before the vows. In one ceremony I conducted—the bride was Armenian Orthodox and the groom Conservative Jewish—the groom did not like idea of a cord being wrapped around his head. So we took the red and white braided cord, provided by the bride's mother, and wrapped it around the couple's hands while I said, "In honor of Armenian tradition, we will wrap the hands of our bride and groom with the traditional red and white cord representing their indissolvable union."

Austrian

Myrtle, the flower traditionally symbolizing life, may be used in the bride's bouquet or arranged around the ceremonial site.

Bulgarian
(See also the Orthodox ritual in the section on Christianity in Chapter 8.)

Jeweled crowns are used in the traditional crowning ritual of the Orthodox service.

Cambodian
(See also the section on Buddhism in Chapter 8.)

BINDING WITH A RED THREAD. In a Buddhist ceremony, the couple's wrists are loosely bound by a red thread or cord dipped in holy water, symbolizing their union. Red is the color of life, joy, passion, and good fortune; water represents life, sanctity, and purity. A contemporary couple may prefer to have their hands rather than their wrists bound. The ritual may be performed just before or after the vows. The celebrant recites a prayer over a small vessel of water, then dips the tip of the red thread in the water before wrapping it around the hands of the bride and groom.

Celebrant: In honor of Cambodian tradition, we bind your hands with this traditional red thread, signifying a joyous and enduring union.

PASSING THE CANDLE. Guests pass a lit candle. If there are many guests, this ritual might be limited to immediate family.

Celebrant: As is tradition in Cambodia, we will now pass around a candle. When you receive the candle, we ask each of you to bestow a verbal blessing or good wish upon the bride and groom.

THE KNOT CEREMONY. A ritual called a ptem ends the ceremony. Knots are tied on a string bracelet by the parents or the parents and grandparents, demonstrating their good wishes for the bride and groom. The bracelet is a keepsake for the couple.

Chinese
(See also the sections on Confucianism, Taoism, and, if appropriate, Buddhism or Christianity in Chapter 8.)

THE USE OF RED. Red is an auspicious color in Chinese tradition, signifying good luck and good fortune. It is the color of joy and love. You may decorate your ceremony site with red flowers, red fruits, red silks and ribbons. Gold accents would also be traditional and most appropriate. Your wedding program may be trimmed with red and gold.

Most Chinese brides today wear a Western-style white dress and change into a traditional red Chinese gown for the reception. Traditionally the bride carried a protective red umbrella or parasol. I remember one bride who honored and combined her Chinese heritage and her modern American life by wearing a contemporary, fitted, white silk, embroidered Chinese-style gown that had countless tiny, exquisite fabric buttons. She looked radiant.

THE SEDAN CHAIR. On her wedding day, the Chinese bride is treated like royalty. Traditionally, she was transported to the groom's house in an elaborate sedan chair. Although most modern brides arrive by car, a couple may choose to incorporate this luxurious ancient custom by having the bride brought to the ceremony site in a sedan chair, if one can be found, or a carriage decorated with red flowers and gold accents. Her parents wait to greet her and escort her down the aisle. Such an arrival, which would work especially well in an outdoor setting, is certainly a dramatic entrance!

A CHINESE LEGEND. Your celebrant can offer the following legend in the opening words or accompanying the sipping of wine. Many couples also choose to print it in their programs.

Celebrant: An ancient Chinese legend holds that a couple is bound at birth by an invisible red thread which continuously shrinks over the years until the couple is united in marriage. The legend states that nothing in this world can sever the thread, not distance or changing circumstances. Marriage is their destiny. [Adapted from *Weddings, Dating, and Love Customs of Cultures Worldwide,* by Carolyn Mordecai]

CHINESE WEDDING CUPS. Before taking their vows, the bride and groom drink wine from two wedding cups that are tied together with a red cord or ribbon. Each first sips the wine individually, then takes a second sip after they have exchanged cups while crossing their arms. If the celebrant has used the Chinese legend in her opening words, she may refer to it at this point with the following words:

Celebrant: The bride and groom will now drink from Chinese wedding cups. These cups are bound by a single red thread, representing the truth of our Chinese legend for [bride] and [groom]. This ritual also represents a prayer that harmony and peace will always rule within their home.

THE BINDING OF HANDS. The celebrant binds the hands of the bride and groom with a length of red Chinese silk. The binding might be done just before or after the vows. She may then state the Chinese legend or use the words of the handfasting, described in Chapter 6.

THE TEA CEREMONY. Traditionally, the bride and groom formally serve tea to each guest at the reception and in return receive from each a monetary gift enclosed in a red envelope with gold letters. The tea ceremony officially establishes the new couple's place within the family. If yours will be a small wedding, the tea ritual could be a lovely way to conclude the ceremony. The celebrant may introduce the ritual this way.

Celebrant: The tea ceremony is an ancient Chinese tradition. It is believed to be witnessed by the couple's ancestors. It formally celebrates and welcomes the couple within the family. We shall therefore conclude our ceremony with the serving of tea by our bride and groom.

FIREWORKS. Traditionally, fireworks, intended to keep away evil forces, greeted the bride. You might adapt this custom by ending your ceremony— right after the kiss!—with a fireworks display. One couple had fireworks from a yacht on New York's Hudson River. It was spectacular! Any outdoor setting, such as a beach, would be wonderfully appropriate. After officially declaring the couple husband and wife, the celebrant may state:

Celebrant: It is an ancient Chinese custom for the groom to greet his bride with a show of fireworks. Today, we honor and adapt this custom. [Bride] and [groom], may there always be fireworks between you. You may kiss.

THE UNITY CANDLE. One Chinese–Anglo-Catholic couple chose to combine the concept of the Christian unity candle with Chinese tradition by using red candles decorated at the base with red flowers. The celebrant may offer these words:

Celebrant: In honor of Christian tradition, the bride and groom will now light the unity candle. In honor of Chinese tradition, the candle is red, signifying good luck and good fortune. This is the symbolic merging of two traditions united in one sacred and profound love. [Bride] and [groom], your lives are now one. Would you please light the center candle symbolizing your blessed union?

HONORING OF PARENTS AND ANCESTORS. Chinese families are usually close-knit, and the honoring of one's parents, elders, and ancestors is intrinsic to Chinese society. In a Chinese interfaith ceremony, therefore, we formally honor the parents, grandparents, and often the ancestors of the bride and groom. This honoring can be done in many wonderful ways, as detailed in other sections of this book.

Cyprian

(See also the Orthodox ritual in the section on Christianity in Chapter 8.)

You may wish to incorporate this lovely legend at a point in your ceremony:

Celebrant: Love, romance, and marriage are reflected for nine thousand years in the history of Cyprus. Legend states that Aphrodite, the Goddess of Love and Beauty, was born in Cyprus. [Adapted from *Weddings, Dating, and Love Customs of Cultures Worldwide,* by Carolyn Mordecai]

Czech

The use of rosemary, symbolizing fertility and loyalty, is traditional in Czech weddings. A bride may want to include a bit of this herb in her bouquet.

Danish

You may want to create the traditional Danish "gate of honor," made of pine, beech, or oak branches. By custom, the bride and groom enter through this archway. One adaptation would be to stand under it for the ceremony.

Dutch

Lavender in the bride's bouquet is said by the Dutch to bring good luck. In a traditional Dutch ceremony, the couple's chairs in the church are decorated with green garlands, and flowers are thrown over the bride and groom at the end of the service.

Egyptian

When Egyptian weddings are celebrated in ballrooms, hotels, or wedding halls, the hotel hosts—standing in two lines—hold torches for the bridal couple to walk between. Typically, the bride and groom enter together holding hands.

THE SHARPAT. After the ceremony, the couple share a drink called sharpat, a rose water juice. Rose water has long symbolized love and romance.

English

In small towns in England (as well as in Italy, Scotland, and several Eastern European countries), brides and their bridal parties traditionally walk to the church, often with all the members of the town following behind. In England young girls walk ahead of the bride, sprinkling flower petals along her path.

There is something quite charming about seeing a bride walk to her wedding. One bride at whose ceremony I officiated married in a pavilion on top of a mountain. To everyone's surprise and delight, her entire bridal party, followed by her father and herself, walked through a large field toward the pavilion. I asked all the guests to stand and witness the magical sight. The pavilion itself was filled with fairy roses and butterflies. Even a hummingbird came to visit! It all felt very reminiscent of a European countryside wedding.

Filipino
(See also the sections on Christianity, Buddhism, and Islam in Chapter 8.)

THE WHITE CORD. In some Buddhist ceremonies, a white silk cord is draped around the couple or white silk scarves are placed around the necks of bride and groom, signifying their union.

SHOWERING OF COINS. Coins are showered on the bride and groom at the conclusion of a Filipino ceremony, to wish them good luck, abundance, and fertility. As an adaptation, coins might be showered over the bride's and groom's cupped hands as a sign of sharing, commitment, and prosperity, and to complete the marriage contract. The showering might be led by your celebrant, who can then invite family members or members of the bridal party to participate.

DOVES. A pair of doves, which have been caged in an elaborate bell made of flowers, are released by the couple after a Filipino ceremony. The doves signify peace and the couple's undying love for each other. You may wish to include the words for the Release of Doves ritual described in Chapter 6.

Finnish

In Finland the bride and groom wed under a wedding canopy, known as the bridal sky. The room is decorated with garlands, ornaments, mirrors, and written messages of good wishes from family and friends.

French

The French groom escorts his mother down the aisle in the procession—a touching moment.

THE COUPE DE MARIAGE. The ritual of the coupe de mariage can take place just before the vows. The bride and groom drink wine from a double-handled goblet, which is passed down from generation to generation. If there is no such heirloom in your family, you may want to purchase one and pass it along to your children, thereby starting your own tradition.

Celebrant: It is a French custom for the bride and groom to drink from the coupe de mariage, or the marriage cup. France is the land of wine, and wine symbolizes all that is good and sweet in life. [Bride] and [groom], in drinking the coupe de mariage, you commit to share all that life may bring, and we pray that your life together will be very sweet.

German

THE HOLDING OF DECORATED CANDLES. In German tradition, the bride and groom may hold candles that are adorned with flowers and ribbons throughout the ceremony. A modern adaptation would be to place the decorated candles upon the ceremony's table or altar.

THE RING EXCHANGE. Protestant German couples place and wear their wedding rings on the right hand instead of the left. If you wish to uphold this tradition, have your celebrant explain it.

Celebrant: It is a German custom for married couples to wear their wedding rings on their right hands. In honor of [bride or groom's] heritage, our bride and groom will therefore exchange rings, placing them upon the ring finger of the right hand.

Greek

(See also the Orthodox ritual in the section on Christianity in Chapter 8.)

IVY FOR THE BRIDE'S BOUQUET. A bit of ivy in your bouquet will echo an ancient Greek tradition—ivy as a symbol of eternal love.

READINGS. You may wish to include a verse from classical Greek literature. You will find some examples in Chapters 7 and 8.

THE CEREMONY OF HONEY AND WALNUTS. In some parts of Greece the wedding ceremony ends with the celebrant offering the bride and groom honey and walnuts on a silver spoon. Honey and walnuts represent sweetness and fertility, and, because the walnut can break into four parts, it also represents the bride, groom, and their two families.

> One word frees us of all the weight and pain of life; that word is love.
>
> —*Sophocles,* Oedipus at Colonus

SHOWERING WITH RICE AND SUGARED ALMONDS. In Greece—as in many other countries—the bride and groom are showered at the end of the ceremony with rice, for fertility, and sugar almonds, for the sweetness and bitterness in life. Because rice is no longer allowed at most wedding sites, for fear of harming birds, many couples opt for a showering of rose petals instead. You may also wish to hand out sugared almonds in fabric pouches as keepsakes for your guests.

Hawaiian

THE KAPPA. Traditionally, a Hawaiian bride and groom wed under a kappa, a native bark cloth, which represents shelter, a new home, and the joining of the couple's lives. Should you use a kappa in your service, your celebrant can give a brief explanation of its meaning and tradition.

LEIS. Leis—gorgeous garlands that often contain exotic flowers—symbolize love. The fragrant wedding lei is entwined with pikake, or white jasmine, and ilima. If you wish to include leis in your ceremony, here are several ways to do so:

Just before or after the vows, the celebrant binds the couple's hands with the garland.

Celebrant: *Leis symbolize love. In honor of Hawaiian tradition, I bind your hands with a lei, signifying your lifelong commitment of love to each other.*

Or the bride and groom may choose to give each other leis just after they exchange rings.

Celebrant: Leis symbolize love. [Bride] and [groom], you may now exchange your leis as a sign of your love and commitment.

Another option: Parents may place leis around the necks of the bride and groom at an appropriate point in the ceremony, as they bestow a personal blessing.

HOLDING HANDS. It is customary for the Hawaiian bride and groom to hold hands throughout their ceremony.

HONI. The delightful custom of honi is the gentle and affectionate gesture of rubbing noses. At the end of the ceremony, the bride and groom may rub noses just before they kiss with their lips!

HULA. The hula can reflect a prayer, a story, or a wish, and there is a hula for every occasion in the Hawaiian tradition. If you are in Hawaii, you can hire native dancers to perform at an interlude during your ceremony. Or you may be fortunate to have a relative or friend who is able to perform this charming dance. Your celebrant may briefly explain its meaning before the dance begins.

Hungarian

MONEY FOR THE BRIDE. In a Hungarian ceremony, the groom presents his bride with a bag of money to demonstrate that he will give her all he has and that he can trust her. The gesture might be done, just before the closing blessing, with an explanation like this by the celebrant.

Celebrant: It is a Hungarian tradition that the groom present to his bride a bag full of money. In this way he promises always to care for her. This is also a ceremony of trust. [Bride] and [groom], may you want for nothing. May you always be generous with each other. May great abundance follow you all the length of your days.

Indian

(See also the sections on Hinduism, Islam, and Sikhism in Chapter 8.)

THE BRIDE'S DRESS. The Indian bride's sumptuous attire is usually fashioned from gold- and silver-embroidered designs rich in symbolism. Red is considered the most auspicious color for the bride, but other colors, including deep pink, may be worn depending on regional tradition. Elaborate jewelry, including bangles, necklaces, earrings, nose rings, and head ornaments, is also worn.

HENNA DESIGNS. In a lovely custom popular throughout India, the bride's hands and feet are decorated with beautiful henna designs.

ROSE PETALS. At the end of the ceremony, rose petals are strewn over the bride and groom by their families. In the Hindu section in Chapter 8, you will find appropriate words for the celebrant to use at this point.

Indonesian
(See also the section on Islam in Chapter 8.)

THE PRESENCE OF FLOWING WATER. Traditionally, the Indonesian wedding ceremony takes place before flowing water, water being the symbol of the ever-flowing love between the bride and groom and for the couple by their families and friends. A contemporary couple may honor this tradition by arranging for their ceremony to be conducted in front of a fountain or beside a river or brook. You may make mention of the symbolism in your wedding program or have your celebrant refer to it in his opening words.

SYMBOLIC FOODS. On a table stands a tray with an arrangement of foods and wine that have symbolic meaning. The celebrant can explain in the opening words:

Celebrant: Before us, on this ceremonial table, are foods that have special meaning in Indonesian tradition. Tumeric rice is a symbol of prosperity, fertility, and love. Candy is for sweetness. Wine represents mirth and abundance, and betel nuts are for strength and harmony.

THE GIVING OF GARLANDS. The bride's mother places a garland of flowers around the groom's neck, signifying acceptance. In a modern version, each mother can give her prospective daughter- or son-in-law a garland, either at the beginning of the ceremony or combined with the parental blessings.

PARENTAL BLESSINGS. In Indonesia it is traditional that the parents formally bless the couple with prayer and good wishes. Your celebrant can call upon your parents to offer their blessings at the appropriate time.

THE SHARING OF RICE SEASONED WITH YELLOW TUMERIC. Following the vows, the celebrant can put a bit of rice in the couple's hands for them to feed each other. Here is an explanation:

Celebrant: The bride and groom will now share rice seasoned with tumeric. Rice is a symbol of prosperity and fertility, while the yellow tumeric represents everlasting love. As [bride] and [groom] share this rice three times, they are making final their marriage bond.

DANCERS SHOWERING THE COUPLE WITH FRAGRANT FLOWERS. What a wonderful way to end or begin a wedding ceremony—to have dancers shower you with fragrant flowers.

Iranian

THE SOFREH. The following material has been adapted from *New Food of Life: Ancient Persian and Modern Iranian Cooking and Ceremonies,* by Najmieh Batmanglij. The sofreh, the marriage spread, is central to the Iranian wedding ceremony, dating back over twenty-five hundred years. Typically arranged on a tray placed on the ceremonial table, the sofreh is beautiful to behold. Its ingredients may vary a bit from ceremony to ceremony; for example, each family creates a different design—perhaps a butterfly, a bird, or a flower—for the esfand, the colored incense. Rose water sometimes is added to symbolize romance and give fragrance. In a religious ceremony, the Koran is placed on the sofreh and quoted. At a nonreligious ceremony, the poet Rumi may be quoted.

A ritualistic element before the sofreh involves the couple's mothers. Using specially designed sugar cones or loaves wrapped in white net, the mothers take turns briefly rubbing the loaves together over the cloth that is being held over the couple's heads. Granules of sugar fall and are collected in the cloth, which the mothers later gather up and put off to the side.

Here are the words I used in one such ceremony:

Celebrant: [Bride] and [groom], would you kindly join me at the sofreh? [They seat themselves at the sofreh.]

The sofreh dates back over twenty-five hundred years in Persia. It literally means "the marriage spread." As you can see, it is truly a visual feast, beautiful to behold and rich in symbolism. Each family places their own personal and artistic touch upon the sofreh in terms of the selection and arrangement of its items.

Here, the mirror is a symbol of purity and clarity.

The candles lit on either side of the mirror, one representing the bride, the other the groom, ensure the couple luminosity and wisdom in all aspects of their life.

Esfand, wild rue, is the incense placed here in a beautiful rendering of a gardenia. It is to protect the couple from all harm.

Noghl is the white sugar candy. Nabat is the crystallized sugar, which is formed into a bowl. These along with the honey and pastries guarantee sweetness.

Bread, herbs, and cheese symbolize abundance and affluence.

The colorfully painted eggs and walnuts bring fertility.

All the races and tribes in the world are like the different colored flowers of one meadow. All are beautiful. As children of the Creator they must all be respected.

—anonymous, taken from the Native American Indian Traditional Code of Ethics; Inter-Tribal Times, 1994

The roses scattered about the sofreh express the hope that beauty and romance shall forever adorn the couple's life together.

A sheer cloth is held by family members over the heads of the couple while the mothers of the bride and groom rub sugar loaves together, as if to say: May only sweet joy and happiness rain upon your lovely heads.

Finally, in the seven brilliant colors of the rainbow, the united threads of love and commitment are carefully sewn into the marriage spread.

We shall now conclude with the words of the Persian poet Rumi: "Lovers do not finally meet somewhere. They have known each other all along."

[Bride] and [groom], would you allow me the honor of proceeding with your wedding ceremony?

[It is traditional for the celebrant to pose this question. The bride and groom reply: *Yes.*]

THE TOSSING OF SWEETS AND COINS. It is traditional for the guests to toss sweets and coins at the bride and groom to wish them good luck, abundance, and joy.

Irish

BLESSINGS. When the bride or groom or both are Irish, I immediately suggest that we incorporate an Irish blessing, which the Irish use often in everyday speech and for which they are delightfully famous. In Chapter 7, you will find several Irish blessings that are wonderfully appropriate for a wedding.

MUSIC. Many an Irish bride and groom have ceremonially processed or recessed led by bagpipers in kilts—one, two, four, or even six bagpipers. The effect is quite dramatic. It stirs the Irish soul!

THE CLADDAGH RINGS. Many Irish couples exchange Claddagh weddings rings. If one or both of you has elected to wear a Claddagh ring, your celebrant may offer the following legend (adapted from theweddingconnection. com) right before the exchange of rings.

Celebrant: According to legend, the Claddagh ring tradition originated with a man in ancient Galway. Soon to be wed, he was taken prisoner by roving sailors and forced into labor in a foreign land. During his imprisonment he taught himself the art of jewelry making. Upon returning to his homeland, he found that his maiden had never married, and in his happiness he fashioned the now famous Claddagh wedding band. The ring depicts a heart, held by two hands, with a crown over it.

TOKENS FOR LUCK. Traditionally, an Irish bride trimmed her wedding dress with Irish lace, famous for its beauty and quality, to ensure good luck. Modern-day Irish brides may carry a dainty handkerchief or wear a veil made of Irish lace.

THE SPRINKLING OF ROSE PETALS. I have been told that it is an Irish custom for all the guests to sprinkle rose petals on the bride and groom as they take their first dance after the ceremony. In adaptation of this lovely custom, I have sprinkled rose petals on the couple after saying the Irish wedding blessing at the close of the ceremony and right before the formal presentation of the newly married couple. In one second marriage we invited the groom's children to participate. In another particularly large gathering—eight siblings on the groom's side, five on the bride's—all the family members were invited to sprinkle the fragrant petals. The celebrant might say words like these:

Celebrant: Rose petals, also an Irish custom, represent love, romance, and beauty—life's sweetest blessings. For your journey, [bride] and [groom], we sprinkle them upon your heads; we lay them at your feet.

Italian

Traditionally, the Italian bride and groom walk to the church on foot.

LE BUSTE. In the tradition known as le buste, the bride carries a silk or satin pouch to hold envelopes of monetary gifts.

FOR THE GUESTS. Bags of sugared almonds (called confetti), symbolizing the bitterness and sweetness of life, are given to the guests as keepsakes.

Japanese
(See also the section on Shintoism in Chapter 8.)

The san-san-kudo, the sharing of sake, is at the heart of the traditional Shinto wedding. In the section on Shinto you will find a description of how the sake ritual can be incorporated in an interfaith ceremony.

THE BRIDE'S DRESS. A traditional Japanese bride wears a regal wedding kimono. Many contemporary brides wear Western-style white gowns for the wedding and change later to traditional Japanese dress.

FLOWERS. White and purple orchids are favorite Japanese wedding flowers, as well as jasmine, lotus blossoms, and cherry blossoms.

A JAPANESE LEGEND. Your celebrant may offer in the opening words this wonderful ancient Japanese legend (it is also considered a Chinese legend), which many couples also choose to print on their programs:

Celebrant: A Japanese legend states that a couple is bound at birth by a red thread, which continuously shrinks over the years until the man and woman are united in marriage.

HONORING OF PARENTS AND ANCESTORS. Honoring one's parents and ancestors is intrinsic to the indigenous Japanese religion of Shinto. Bowing demonstrates respect in Japanese society. When I conduct a ceremony for a Japanese family, therefore, I usually formally honor the parents, and often the grandparents, by bowing deeply and solemnly. You may also wish to present your parents with a gift of white or purple orchids (purple is considered the color of love). Elsewhere we have suggested other ways, including readings, to honor family.

DEPICTION OF CRANES OR GEESE. In a traditional Japanese ceremony, live pairs of cranes or geese were sometimes part of the bridal procession! Geese mate for life and thus are often associated with marriage. One Japanese couple had printed programs that featured two geese flying into the horizon. Cranes are another popular image. It is said that the crane lives for 1,000 years, so 1,001 origami cranes symbolize long life. An origami crane might be a delightful keepsake for each guest.

Korean
(See also the sections on Buddhism, Christianity, and Confucianism in Chapter 8.)

THE BRIDE'S DRESS. The Korean bride may choose to wear a traditional gown, which is a full silk, kimonolike dress with large sleeves. Most Korean brides today wear Western-style white gowns, perhaps changing later into traditional Korean dress.

SYMBOLS. Peonies, symbols of beauty, love, and joy, are traditional elements in Korean wedding ceremonies. The goose and gander are also favorite symbols, because they mate for life. Your celebrant can include in her opening words a brief description of these elements.

THE KUNBERE. In the kunbere ritual the couple share a special white wine. The kunbere is done in reverent silence, before which the celebrant can offer the following explanation:

Celebrant: In a Korean tradition known as the kunbere, the bride and groom share a special white wine—jung jong—from cups fashioned from the two halves of a gourd. Each will take a sip from his and her own cup, after which our bridesmaid will mix the wine from both cups together. Then the bride and groom will drink again, signifying their vow to each other and their consent to the marriage. Their lives are now joined.

SHOWERING OF THE BRIDE WITH DATES AND CHESTNUTS. Traditionally, the groom's mother scatters dates and nuts over the bride's dress for fertility, and the bride tries to catch them in her skirt. Since dates are sticky and chestnuts hard, a modern, and less messy, adaptation would be to serve these foods to your guests.

Laotian
(See also the section on Buddhism in Chapter 8.)

THE BINDING OF WRISTS. The celebrant in a Laotian wedding binds the bride's and groom's wrists with white cotton threads. A modern couple may wish instead to have their hands bound according to the handfasting ritual described in Chapter 6. White cotton threads, which represent blessings and good luck, are also passed out to all the guests. Shortly before the couple exchange vows, the celebrant holds the threads high in her hand and says something like this:

Celebrant: These white cotton threads are a Laotian tradition. They symbolize blessings for the bride and groom. [Bride] and [groom], remember this: "Pains do not hold a marriage together. It is threads, hundreds of tiny threads, which sew people together through the years." [These are actually the words of Simone Signoret.] May these threads symbolize the joining of your hearts, minds, bodies, and souls.

Latin American, Central American, and Spanish
(See also the section on Christianity in Chapter 8.)

CLOTHING. A Spanish groom traditionally wears a tucked shirt that has been embroidered by the bride. In a modern adaptation, the bride might give her groom a (purchased) embroidered shirt to wear on their wedding day.

ARRAS. The delightful tradition of arras originated in Spain and is also celebrated in Central and South America. Thirteen gold coins, placed in a small and beautifully decorated treasure chest or on a silver tray, are given to the bride by the groom, signifying that he will always provide and care for her. More broadly, the chest of coins symbolizes abundance for the couple. The sound of the clattering coins is important! (Traditionally, sound has been a significant element in many rituals, as a means of warding off evil. Today, the clattering of the coins is simply considered to provide dramatic effect, and to be a demonstration to the guests that the exchange is taking place.) Often these treasure chests are family heirlooms. If your family does not have one, you may wish to purchase a chest—perhaps engraved with a special verse—and start the tradition to pass along to your children.

The celebrant holds the chest high, explains the tradition, then gives the chest to the groom, who removes the coins and passes them to his bride; she in turn passes them back to him. I have also seen the ritual performed with loose coins, sort of flowing between the couple's hands with lots of cha-chinking sounds.

Celebrant: [Bride] and [groom] wish to honor the tradition of arras. It is the sharing of wealth symbolized by the passing of thirteen coins between the bride and groom. [Bride] and [groom], as you pass these coins between you, may you want for nothing. May you always be generous with each other. May great abundance follow you all the length of your days.

COMPADRES. Compadres, or godparents, are held in high esteem in Latin America and are expected to participate in the wedding ceremony. Your compadres may be asked to stand as the best man and matron of honor and/or to sign the wedding license.

Latvian

Instead of a maid of honor and best man, a Latvian bride and groom choose a married couple who are close to them to represent them at the ceremony.

Malaysian
(See also the section on Islam in Chapter 8.)

HENNA DESIGNS. The Malaysian bride's hands and feet are decorated with designs done in henna.

THE SUAP-SUAP, THE SHARING OF RICE. In a ritual of mutual sharing and nourishment, the bride and groom feed each other rice, called adab-adab. A close relative or the celebrant places a small lump of (cooked) rice in the groom's hand and then in the bride's hand. This ritual would fit well just before or after the vows.

Celebrant: In a Malaysian custom known as the suap-suap, the bride and groom feed each other rice, adab-adab. By doing so, they agree to share all that they have. They commit to nourish each other always.

Mexican
(See also the section on Christianity in Chapter 8.)

Mexican wedding traditions include the arras, or sharing of gold coins, and the inclusion of godparents (padrinos) as an honored and integral part of the wedding ceremony. Both are described in the earlier section on Latin American customs.

THE LAZO. A lazo, a large rosary, is draped around the couple, figure-eight style, as the celebrant offers a brief prayer, perhaps before or after the vows. The padrinos may be called on to arrange the lazo, which can be intricately designed and quite beautiful.

Celebrant: Let this union be binding. Let this union serve as an inspiration. Remember the sanctity and love necessary to preserve your new family as a family of God.

Moroccan
(See also the section on Islam in Chapter 8.)

HENNA DESIGNS. In a lovely custom popular in Morocco and throughout the Middle East, the bride's hands and feet are decorated with designs painted in henna. At one intercultural wedding, the American bride surprised her Moroccan groom by presenting to him her henna-designed palms.

THE PROCESSIONAL. In Morocco women walk down the aisle carrying lit candles. In a Western adaptation, the bride may wish to process with her female friends and relatives carrying candles before or behind her.

THE SHARING OF SWEET MILK AND A DATE. The custom of sharing sweet milk and a date, also practiced in other Middle Eastern cultures, can easily be incorporated in your ceremony, ideally right before the vows.

Celebrant: It is a delightful Moroccan tradition that a bride and groom shall drink sweet milk together and share a date. In doing so, they partake of the nourishing sweetness of life.

[The celebrant first pours milk, which may be sweetened with honey, from a pitcher into a cup and gives it to the groom, who then shares it with his bride; the ritual follows in the same manner with the date. The celebrant may conclude by saying this particularly appropriate blessing from the poet and mystic Rumi, which begins, "May these vows and this marriage be blessed. May it be sweet milk. . . ." The full verse is on page 128.]

SHOWERING OF DATES, FIGS, AND RAISINS. At the end of the ceremony, the guests shower the bride and groom with dates, figs, and raisins, symbolizing fertility. A modern adaptation would be to serve your guests these dried fruits at the reception, or perhaps to hand out little fabric pouches of them.

Norwegian

The Nowegian bride wears a crown of silver and gold that softly rings. Green is the preferred color in a traditional Norwegian wedding.

Pakistani
(See also the section on Islam in Chapter 8.)

Firecrackers and musicians traditionally announce the groom's arrival at a Pakistani wedding, and strings of white lights adorn the outside of the ceremony site. The bride often wears a red sari, perhaps with henna floral designs on her hands and feet. After the vows the Koran is held over the heads of the bride and groom.

Polish
(See also the section on Christianity in Chapter 8.)

SALTED BREAD AND SWEET WINE. Traditionally, the Polish bride and groom share bread and wine, after which their parents bless and embrace the couple. You may wish to include this ritual as part of your ceremony just before exchanging vows, or at the reception. The celebrant may explain it this way:

Celebrant: As is Polish custom, the bride and groom will now partake of salted bread and sweet wine, as a reminder of the sweetness and bitterness in life. [Bride] and [groom], bread is the sustenance of life, and this bread represents our hope that you will always be nourished physically and spiritually. The salt represents life's difficulty, for which you must remain united and strong—and the wine, our hope that life will be for you full of happiness and good cheer. We now invite the parents of the bride and groom to come forward and bless their children.

Portuguese
(See also the section on Christianity in Chapter 8.)

BINDING OF THE HANDS. The Portuguese couple's hands are wrapped loosely with a prayer vestment before the exchange of rings, following the handfasting ritual described in Chapter 6.

DRINKING OF PORT. The bride and groom may choose to drink port—a sweet wine that comes from Portugal—as part of their ceremony.

SONNETS FROM THE PORTUGUESE. Some couples include a reading from *Sonnets from the Portuguese* in their wedding.

A SHOWER OF BONBONS. At the end of the ceremony, guests throw bonbons over the bride and groom. A modern adaptation would be to hand the sweets out in fabric pouches, as keepsakes for your guests.

Romanian
(See also the Orthodox ritual and Catholic elements in the section on Christianity in Chapter 8.)

In Romanian weddings metal crowns are used for the crowning, symbolizing an enduring and peaceful rule within the family.

Russian
(See also the Orthodox ritual and Catholic elements in the section on Christianity, and the section on Islam in Chapter 8.)

To honor your heritage, you may wish to incorporate verse from the rich proliferation of Russian literature.

One unconventional couple decided to develop their own tradition by sharing vodka and caviar, with soft Russian folk music playing live in the background, as part of their ceremony.

Samoan

The Samoan bride wears a mother-of-pearl crown, as well as flowers in her hair.

Scandinavian

The Scandinavian bride wears a jeweled crown, representing her innocence. If one of the bride's parents is deceased, a poignant tradition is to save the bridal bouquet so that she may later place it on the grave of her late parent.

Scottish

CELTIC WEDDING BANDS. Wedding bands with Celtic designs are enjoying renewed popularity.

CELTIC HANDFASTING. See the description in Chapter 6.

A KILT FOR THE GROOM. The groom may wear a kilt in the colors of his clan's tartan.

A PIPER. In a traditional Scottish wedding, a bagpiper leads the processional.

THE QUAICH CUP. Immediately after they say their vows, the bride and groom drink from the quaich "cup of life."

Celebrant: The bride and groom will now drink from the Quaich, a Scottish custom. The drink from these glasses is the embodiment of your families, your ancestors, and your bloodlines. It represents your lineage and symbolizes that which you are.

[Celebrant then instructs the couple to pour the wine or liquor from the two individual glasses into the Quaich. Holding the cup up high, she continues:] *This quaich symbolizes the merging of two lives or two traditions, united in one sacred and profound love. You may drink.*

Spanish

A lace mantilla, a symbol of purity, is traditional for the Spanish bride.

Orange blossoms are considered the wedding flower of everlasting love in Spain (because the orange tree is an evergreen), and Spanish brides carry orange blossoms in their bouquets.

THE EXCHANGE OF COINS. Please see the section on Latin American customs for the exchange of coins.

One Castilian bride, wearing a Spanish-style gown with a mantilla, had gold coins in a velvet pouch placed on an ornate silver tray. At the end of the ceremony, just before the closing blessing, I held the tray high and explained the symbolism with the words included here. The groom poured the coins into the open palms of his bride, making loud clattering sounds. She then poured them back into his waiting palms. Everyone laughed when he then slipped the coins into his pockets, as she shrugged her shoulders and raised her hands.

Celebrant: There is a Spanish tradition that dates back to ancient Castile [you may adapt the region]. *It is the sharing of wealth, symbolized by the passing of thirteen coins between the bride and groom. [Bride] and [groom], as you pass these coins between yourselves, may you want for nothing. May you always be generous with each other. May great abundance follow you all the length of your days.*

Sudanese

The Sudanese groom presents to his bride a red and gold shawl, which she wears on her wedding day. Her hands and feet are decorated with henna designs.

Swedish

The Swedish bride wears a jeweled crown. As in so many cultures, the Swedish bride and groom are treated like royalty on their wedding day.

Swiss

Edelweiss, the symbol of love and strength, may be incorporated in the Swiss bride's bouquet.

Part III

IN THEIR OWN WORDS:

Eight Interfaith,
Intercultural Couples,
Their Love Stories and
Wedding Ceremonies

Leah and Zack
a Jewish–Iranian couple
a personalized humanist ceremony

Leah's spirited voice rang clear as a bell over the telephone. Her mother had read about my interfaith work in a wedding magazine, and Leah and her fiancé would be in New York for Halloween. "Could we meet?" Leah asked. And so we did, a couple of hours before I had to dash off to don costumes and paint my son's face for our participation in our local community Halloween parade. Later I would find out just why the idea of it tickled this couple so.

"Leah and Zack are two of the most genuinely happy people that I have ever met," one of this couple's dear friends wrote to me. "When I picture Zack, I think of him in one of two ways: with the devilish smile he gets when he laughs, or in full Halloween costume regalia, as Baryshnikov or Mighty Mouse or a genie. After college graduation, as our group of friends became separated by geography and we struggled with how to keep connected, Zack single-handedly convinced us that we were to reunite at Halloween every year. Of course, the day itself wasn't the important thing. What was important was that Zack had the vision to see the value of picking one specific, easy-to-remember day, and marking it as the day we would all hold aside for traveling across the country to see each other.

"As for Leah, to see her passion for life all you need is to have a conversation with her. Her eyes light up and she bubbles with enthusiasm when engaged in a discussion about almost everything. Leah is one of my favorite people in the world to talk to on the phone or to sit next to at dinner. The love Leah and Zack bring to the world is equaled perhaps only by what they get from each other."

Their passion, happiness, and high spirits this friend talked about were so very evident in the questionnaires Leah (a historian and teacher) and Zack (a radiologist) had completed.

He wrote, "Traveling and living with her is unbelievable, amazing. It's easy without ever being boring; we laugh at everything, never taking ourselves or others too seriously. I went through a period before Leah where I doubted I would ever find a woman I wanted to marry and, even if I did, I doubted that she would ever be my true 'best friend,' especially given my long-standing and deep male friendships. But Leah really is my best friend. Every experience I have I want her to share. I don't think there has been one specific moment that made me realize we would be together forever. I am too measured for that and not given to dramatic revelations very often. But during my medical internship, when I saw patients at the end stages of their lives surrounded by generations of family and their spouses, I knew I wanted to be with Leah when I got to that point."

From Leah, I read, "He is an extraordinary person—so healthy, strong, and insightfully smart—and I feel unbelievably lucky (not undeserving, mind you, but tremendously fortunate) to have been able to connect so intimately with him as a friend and a lover. The intensity of my feelings for him goes far beyond the paltry words used to try to describe them. I can only say that it is a strong, boundless love filled with hope, respect, admiration and, frankly, awe for the gift I have been given. With or without this ceremony, I feel that my commitment to Zack and my love for him would stand as one of the greatest forces in my life. One of our greatest strengths as a couple is our shared trust in each other's commitment to our relationship—it is a safe place where problems can be discussed and dealt with, without fear of the center or our commitment to each other giving way. I imagine that this, more than desire, more than laughter, more than any of the other wonderful qualities that nourish our relationship, will sustain us in difficult times and inspire us when things are good."

Zack made it clear to me that he did not consider himself a Muslim. He was raised as such, he said, in name only, and although his parents were Muslim and he believed in God, he was not religious. But, culturally, he called himself "very Iranian." Leah, too, stated that she was not a religious person, but felt strongly connected to her Jewish culture. So they wanted a humanist ceremony, spiritual at heart, celebrating their traditions and honoring their families—"both our immediate family," she wrote, "and our extended family, whose origins and cultural roots in Iran, Poland, Germany, Austria, and Russia are integral to our being here today."

The ceremony should be, she said, "intimate and touching while at the same time more festive, relaxed, and upbeat—a celebration—than a solemn or serious event." And she hoped it would be "a moment during all the usual rush that surrounds our lives for Zack and me to take some time, some breaths, some space for ourselves and our relationship—and to reaffirm our sense of awe and sacredness that comes from the other's daily gift of love."

In planning the ceremony, I met with both sets of parents. Both were a little concerned that the service be balanced. As we talked about how that could be accomplished and as they saw the beautiful possibilities unfold, Zack's father turned to me and said, "I have just one question. How will I keep from crying?"

Just before the ceremony, the bride and groom were scheduled to take photographs. I remember Zack gazing at his bride as she posed for her formal portrait, resplendent in a beaded sheath that seemed Persian-inspired. I quietly slipped behind him and whispered in his ear, "Zack, are you drinking her in?" Poignantly, he answered, "I can't. It is just too much."

The ceremony took place in the garden room of a luxurious old hotel in Washington, D.C.; the guests had arrived from all over the United States, from Canada, England, France, Belgium, Wales, and the groom's native Iran. They saw a gorgeous setting—the ceiling draped with fabric, candlelit lanterns, urns of flowers everywhere, and the wedding canopy a work of art, with twigs, foliage, flowers, and sumptuous fabric. A small table under the canopy held the antique kiddush cup, for the blessing over the wine, which had belonged to Leah's great-grandmother, the family matriarch. On the floor was the Iranian sofreh, a sumptuous spread of a variety of items on a Persian rug, all rich with symbolism and artistry.

> Two souls with but a single thought, two hearts that beat as one.
> —*Friedrich Halm*

Here, the wedding of Leah and Zack.

Procession

In the Jewish tradition, the bride and groom walked in with their parents, followed by grandparents, siblings, and the bridal party. A soloist sang, "My Baby Just Cares for Me," a Nina Simone song: Leah had decided that she wanted her guests to smile as she walked down the aisle, and she said that the song, "though a bit untraditional, captures the happy mood I wish to set, and suggests that I am not taking my 'grand' entrance as the bride all too seriously." Both sets of parents took their places under the canopy, surrounded by the bridal party.

Opening Words

In welcoming everyone on behalf of the bride and groom, I began by reading a few excerpts from the letters written to me by family and friends. Here are two of them.

The bride's mother writes, "To share space and time with Leah and Zack is truly a gift. When they are together, they are a definitive unit that both encloses them in their private feelings for each other and at the same time invites you in and warms you."

From a friend: "I look forward to watching Leah and Zack walk into the future. I know they will be hand in hand, never one in front and the other behind, always side by side, finding fun and frivolity along the way."

Celebrant's Address to the Parents

Here is a portion of my address to the mothers and fathers.

I know it feels like only yesterday that Leah and Zack were born. Time goes by so quickly! When you first gazed at these two faces, I know you marveled at their perfection and you felt truly blessed. In your children you saw infinite potential and placed great hope. You guided them, nurtured them, educated them, loved them. You gave them all you had to give, so that they would grow up strong and independent, capable of great love, capable of what they are doing here today. Without you, this marriage would not, could not be possible.

Leah, with her usual exuberance, wrote me pages and pages about her family, all with the greatest admiration—using many superlatives and exclamation points. My fax machine ran out of paper! Leah summed up her feelings for her mother with these words: "She is my core, my guide." She refers to her father as "extraordinary. A father who is a tremendous caretaker, whose generosity, tenderness, and unwavering beliefs in my abilities have made me confident and given me security." These are her words, parents, not mine! She is a very happy young woman. You have done a great job!

Dr. and Mrs. [Zack's parents], Zack has great appreciation and admiration for what it must have meant for you to leave homeland and family behind to make a new life for your children here in a Westernized culture. And you have done such a good job! He writes, "My very essence originates from their close nurturing while I was growing up and from seeing how they interact with each other." [Zack's mother], your son remembers that when he was very young you would sit in his room, on the floor with your back against the wall, until he fell asleep. A selfless act that he attributes to your later needing back surgery! He admires your resiliency and inner strength.

Dr. [Zack's father], your son sees you as a generous and selfless father, and a professional mentor. I don't think he will ever forget his graduation from medical school, when you placed the hood around his neck. Or when he was in high school and told you that football was the most important thing in his life, and you raised an eyebrow and said, "Really?" And how, after that, you left work early one day every week to come and watch him play football. Through these selfless acts, Zack learned to love.

So it is with much gratitude, in honor of Zack's and Leah's parents, and their siblings, and their beloved grandparents, that we offer this saying by Linda Hogan:

Walking. I am listening to a deeper way. Suddenly all my ancestors are behind me. Be. Still. They Say. Watch and Listen. You are the result of the love of thousands.

Celebrant's Address to the Couple

Among my comments to the couple was this one: "You don't need my advice, because you have your priorities in order. Leah, you said it all with your inscription on the watch you gave Zack—'My friend, my love, my life.' That's it!"

The Sofreh and the Blessing over the Wine

Ladies and gentlemen, today we witness the joining of two lives, two families, two ancient and equally rich cultures. In honor and in celebration of this union, the bride and groom have chosen rituals from each tradition for their wedding ceremony.

Leah and Zack, and your mothers, would you kindly join me at the sofreh?

The sofreh dates back over twenty-five hundred years in Persia. Literally, it means "the marriage spread." As you can see, it is truly a visual feast, beautiful to behold and rich in symbolism. Each family places their own personal and artistic touch on the sofreh in terms of the selection and arrangement of its items. I'd like to explain them to you now.

The mirror is a symbol of purity and clarity.

The candles lit on either side of the mirror—one representing the bride, the other the groom—ensure the couple luminosity and wisdom in all aspects of their life.

Esfand (wild rue) is the incense placed here, beautifully rendered in the shape of a gardenia. It is to protect the couple from all harm.

Noghl is the white sugar candy. Nabat is the crystallized sugar, formed here into a bowl. These along with the honey and pastries guarantee sweetness.

Bread, herbs, and cheese symbolize abundance and affluence.

The colorfully painted eggs and walnuts bring fertility.

The roses scattered about the sofreh express the hope that beauty and romance forever adorn the couple's life together.

In the seven brilliant colors of the rainbow, the symbol of hope, the united threads of love and commitment are carefully sewn into the marriage spread.

As you see, the bride's and groom's mothers have throughout been rubbing sugar loaves together above the couple, as if to say, "May only sweet joy and happiness rain upon your lovely heads."

We will conclude the sofreh with the words of the Persian poet Rumi: "Lovers do not finally meet somewhere, they have known each other all along."

Leah and Zack, would you allow me the honor of proceeding with your wedding ceremony? (*It is an Iranian custom for the celebrant to pose this question.*) [Adapted from *New Food for Life* by Najmieh Khalili Batmanglij]

Now in honor of the Jewish tradition, the bride and groom will drink from the kiddush cup, the cup of life. Within it is wine that symbolizes all that is good and sweet in life. This kiddush cup has special family significance, as it was passed down by Leah's great-grandmother, who lived to be 101. So perhaps in this case it also signifies longevity! Leah and Zack, before you take your wedding vows, I ask you both to drink from the cup of mirth and abundance. Whatever seeds of bitterness it may contain shall be all the sweeter because you drink it together.

Reading

*Following the **declaration of intent**, I explained to the guests that the bride and groom chose to read Sonnet 89 by Pablo Neruda that expressed eloquently how they felt about marriage.*

> *[Leah]*
> *When I die, I want your hands on my eyes:*
> *I want the light and wheat of your beloved hands*
> *to pass their freshness over me once more:*
> *I want to feel the softness that changed my destiny.*
>
> *I want you to live while I wait for you, asleep.*
> *I want your ears still to hear the wind, I want you*
> *to sniff the sea's aroma that we loved together,*
> *to continue to walk on the sand we walk on.*

[Zack]
I want what I love to continue to live,
and you whom I love and sang above everything else
to continue to flourish, full-flowered:

so that you can reach everything my love directs you to,
so that my shadow can travel along in your hair,
so that everything can learn the reason for my song.

Vows

In turn, Leah and Zack repeated the vows as I read them. Each had selected
slightly different vows.

    [Leah]
    With this ring,
    I give you my heart.
    I have no greater gift to give.
    I promise I shall do my best.
    I shall always try.
    I feel so honored to call you my husband.
    I feel so fortunate to call you mine.
    [Zack]
    With this ring,
    I give you my promise that from this day forward you shall not walk alone.
    May my heart be your shelter,
    And my arms be your home.
    May we walk together through all things.
    May you feel deeply loved, for indeed you are.
    I feel so honored to call you my wife.
    I feel so fortunate to call you mine.
    [Adapted from *Illuminata*, by Marianne Williamson]

During these vows, Zack at one point had to stop and compose himself. Leah,
herself deeply touched, reassuringly and gently caressed his arms. These moments
for me remain emblazoned in memory.

Do you, Leah/Zack, take this man/woman, to be your lawful wedded
husband/wife, to have and to hold, to love and to cherish, to be true to
him/her, through times of sorrow as well as joy? Do you promise this heart,
body, and soul? Do you commit to honor this vow all the days of your life?

*After **the pronouncement** and **the kiss**, I addressed the guests, asking them to offer their support to this intercultural, interfaith union, ending with the words "And perhaps they bring us one step closer toward world peace." Somewhat to my surprise, all two hundred guests clapped and cheered!*

Closing Blessing

For the final blessing, I ask you all now to take a moment, go inside yourselves, and fill yourselves with all your good wishes, all your hopes and dreams for Leah and Zack in the years to come.

Zack and Leah, you will now go into the world as husband and wife. May you grow glorious in each other's arms. May laughter and warmth reign supreme in your home. May you have fine healthy children whom you shall cherish, and they you in return. May you be graced with the joy of family and friends. May you live long. May you live well. Go in peace. Go with love.

*After the **breaking of the glass** and shouts of "Mazel tov!" the new husband and wife and their families, followed by all their guests, headed to the main lobby and champagne. Later, at the reception, Leah delighted Zack's family— especially his parents and elderly grandmother, who had flown in from Iran— with a speech she read in Farsi as well as English. A fitting end to this day was a dance between the bride, her mother, and myself—for the entire experience was a dance, a delightful, sacred, and passionate dance.*

Some time later, Leah's mother wrote me, "Will we meet again? I hope so. But if by some mistake we do not, please know that we will not forget your presence on this earth, we will look for your footprints along that way. We will think of you often with smiles and with grateful tears, and we hope your future is everything you hope it to be." To the families of Leah and Zack, I humbly and gratefully, say: Ditto. Emerson wrote that when there is true giving there is neither giver nor receiver. I believe it was so in this case. We experienced a pure and mutual sharing.

Natasha and Phillip
a Hindu–Jewish couple
a religious ceremony celebrating cultural traditions

Natasha and Phillip—a schoolteacher and an accountant—did not want a highly personalized ceremony. They had decided not to answer the questionnaire, preferring to create a formal and complex service that focused on blending the sacred rituals and words of their two ancient traditions.

Their wedding was a feast for the eyes. Their guests came from India, Panama, and many other exotic and not so exotic parts of the world. At the evening ceremony, held in a spacious banquet room in a New York hotel, the women arrived dressed in splendid, luminous saris. Chairs had been arranged in a circular pattern, with the chuppah/mandap in the center. Under the canopy were two chairs, for the bride and groom, and a table on which (and under which) we had arranged a number of items that would be used in a series of rituals: One tray held the tea lights or candles we would light, symbolizing the fire central within a Hindu ceremony (the hotel could not allow the traditional open fire for safety reasons); another tray contained bowls of rice, coconut, sweets, and flowers. Also on the table were the kiddush cup, a carafe of wine, a small pitcher of water, a sacred thread for the tying of the hands, a silver bowl, matches, several cloth napkins, and two roses the bride and groom would present to their mothers. Under the table we had placed the flower garlands to be exchanged. A bowl of rose petals was at the end of each row of chairs for the guests.

> Love is our true destiny. We do not find the meaning of life by ourselves alone.... We find it with another.
>
> —*Thomas Merton*

Throughout the service, we included a great deal of explanation, so that all in attendance would understand the meaning and symbolism behind each ritual.

Here, Phillip and Natasha's wedding.

Procession

Wearing my civil clothes, I waited under the chuppah/mandap as the groom entered—looking most handsome in his tuxedo and with a parent on each arm—walked to the chuppah, and kissed his mother and father, who took their seats in the first row. All eyes then were on the bride, who wore a stunning silver-and-pale-pink-embroidered gown and veil complete with exquisite jewelry and a diamond bindi (worn in the center of the forehead), as she walked in with her parents. The bride's departure from her parents was quite emotional, and her tears flowed freely while Dad gently consoled her. The groom then gallantly offered his arm and escorted his bride to two waiting chairs (as is Hindu tradition), which stood before me.

Opening Words

Here is an abbreviated version of my welcoming address.

Namaste and Shalom!

Today, we witness the joining of two lives, two ancient and rich cultures united in one sacred love. And God is smiling! The Kabbalah states that God is continuously creating new worlds by causing marriages to take place. Today we are privileged to witness the birth of a new world. It is the dawn of Natasha and Phillip's marriage. It is from this world that children shall come forth—more new worlds.

In the Kama Sutra it is said that when the one man loves the one woman and the one woman loves the one man, the angels abandon heaven and go sit with the couple and sing for joy. Just look around you; look into the face of the person next to you. The angels are here! For you have come with joy and love in your hearts. Your light, the light of your soul, has touched their light. Your presence adds sanctity to this occasion. It is a great gift you give to Natasha and Phillip, one for which they are most grateful.

You are about to witness a ceremony perhaps unlike others you have seen. We have tried to merge the most significant aspects of both traditions in a sacred dance, a Hindu-Jewish dance. We have also incorporated personal elements selected by the bride and groom to create a ceremony that is unique and reflective of our couple and their families.

We begin with the gift of a flower to each of the women who gave the bride and groom life, their mothers—a gift symbolic of beauty and gratitude. Will the mothers please rise?

Phillip's and Natasha's mothers came up to the chuppah/mandap, where they received their flowers, an embrace, and a kiss from their son and daughter.

Today we bless this union under a wedding canopy, called a chuppah in the Jewish tradition and a mandap in the Hindu tradition. In both cultures the meaning is the same. The canopy represents shelter, sanctity, and peace. The four poles correspond to the four directions—north, south, east, and west—as the couple's love reaches to the four corners of the earth. The sides are open, for the couple's home and arms will remain open to their family and friends. "The chuppah," the mandap, "is the house of promises. It is the home of hope." (by Debra Cash) We will now hear a poem about the chuppah, written by Marge Piercy, a poem that applies to the mandap as well.

Reading

A member of the bride's family stepped forward to read the chuppah poem, which
contains the following much-loved lines:

O my love O my love we dance
under the chuppah standing over us
like an animal on its four legs,
like a table on which we set our love
as a feast, like a tent
under which we work
not safe but no longer solitary
in the searing heat of our time.

(See page 183 for the complete text.)

Prayer

In Hindu tradition every auspicious occasion begins with an invocation to
Lord Ganesh. This is a prayer to ensure that the ceremony is free from
impediments and, at a wedding, that the marriage be free from all hardships,
evils, and obstacles. Prayers are offered also to Nava-Graha, the nine planets,
symbolizing the cooperation and welcoming of the universe. These prayers
ask for continuous happiness, peace, friendship, and prosperity in the marriage.

The bride's father will recite the holy invocation in Sanskrit, and I will
then recite it in English.

Natasha's father walked up to take a place under the canopy, and said the
prayer.

Ajam nirvi kalpam niraa kaara mekam
Niraa nandam anandam advaita purnam
Param nir gunam nirvi shesham nireeham
Para bhrama rupam ganesham bajemam [Provided by Pandit Harkishin Sharma]

Unborn, absolute, and formless Thou art,
Beyond bliss and yet infinite bliss Thou art,
From attributes and desires Thou art free.
Ganesh, O Supreme Spirit, we worship thee.

Hindu Fire Lighting and Offerings

At this time we light the sacred fire—the vivaha homa. Fire is a symbol of the illumination of the mind and also serves as a pure, holy witness to the marriage ceremony. The offerings include flowers for beauty, a coconut for fertility, rice for sustenance, and sweets for the sweet things of life. I now invite both sets of parents and the bride and groom to light the sacred fire.

Natasha and Phillip, their four parents, and I lit the sacred fire, then stood together for a moment of prayer.

O Lord Fire, First Created Being! Give food and drink to this household. O God, who reigns in richness and vitality over all the worlds, come take your proper seat in this home. Accept the offerings made here, be their protector on this day. O you who see into the hearts of all created beings, bring them together as one.

I asked Phillip's mother and Natasha's parents then to be seated, while Phillip's dad remained standing under the chuppah.

Prayer

Natasha and Phillip, as you nurture these gifts with each other—consecrating your blessings to God, humanity, and the natural world—we pray you achieve life's richest rewards: true happiness, health, and devotion. May your lives be bound together in sanctity, and may God be with you in this sacred hour and in all the sacred hours in all the days and years to come.

[Phillip's father, welcoming all present]

Barukh Haba b'sheym Adonai. Welcome in the name of Adonai. O God, source of life and joy, bless this loving gathering that has come to witness this marriage. Bless the covenant this bride and bridegroom are about to create in Your name.

Ni Adir el hakol
Mi Gadol el bakol
Hey'varesh b'hatan v'hakallah

Splendor is upon everything.
Blessing is upon everything.
Eternal who is full of this abundance,
Bless this bride and groom.
[*The New Jewish Wedding*, by Anita Diamant]

Celebrant's Address

Phillip's father returned to his seat, Natasha and Phillip sat in the chairs placed under the chuppah/mandap, and I then addressed the parents and the couple themselves. Following are a few of my words.

Phillip's mother and father, Natasha's mother and father, it was Emerson who gave my favorite definition of success. He said that success was to leave this world a better place—by virtue of a redeemed social condition, by way of a patch of garden, a kind word, or a child. I congratulate you on your success. So it is most appropriate that on your children's wedding day we say thank you. We honor you. And God blesses you.

Phillip and Natasha, if I could give you one thing, one gift to keep in your marriage, it would be this: kindness. The Talmud states that kindness is the beginning and the end of the law, and the older I get, the better I understand the meaning of that statement. Remain kind to each other. Use your words gently and wisely. Commit to do whatever it takes to make your marriage strong and healthy.

I conclude with words from the Hindu Bhagavad Gita: "He who offers to me with devotion only a leaf, or a flower, or a fruit, or even a little water, this I accept from the yearning soul, because with a pure heart it was offered with love."

Natasha and Phillip, offer up your marriage to God with a pure heart, with love.

Offering of the Bride and Joining of the Hands

*After the couple spoke the **declaration of intent**, the ceremony continued with the following words:*

At this time we invite the bride's parents to come forward to perform the kanyadhan and hathialo. In the custom of the Hindu kanyadhan, or offering of the bride, the bride's parents will place her hand in the right hand of the groom, symbolizing their approval and blessing of this union. Her hand in marriage is one of the greatest gifts that parents can offer. Holy water flows from the parents' hands through the bride's hand to the groom's hands.

In the hathialo, or joining of the hands, the right hands of the bride and groom are tied with a thread, signifying their eternal bond.

I poured a small amount of the blessed water through their hands, and the water was gathered into the silver bowl below. This is when the cloth napkins came into use! Natasha's dad then tied the sacred thread around the hands of

Natasha and Phillip. The groom's parents joined us, both moms and both dads placed their right hands on their children's hands, and we had a moment of silent prayer. The parents returned to their seats. I then removed my red prayer shawl— red is considered auspicious in Hinduism—and connected it loosely between the bride and groom.

Circling of the Sacred Fire

The couple will now circle the sacred fire four times. This is the mangal fera, one of the main aspects of the Hindu ceremony. With each round, they seek the four goals of human life: Dharma—moral values, the wisdom to lead a good life; Artha—prosperity to make life as happy as possible; Kama— energy and passion in life, family, and children; Moksha—being one with God and attaining the state of completeness.

Natasha led the first two circles around the table holding the sacred fire; then Phillip took the lead and Natasha followed.

The Seven Steps and Seven Blessings

In both the Jewish and Hindu traditions seven is a mystical number. The Kabbalists, the Jewish mystics, claim that circling helps the bride and groom enter the seven spheres of the soul, which correlate with the Hindu seven levels of consciousness, or the seven chakras.

In Hinduism, this is the satapadi—the seven steps—which symbolize the beginning of the bride and groom's journey through life together. These steps represent seven principles and promises to each other. It is said that if the bride and groom walk the seven steps together, they will become lifelong friends. Blessing upon them as they begin their journey.

Phillip and Natasha took the steps around the table simultaneously, as I handed them cards to read from in sequence. Before each I said, "Natasha and Phillip, please take the first step . . . take the second step," and so on. In unison, they recited the following pledges.

[Natasha and Phillip]

We shall cherish each other in sickness and health, in happiness and sorrow.

We shall be lifelong friends.

Together we shall share each other's ideals.

We shall nourish each other's strengths, powers, and fortune.

Together we shall make each other happy.

Together we shall love, provide, and care for our children, our parents, our brothers and sisters, and friends.

Together we will look toward the mysteries of the future with awe, open-mindedness, and inspiration.

I now introduced the Jewish seven blessings. During my words, Natasha and Phillip discreetly removed the tying hand thread and the shawl.

In Judaism, the bride and groom have histori-cally been blessed with seven wedding blessings, the number seven symbolizing creation and completion. According to the Bible, God created the world in seven days; and marriage is a seven-day-a-week creation. As a man and woman join together in love, they make each other feel more complete and whole. [Adapted from *Celebrating Interfaith Marriages,* by Rabbi Devon Lerner]

[Phillip's father], would you honor us by pre-siding over the seven blessings.

Phillip's father came forward and read the bless-ings in Hebrew; after each, a family member or friend read the English translation. The blessings were as follows:

> I grew tired of
> the road
> when it took me
> here and there.
> I married it in love
> when it took me
> Everywhere.
>
> —Rabindranath Tagore

May the Lord God, who created our parents and established them in mar-riage, establish and sustain you, that you find delight in each other and grow in holy love until your life's end.

Let us bless God for all the gifts in which we rejoice today.

Lord God, constant in mercy, great in faithfulness: With high praise we recall your acts of unfailing love for the human family, and for all your people.

We bless you for the joy which your servants, Phillip and Natasha, have found in each other, and pray that you give to us such a sense of your con-stant love that we may employ all our strength in a life of praise of you, whose work alone holds true and endures forever.

Let us pray for Phillip and Natasha in their life together.

Faithful Lord, source of love, pour down your grace upon Natasha and Phillip, that they may fulfill the vows they have made this day and reflect your steadfast love in their lifelong faithfulness to each other.

Gracious God, you bless the family and renew your people. Enrich hus-bands and wives, parents and children more and more with your grace, that strengthening and supporting each other, they may serve those in need and be a sign of the fulfillment of your perfect kingdom.

Blessing over the Wine

The blessing over the wine, which is in the kiddush cup, is part of many Jewish celebrations and holidays. The word *kiddush* means sanctification, so as we recite this blessing, we symbolically sanctify this couple on their wedding day.

Phillip and Natasha, as you share the one cup of wine, you undertake to share all that the future may bring. All the sweetness life's cup may hold should be sweeter because you drink it together. Whatever drops of bitterness it may contain should be less bitter because you share them.

[Phillip's father]:

Baruch ata Adonai Eloheynu Melech Ha-olam, borey p'ree ha-gaffen.

Holy One of the Blessing, your presence fills creation forming the fruit of the wine. Let us bless the source of life that nurtures the fruit of the vine as we weave the branches of our lives into the tradition.

*Phillip's father then offered the cup of wine to Phillip and Natasha. We followed with **the blessing and exchange of rings** and **the vows.** Before the couple gave each other the rings, I explained what they were doing.*

The bride and groom will honor an old Jewish tradition of first placing the ring upon the index finger. It is believed that there lies an artery that leads directly to the heart, and so the bride and groom symbolically join their hearts. The ring is then moved to the ring finger, signifying acceptance.

Exchange of Garlands

The bride and groom will now exchange flower garlands, symbolizing in the Hindu tradition the acceptance of the marriage by both parties. The exchange of garlands is similar to the ring exchange.

Natasha and Phillip removed the garlands from under the table and placed them around each other's necks.

From every being there rises a light that reaches straight to heaven. And when two souls destined to be together find each other, their streams of light flow together, and a single brighter light goes forth from their united being. This covenant is now sealed in truth and devotion. [by the Ba'al Shem Tov]

*Following **the pronouncement** and **the kiss,** I asked the gathered family and friends to support this young couple.*

Closing Blessing

We now invite [Natasha's father] and [Phillip's father] to recite the final blessings of peace, in Sanskrit and in Hebrew, which I will repeat to you in English.

[Natasha's father]:

Aum sarveshaam swasthir bhavatu
Sarveshaam shaanthir bhavatu
Sarveshaam poornam bhavatu
Sarveshaam manglam bhavatu
Om shaanti, shaanti, shaanti

May perfection prevail on all.
May peace prevail on all.
May contentment prevail on all.
May auspiciousness prevail on all.
Peace, peace, peace.
[Sanskrit and translation provided by Pandit Harkishin Sharma]

[Phillip's father]:
Y'varechecha Adonai v'yishmarecha.
Yaer Adonai panav aylecha veechuneka.
Yeesa Adonai panav aylecha v'yasem lecha shalom.

May God bless and keep you.
May God's presence shine upon you and be gracious to you.
May God's presence be with you and give you peace.

Breaking of the Glass and Showering of Rose Petals

We conclude this ceremony with the breaking of a glass, a joyous Jewish tradition that reminds us marriage is a transforming experience. A broken glass cannot be mended; likewise, marriage is irrevocable. The bride and groom have asked that it also symbolize the breaking down of barriers between people of different faiths and cultures. At the moment the glass is broken, we invite everyone to shout "mazel tov!" which means "congratulations!" and "good luck!"

"In India, the bride and groom are showered with flower petals, as if to say through the extravagance of spilled flowers: May your life together be filled with the beauty and romance of flowers, and may you want for nothing." [From *Weddings from the Heart,* by Daphne Rose Kingma] As they leave, we invite you to shower the couple with petals after the glass is broken.

As tabla players devotedly performed their music, Natasha and Phillip recessed under a shower of flower petals, followed by their parents. As the bride and groom had written in their program: "This is the end of the ceremony, and the beginning for Natasha and Phillip!"

Mercedes and Jack
a converted Buddhist–Jewish couple
a humanist ceremony in the Buddhist tradition

"I am a Latina from a traditional Catholic family," said Mercedes. "My mother is Chilean of European lineage. My father is Argentinian of Paraguayan lineage. They say our last name is Basque, which I've yet to investigate." But Mercedes had converted to Buddhism. "The thing I hold sacred is the Dharma [truth, ultimate reality]. When I first began reading these scriptures, it was some sort of epiphany. I finally understood what I needed to do to change my behavior and to affect the world—by becoming a better person through the Dharma. The Buddha's words are so inspiring to me. Whenever I read the sutras [teachings], I practically start to weep, because they're so simple and beautiful and I feel so inadequate and unworthy of them."

Jack grew up in a culturally Jewish household, with seders, Hanukkah celebrations, and Hebrew school for a short time. Now he considered himself essentially nonreligious. His favorite place to be, he told me, was anywhere he could think; libraries, quiet, and owls were among the things that touched his heart. (Mercedes's favorite things were tigers. She had a collection of them—inanimate, of course!) Jack wrote that he had been on "a philosophical quest, to find how we can develop character, both as individuals and a society"; since knowing Mercedes he had been drawn to Buddhist literature as well, although he didn't consider himself Buddhist as such. They both saw themselves on a spiritual path—of reading, self-educating, a search that they felt they were in some sense just beginning.

Mercedes worked as a journalist; Jack was writing a science-fiction novel and working full-time at a prestigious New York museum. These two very verbal young people wrote about themselves and each other with great eloquence. Mercedes wrote, "What's special about Jack and me is that we can talk about anything, anytime. We always have fun. No more different people could have fallen in love—that's what's funny. Socioeconomically, politically (he's the defender of the Constitution, I want the people to rise up and create a new paradigm), he likes to stay in, I like to go to clubs and dance . . . and on and on. I most admire his clearheadedness, calmness. He's my rock, and I'm the sea crashing, waves up and down. But the sea has to meet the land, and vice versa. They're joined."

About her, Jack wrote, "She's so her. She's not a collection of fashions and attitudes and beliefs, which I can be sometimes. She's not afraid to be contradictory. She's everything that modern society is not, and thus is she incredibly modern. We balance each other. I'm the optimist, she's the pessimist. I'm the amiable get-along, she's the driver, my-way-or-the-highway. We get nervous about totally different things. I'm a Hamlet debater, she rushes in. She can decide to change her life in the blink of an eye. I'm a ditherer. A friend of ours once said to me that Mercedes's character is so strong because of her refusal to 'play nice' in a world that pays so much lip service to politeness. Her honesty burns like a bonfire."

For their wedding, which they would be mostly paying for themselves, Jack and Mercedes knew what they didn't want. It should be, they told me, "a quiet time, touching, spiritual, celebrating the power of fate and love and unity. No references to any deity at all. No traditional ceremonial elements (nothing Jewish or Christian) at all. It should be new, and unique." Jack wrote, "I'd like to avoid things that sound like prayers in favor of analects (Confucian-style) or suttas, which are more universal in my mind." Mercedes wrote, "I see my ceremony as a reflection of my Buddhist self. It's also my commitment to Jack as my life partner. I'm very unsentimental as well, so I don't want the ceremony to get bogged down in treacly, flowery words or rituals." They wondered: Could we design a ceremony like this? Was there a way they could show their families who they were *and* help them understand and reveal their love as well? And so we began.

Mercedes and Jack were married on the penthouse terrace of a Manhattan hotel, one with a Japanese sensibility. About forty people were invited to the ceremony; many more came for the reception. We had set up a table, an altar, on which we placed a small Buddha statue, the Buddhist rosary (the mala), and flower offerings and fruit. It was sunset, with the terrace framed in the background by both the spires of a church (a sight that pleased the bride's mother) and the Empire State Building! To splendid music (including the Triumphal March from Verdi's *Aida*), I led the procession up to our small altar, followed by the bride and groom walking with both sets of parents and the bridal party behind. Jack and Mercedes each placed a flower on the altar, an offering to the Buddha; their parents took seats; and I began the ceremony, and set the tone, by ringing Tibetan bells. (They are loud and quite distinct!)

Here, Jack and Mercedes's Buddhist wedding ceremony.

Opening Words

Often, when I am aware that the ceremony to come might seem unusual or for-
eign, I put that issue right out at the beginning. I sought to prepare the guests in
my opening words, some of which follow.

On behalf of Jack, Mercedes, and their families, I would like to welcome
you all here today. You are about to witness a Buddhist ceremony. Since most
of you have probably never before witnessed one, I thought I would read two
quotations. The first is from the Dalai Lama: "There is no need for temples;
no need for complicated philosophy. My own brain, my own heart is my
temple; the philosophy is kindness." Albert Einstein said that Buddhism
"transcends a personal God, avoids dogmas and theology; it covers both the
natural and spiritual, and is based on a religious sense aspiring from the
experience of all things, natural and spiritual, as a meaningful unity." Perhaps that is, in part, why our bride and groom, these two intelligent, caring,
thinking people are so drawn to its philosophy.

When I asked Jack what he held sacred, he answered, "Everything and
nothing. The butterfly-flapping-its-wings-in-Africa circumstances that led
Mercedes and me to meet. The idea that we might be connected on a level
beyond what we can see or even feel. The telepathy that leads us to call each
other at exactly the same time (or is it just the fact that we know when to
call?). Mercedes is my family, has been since the day I met her. To me, our
marriage is a sacred partnership. I will treat it as such."

When I asked Mercedes when she knew that Jack was her partner for life,
she answered, "We were outside of the city one day, in an area where there
are few streetlights, and Jack realized that he could look up and see constella-
tions much more clearly than in Manhattan. We shared this moment, and
later, that's when I knew I loved him. Three months in. It was that quick,
and I had no doubts whatsoever."

Marriage is not an exclusive act. Nor is Buddhism exclusive. Each of you
has been invited here because you have touched the lives of Mercedes and
Jack in some significant way. Some of you have been there from the very
beginning. Others have come to know them more recently. Whichever the
case, your presence adds meaning and sanctity to this occasion. Your presence is their gift. As is their love our gift. These are gifts for which we are very
grateful.

Suzuki Roshi once said, "To be human is to be a Buddha." Let us join in
our humanity. And let us now join together in a holy bond of intent, to
honor and celebrate with Jack and Mercedes as they join together as husband
and wife in marriage.

First Reading

After acknowledging Jack's grandmother, who had died just the week before, a bridesmaid read the first reading, which I announced to the guests was the Metta Sutta, Buddha's Teaching on Loving Kindness. These beautiful and truly universal words are to Buddhism what 1 Corinthians 13 is to Christianity.

This is what should be done by one who is skilled in goodness and who knows the path of peace: Let them be able and upright, straightforward and gentle in speech. Humble and not conceited, contented and easily satisfied. Unburdened with duties and frugal in their ways. Peaceful and calm, and wise and skillful, not proud and demanding in nature. Let them not do the slightest thing that the wise would later reprove.

Wishing: In gladness and in safety, may all beings be at ease. Whatever living beings there may be—whether they are weak or strong, omitting none, the great or the mighty, medium, short or small, the seen and the unseen, those living near and far away, those born and to-be-born—may all beings be at ease!

Let none deceive another, or despise any being in any state. Let none through anger or ill-will wish harm upon another. Even as a mother protects with her life her child, her only child, so with a boundless heart should one cherish all living things: Radiating kindness over the entire world, spreading upwards to the skies and downwards to the depths, outwards and unbounded, freed from hatred and ill-will.

Whether standing or walking, seated or lying down, free from drowsiness, one should sustain this recollection. This is said to be the sublime abiding: By not holding to fixed views, the pure-hearted one, having clarity of vision, being freed from all sense desires, is not born again into this world. [From www.members.tripod.com]

Taking of the Threefold Refuge and the Precepts

The Taking of Refuge and the Precepts are among the central elements of a Buddhist wedding.

Mercedes and Jack, will you take the Threefold Refuge? [They replied, "We will."]

[Mercedes and Jack, in unison]

With great devotion of body, voice, and mind, we take refuge in the Source of all being. This is our unconditional nature and the nature of all things.

With great devotion of body, voice, and mind, we take refuge in our Seeking and in our Life Lessons. This is the path of the heart and the enlightened mind.

With great devotion of body, voice, and mind, we take refuge in our Humanity and in the Boundless Interconnection of all Beings. [Provided by Rev. Tozan Hardison]

Jack and Mercedes, are you able to accept these as guidelines for your life? [They replied, "Yes we are."]

We now ask the bride and groom to observe the basic Buddhist precepts for sacred living. Mercedes and Jack will each in turn read the precepts.

[Bride and groom, alternating lines]

I will seek my strength in purity of life.

I will seek my honor in sincerity of speech.

I will seek my joy in readiness to serve.

I vow to abstain from cruelty.

I vow to abstain from taking things not given.

I vow to encounter all creations with respect and dignity.

I vow to listen and speak from the heart.

I vow to cultivate a mind that sees clearly.

Therefore I promise to myself:

To do what I think to be my duty.

To speak what I think to be the truth.

To help others in what I think to be fair.

I accept full responsibility for action and reaction, for motive and effect.

May the sincerity of this resolution give me strength to nurture and support
    myself and others.

Celebrant's Address

In their questionnaires, Mercedes and Jack had written volumes about their love, about how and why each found in the other the perfect mate. I enjoyed using so many of their words in my address, a portion of which follows.

Mercedes, something you wrote impressed me. You said, "Now that I have learned something of personal, private, romantic love, I can begin to work on loving everyone else and developing my compassionate heart. I think I will be able to do this because I have such a good relationship with Jack. If it wasn't for that personal basis of knowing what it's like to love at least one person unconditionally, I could not hope to learn to expand it beyond to everyone else. This gives me hope and helps me renew my efforts every day."

Jack, what a wonderful gift you have given to Mercedes—and Mercedes to herself! Now, flanked by your love for Jack and your love of Buddhist teachings—remember the spiritual epiphany—you are well on your path. I want to answer a question you asked: "How do I write, see the rest of the planet, and help people, all in one?" The answer? A step at a time. Then at the end of your life you will view it as a whole. Right now, begin with this step. This marriage has ramifications more than you know.

Continue your philosophical search. Write. Love. Play. Think. Talk. Be aware. Cherish the moments. Continue to help each other realize who you really are. That is your duty as a spouse. Only then will you live the life you were meant to live.

The following is an adapted version of a Buddhist marriage homily, and it is the closest thing to advice that I will give you: "Nothing happens without a cause. The union of this man and woman has not come about accidentally. This tie can therefore not be broken or dissolved. In the future, happy occasions will come as surely as the morning. Difficult times will come as surely as night. When things go joyously, be compassionate. When things go badly, be compassionate. Compassion and meditation must guide your life. To say the words 'love and compassion' is easy, but to accept that love and compassion are built upon patience and perseverance is not easy. Your marriage will be firm and lasting if you remember this." [Adapted from *Wedding Readings* by Eleanor Munro]

> You are part of me.
> I do not know
> By what slow
> chemistry you
> first became
> A vital fiber of
> my being.
> —*Frank Yerby, "You Are Part of Me"*

Reading

We will now hear our second reading, chosen by the bride and groom—more specifically, Jack—a passage from the novel *Valis* by the writer Philip K. Dick. It will be read by Jon.

Read by the best man, this passage had great meaning for Jack because of its message of love and truth, and the need to reach out to others for the wisdom that is in all of us.

Declaration of Intent

After Jack and Mercedes answered "yes" to my question "Have you come here freely and without reservation to enter into marriage?" I wrapped their hands loosely with the mala, the Buddhist rosary or prayer beads, which I took from the altar. After a moment of silent meditation, I placed the mala around the neck of the statue of the Buddha.

Vows

Mercedes and Jack, please repeat after me.
I, Mercedes/Jack, take you, Jack/Mercedes, to be my husband/wife, in equal love, as a mirror for my true self, as a partner on my path, to honor and to cherish, in sorrow and in joy, till death do us part.

Blessing of Rings

I ended my statement about the symbolic meaning of the rings with a quotation I believed would have special meaning for this couple because of the groom's stated attraction to Confucian and Taoist thought.

I give you the words of Confucius: "The moral man and woman will find the moral law beginning in the relation between husband and wife, but ending only in the vast reaches of the universe."

These rings are hereby blessed. Jack, take Mercedes's ring and place it upon her left hand and repeat after me: "I give you this ring as a symbol of my vows." Mercedes, take Jack's ring and place it upon his left hand and repeat after me: "I give you this ring as a symbol of my vows."

To everyone's delight, precisely at the moment they exchanged rings the Empire State Building, which was behind me, lit up all in white!

This marriage is sealed in truth and devotion. By this truth let there be happiness.

Closing Blessing

After I asked the congregants to support this couple in the future, I read two closing blessings: the lovely verses by Wendy Egyoku Nakao, "The Blessings of Unknowing," and "Four Boundless Meditations," translated by Sogyal Rinpoche.

On this day, two lives join as one. Who can know from where this union comes? Who can know how far into eternity this will go? These are the blessings of Unknowing.

On this day, two hearts beat as one. Who can know how many other hearts this joins? Who can know how far this love will flow? These are the blessings of Unknowing.

On this day, two eyes shine as one. Who can know how many are the gifts of joy? Who can know how far this light will glow? These are the blessings of Unknowing.

On this day, two hands meet as one. Who can know how many other beings this holds? Who can know how far this touch will grow? These are the blessings of Unknowing.

On this day, one is no longer one. Two are no longer two. Who can know how far these blessings go? Who can know? Who can know? Let us rejoice in the blessings of Unknowing.

The Four Boundless Meditations
By the power and the truth of this practice, may all beings have happiness,
    and the causes of happiness,
May all be free from sorrow, and the causes of sorrow,
May all never be separated from the sacred happiness which is sorrowless,
And may all live in equanimity, without too much attachment and too much
    aversion,
And live believing in the equality of all that lives.

*We concluded with **the pronouncement** and **the kiss,** and as a final ritual, I rang the Tibetan bells with which we had begun. To much clapping, a shower of rose petals, and the music to "All You Need Is Love," by the Beatles, the beaming bride and groom walked out to receive their guests among an abundant supply of champagne and sushi.*

Vicki and Karl
a Greek Orthodox–Jewish couple
a religious ceremony co-officiated by a minister and a rabbi

From the beginning, there was something special between Vicki and Karl. Their relationship began on a blind date over brunch, during which they talked and after which they walked—for six hours. Vicki jokes that there were two moments when she knew "this would be different." At one point on their second date: "I was describing an instinctive negative and avoiding reaction I had to something or someone. To illustrate the point, I quoted the robot in the TV show *Lost in Space,* which always said, 'Danger, Will Robinson! Danger!' Karl laughed and said he loved that too and actually had a toy robot that was programmed to say those words. His first gift to me was my very own B-9 toy robot, just like his!" The second moment came when Vicki introduced Karl to her pet ferrets. Most people were frightened of the little critters, so Karl's response—"Hmmm, interesting . . ."—pleased her enormously.

Vicki and Karl looked me up after reading about my work in a magazine article. I was impressed to hear Karl say, "I believe that an interfaith ceremony, done properly, can be an enlightening experience." They had already engaged Rabbi Joel Braude, a Reformed rabbi, but since an Orthodox priest would be unable to perform a Jewish-Greek wedding, it was arranged that I would co-officiate with the rabbi.

Karl described himself as "Jewish, raised in the Conservative tradition. I feel my Judaism mostly in the sense of history, culture, and humor. The spirit of Jewish ethics, but not the religious rites." Vicki explained, "I was brought up in the Judeo-Christian tradition and hold very strongly to the values of community, ethics, caring for others. The concept of peace and being at peace with nature and the world around has always appealed to me."

Vicki's mother and much of her family were born and raised in Greece. They were members of the Greek Orthodox Church and respected it, even though they had some differences with it. Consequently, Vicki did not want the ceremony to suggest to her family that she and Karl were becoming more Jewish than Greek. Karl agreed: "My greatest sensitivity is that no one should feel in any way threatened by our interfaith relationship, ceremony, and marriage. Most of all, we want people coming away feeling good about themselves, and about life's unexpected possibilities." And so they knew at the outset that a few rituals would be important to them—the chuppah ("a somewhat modern one with an ethereal quality, perhaps with tulle," the bride said), in the Jewish tradition; walking down the aisle together, in the Greek fashion—"but all done with explanation of their origin, of their meaning to us and our guests." The drinking of wine and the breaking of a glass would be included; these rituals are common to both traditions.

The gathering would be a large one—about two hundred guests were expected, arriving from eleven states as well as from Greece, Austria, Hong Kong, Great Britain, and a sizable contingent from Australia. The rabbi would recite certain blessings in Hebrew; we would use some readings from Greek literature. Bit by bit, and with a good deal of discussion, we achieved a harmonious balance. Initially, these two young people were concerned about how matters would go between the interfaith minister and the rabbi. But when he and I were able to confer with all involved, we turned out to be a splendid team. Indeed, we spoke the pronouncement—"By the power vested in me . . ."—in tandem. At the rabbi's kind suggestion, I as well as he signed the ketubah, the Jewish marriage contract.

In my address to the couple, it was my pleasure to share some of their own words from the questionnaire with their families and guests.

Karl wrote, "I'm sometimes fond of saying that I never fell in love with Vicki but shot past that to a higher plain of some sort, an almost translucent and intimate understanding of her and our life together. I don't really know how to describe it, other than to say it exists. We finish each other's sentences, and have since very early on. We share values and laughter. We hate being apart for any length of time. She is my first thought in the morning and last at night. We are true partners in every sense of that word. I get a charge from her presence in my life. All the time. The threshold was crossed beyond friendship and beyond love, and I've been certifiably bursting with happiness ever since. And not just for myself, but for how happy she says (and I can feel) I make her. That, to me, is the greater gift."

From Vicki, I read, "Karl is the only person I feel completely comfortable with. I can be myself in ways I had never before experienced. He makes me feel safe and secure in a way I never thought imaginable. I love Karl without reservation, with my heart, my head, and my arms. I want to go skipping through life, holding his hand for a hundred years. He makes me feel strong and powerful. Like a natural force. [As I was reading these words at their wedding, I spontaneously interjected: "Just wait until you have a baby!"] He also makes me feel very, very protective, and I want to soothe every stubbed toe and ache. I try to remember every day how life was before I met him. Not bad, but not wonderful like it is now. I never want to take what we have for granted. I will take care of it like a precious jewel."

Here, then, the ceremony of Vicki and Karl.

Procession

The ceremony took place in the courtyard of a historic National Trust home. They had arranged a small table with the kiddush cup, the wrapped glass to be broken, the stephana or traditional Greek crowns, and a bowl of sugared almonds and rice, representing fertility and good luck. Behind the small table were floor-standing candles, in the Greek tradition.

To the music of a string quartet, four chuppah bearers came forward from the front row, gathered the chuppah from the side, and walked it into position before the table. The rabbi and I together led the procession. Vicki's brother and Karl's sister then walked down the aisle, lighted the candles, and stood on either side of the chuppah, where they were joined by the maid of honor and the best man. Finally, Vicki and Karl walked in together.

Opening Words

Rabbi Joel Braude and I, in turn, welcomed the guests, after which the rabbi offered the following words of explanation:

Vicki and Karl have entered our assembly walking arm in arm in the Greek tradition, in demonstration of their commitment to each other, and to us, as a loving couple. They now stand before us under this canopy, called a chuppah, in the Jewish tradition of shelter, home, and peace. This is the blending in which they ask us to share. Your lives are part of their home, the home symbolized by this chuppah. The chuppah is itself poetic, as we shall hear in the words of Marge Piercy, read to us by Karl's sister.

Readings

[Karl's sister]
The Chuppah stands on four poles.
The home has four corners.
The marriage stands on four legs.
Four points loose the winds
that blow on the walls of the house. . . .
(See page 183 for the complete text.)

Now Reverend Macomb will read from the New Testament, 1 Corinthians, chapter 13.
[Susanna]
If I speak in the tongues of mortals and of angels, but do not have love, I am a noisy gong or a clanging cymbal. . . .
(See page 152 for the complete text.)

[Rabbi]
Vicki and Karl, as you nurture these gifts with each other—consecrating your blessings to God, humanity, and the natural world—we pray you

achieve life's richest rewards: true happiness, health, and devotion. May your lives be bound together in sanctity, and may God be with you in this sacred hour and in all the sacred hours in all the days and years to come.

Barukh Haba b'sheym Adonai.

O God, source of life and joy, bless this loving gathering that has come to witness this marriage. Bless the covenant this bride and bridegroom are about to create in Your name.

[Susanna]

O eternal God, you have brought this bride and groom to unity. May their love be an indissoluble bond. Preserve them in oneness of mind and steadfastness of faith. Guide them unto every good work. O eternal God, grant them peace. Amen.

We ask each of you now to go into your hearts. Feel the warmth, the love you have for these two people as they say the most powerful words they can to each other: their wedding vows. This act, my friends, is magnificent and so very tender to behold.

Honoring of Family Members

We acknowledged the spirits of Vicki's father and Karl's father, both long passed away. We also paid tribute to the mothers of the bride and groom based on their words from the questionnaire.

I will end by offering the mothers of the bride and groom a quotation from classical Greek literature:

It is she, who nourished you
she, out of her treasures.
Beautiful children
beautiful harvests
are achieved from you,
the giving of life itself. [From Homer's Hymns]

Celebrants' Addresses

Here is a portion of the rabbi's address.

In the Holy Book, the story of Ruth is a beautiful metaphor for the life of Vicki and Karl. It is a story of mutual acceptance, respect, and enduring love. It is a story of two people from different backgrounds who drew strength and pleasure from their cultures—with no fear of blending their worlds and making one world of their own. As Vicki and Karl now reach out to each other, and to us, they do so with respect and with traditions of importance to each.

All, everything that I understand, I understand only because I love.

—*Leo Tolstoy*

Vicki and Karl, as your life together proceeds along its joyous course, allow me to suggest another avenue through which the spirituality of this ceremony can resonate throughout your lives. Make use of sacred rituals you both find meaningful. Holiday observances with your family and friends. Shared expressions of charity and other sacred deeds.

My message to you is a simple one. As long as your love is complete and continuous, as rounded and continuous as the rings you are about to exchange, your future will be assured. All of us gathered here wish this for you. And we pray that you will now go forth together to many, many years of happiness, health, and love.

Here is a portion of my address.

Life can be delightful, sprouting adventures at each turn, or can become quite cruel. How you are with each other in the good times, and also in the difficult times, will determine the closeness of your relationship.

You are two people of quality. You have your priorities in order. Therefore, in lieu of advice, I wish to give a gift, a gift inspired by the two of you: When times get tough—and I pray they will not, Vicki and Karl—and if things are ever strained between the two of you, I want you to turn to each other and say those famous words of the robot in *Lost in Space:* "Danger, Will Robinson! Danger!"

Ladies and gentlemen, this is an inside joke!

It will make you laugh. It will make you aware. Then remember to reach deep within your hearts and become greater than yourselves. Go to that higher plane of translucent understanding. There is always more there than you think.

Blessing Over the Wine and the Stephana

[The rabbi]

The sharing of a cup of wine by the bride and groom is a tradition common to Jews and Greeks. In Judaism, wine is a symbol of the joy and richness of life. Of the sweetness of love. On this joyous occasion, we make a toast together—*l'khayim*—to life and to love. May you find life's joys heightened and its bitterness sweetened. May there always be peace in your home and confidence in your hearts. And as you share wine together from this cup, so may you share joy and fulfillment from the cup of life.

We praise God, Creator of the fruit of the vine. Baruch ata Adonai, Eloheynu Melech Ha-olam, borey p'ree ha gaffen.

As the rabbi offered the kiddush cup to them, Vicki and Karl each took a sip of wine.

[Susanna]
For thousands of years, people in Greece have been crowned with floral wreaths, signifying achievement, on important occasions. At weddings, the wreaths—the stephana—signify mastery of the bride and groom's home. The stephana are bound by a single cord, a cord of love and commitment. The flowers represent romance and life's sweet blessings. As they are crowned, they are forever united.

We now call on Vicki's brother, who will exchange the stephana three times as is custom and offer a personal blessing.

Vicki's brother recited a short blessing in Greek and in English.

Declaration of Intent and the Vows

*Following the **declaration of intent**, I invited the rabbi to hold the couple's hands along with me in a moment of silent prayer.*

Karl/Vicki, do you take Vicki/Karl to be your wife/husband, promising to cherish and protect her/him whether in good times or in adversity, and to seek together with her/him a life hallowed by the love you share?

[Each responded, "I do."]

[The rabbi]
The Shehekhiyanu blessing is recited at many important events in life—at joyous occasions, like holidays or weddings; at special events of gratitude each year, as when we enjoy the first fruits of the season. And so, we praise God, who had given us life, sustained us, and brought us to this joyous time.

Barukh Ata Adonai, Eloheynu Melekh HaOlam, shehekhiyanu vkiyimanu, v'higiyanu lazman hazeh.

From the earliest times, the circle has been a symbol of committed love. An unbroken and never-ending circle symbolizes a love commitment that is also never-ending. These rings represent the ties that bind you together as

husband and wife, as partners in life. They are of gold, a metal that is enduring and does not tarnish. As often as each of you looks upon these rings, we
hope you will be reminded of your enduring commitment, to love each other
always, and that together you will be the perfect bearers of God's blessings.

Karl/Vicki, place the ring upon Vicki's/Karl's index finger and repeat
after me:

You are my love. You are my life. This truth is with you now, and always.

[The rabbi and Susanna]

And now, in the company of these loving witnesses, and by your words
and actions that do unite your lives, I therefore declare you, Karl and Vicki,
husband and wife, married under the laws of this state and in the presence of
the Almighty.

After the Kiss, I offered these words:

Linda Hogan, a Native American writer, offers a spiritual path to Karl and
Vicki's future that is as Greek and as Jewish as it is Native American: "Walking,
I am listening to a deeper way. Suddenly, all my ancestors are behind me. Be
still. They say. Watch and listen. You are the result of the love of thousands."

Closing Blessing

[The rabbi]

Most gracious God, we thank you for the beauty of this moment. Look
favorably upon Karl and Vicki, that their home will be a haven of peace.
Guide them by your wise counsel and grant them the fullness of years to
enjoy their children's children. And grant them entrance into your everlasting realm.

Y'varechecha Adonai v'yishmarecha.

May God bless and protect you.

Breaking of the Glass

[The rabbi]

We conclude with the breaking of a glass, a ceremony similar in both Jewish and Greek traditions. It reminds us that marriage is a transforming experience. And Karl and Vicki ask that it also symbolize the breaking down of
barriers between people of different faiths and cultures.

Karl broke the glass as the guests applauded and shouted, "Mazel tov!"

At the **recession**, the new bride and groom walked down the aisle to the sounds of the Wedding March from Mendelssohn's A Midsummer Night's Dream.

After the ceremony, Karl, with Vicki still on his arm, turned to me as he fingered his wedding ring and said, "Do you see this? I could not wait to get this on my finger!" To which Vicki responded with a multitude of small kisses.

Stardust. Simply stardust.

Marie and Luigi
an Italian-American Catholic couple
a Christian ceremony

"A few years ago, if someone had predicted my future, and told me I'd be where I am now, I would have said they were sadly mistaken," Luigi wrote. "Never in a thousand years would I have believed that there is life after broken hearts. You don't trust anyone. You think people are out to use you. Love is a word used to describe your car, your vacations, the days at the beach. Counseling is no more an option, loneliness is an excuse for comfort. Sleep is a hobby in the past. You swear off your life."

Luigi was referring to one of his darkest times, and by amazing coincidence, Marie—who would become his wife—had been through an almost identical experience. Each had been in a short-lived, unhappy marriage that ended when Luigi and Marie discovered their respective spouses had been unfaithful to them. Adultery was a sin and a profound betrayal to these two deeply moral, religious individuals. Almost from the moment they met—introduced by a facilitating angel who happened to be Luigi's brother-in-law—they saw what Luigi described as "the sparkles." Yet they could hardly trust their good fortune. "When we met," he wrote, "at first we dated once a week. Never believing that we were facing our greatest gift." When Luigi turned to Marie one day, looked right into her eyes, and said, "Could you be the one?" she answered, "The one *what?*" (I told that story in my opening remarks.)

But it didn't take them too long to start believing. Describing how he was all ready to propose to her one night over dinner, Luigi said, "I remember asking God, 'Please help me. Find the right time for me to do this and guide me.' Amazing how fast sometimes prayers are delivered. That moment, she stopped eating, looked at me, and with the sparkles in her eyes, admitted that she had never been happier. She came around to where I was sitting and with a big hug she said, 'It doesn't get better than this.' Talk about an answer from above! I laughed to myself, and thanked the Lord." And so he proposed. Marie cried and cried and didn't even bother to look at the ring; five minutes later she said, "Yes!"

The wedding would be a problem, however. They wanted so much to be married in their church, on sacred ground, but felt that would be impossible for them as divorced Catholics. "We wanted to be able to walk down the aisle of a Catholic church," Luigi said, "but if we were granted annulments, we would also be giving back to our ex-spouses the same rights. So, perhaps out of anger, or stubbornness, or just the fact that we felt this was very unfair, we decided to seek other options." Luigi did approach a priest he knew to ask him to bless the rings the couple would use, but the priest was unwilling to offer such a blessing.

> Love is our highest word and the synonym for God.
>
> —*Ralph Waldo Emerson*

One day Luigi was telling a client how he wished he could remember the name of a particular interfaith minister who had presided years earlier over a wedding at which he had played the piano. His client said that a friend of hers was an interfaith minister and perhaps he should look her up. When we met Luigi's eyes widened with wonder: "It's you!" Thus we began to plan a ceremony that would satisfy their deepest wishes: "To capture the feeling of how our prayers have been answered. God was listening and brought two people meant to be together. A spiritual ceremony, with a Godly presence. A little humor is good too."

Reading their questionnaires, I had no doubts that these two enjoyed riotous times! "We balance one another with lots of laughter," Marie wrote. "Luigi is completely off the wall. When you least expect it, he'll do or say something that will make your stomach cramp in laughs." "Watching her laugh is one of my best turn-ons!" he wrote. "I'm going to make her laugh till the day I die, and when I do, before I go, I'm going to look at her and point up to the sky and wink! I'm going to break their chops up there too!"

Their large Italian-American families would be present at the wedding, and both Marie and Luigi very much wanted to honor their long-married, hardworking, loving, and supportive parents. After I suggested a number of churches and chapels that would welcome them, they found an Episcopal church not far from their home and felt comfort in the fact, they said, "that the Episcopal religion is the one closest in resemblance to the Catholic religion."

Here, the wedding ceremony of Marie and Luigi.

Procession

After Marie's father escorted her down the aisle, both Luigi and Marie presented roses to their parents.

Opening Words

Here is a shortened version of my opening words.

I'd like to begin with a story. It is said that forty days before a child is born, his or her spouse is selected in heaven. These two souls are created, and an angel cries out, "This man is made for that woman." Now should these two souls, these two people, meet on earth, should they recognize each other for who they really are, they will fall in love. From that moment on they shall become as one. The legend says, "Then no hardship, absolutely no hardship can alter the strength of their enduring love. Everything they do shall succeed."

I tell you this legend today, because these two people, Luigi and Marie, knew from the very beginning that they were meant to be together. To quote Marie, "When God put Luigi in my life, I knew he had listened to my prayers." They are so very grateful. They feel so blessed. And God is smiling.

Let us come together now in reverence. Let us form a symbolic circle around the bride and groom, a sacred bond of the heart to honor and celebrate Marie and Luigi as they join together in the most holy state of matrimony. This is a sacred act, one that is blessed by God. Heaven and earth are rejoicing in his glory. Amen.

Reading

I announced to the guests that our first reading was written by a Renaissance man with a soft heart and an artist's soul—our groom. One of Luigi's nephews then read what Luigi had entitled "A Reading from the Book of Our Lives," a sort of prayer of thanks to God and an expression of love to all present. It included these words: "Today, in a world created with beauty in mind, regardless of man's imperfection, you are all made witnesses to two lives, which in the joining have realized the greatest truth—to love and to give is to receive."

Honoring of Family Members

Both Luigi and Marie had expressed in the questionnaire their great admiration and appreciation for their parents, and their love of family, including Luigi's "huge tribe." I read to the parents their children's own words.

Reading and Prayer

I announced to the guests that Luigi's brother-in-law would read in Italian a passage from the Bible, St. Paul's letter to the Ephesians, chapter 5, verses 22 through 33. The entire congregation then recited the Lord's Prayer.

Celebrant's Address

Here is an abbreviated version of my words to the couple.

Luigi and Marie, there is a saying that God continually creates new worlds by causing marriages to take place. This is the beginning of your new world. It is in the dawn of its creation. And God is saying, "It is good." Just like he did in Genesis. Shall I tell you why God causes marriages to take place, the reason you were brought together? Some would say to procreate. However, there is another spiritual reason. You were brought together because it is together that you can more fully manifest and fulfill your inner potential, God's potential, the majesty and glory that lies within each of you. You can do this far better together than apart. As husband and wife you will have the privilege of evolving together as soul, on the path of the human being.

Together you are healing each other, balancing each other, helping each other grow, filling in each other's gaps. That is why you feel so happy, whole, and at peace. And this is just the beginning! You have a lifetime to play, to study, to relish and learn about each other's universe. What a gift you've been given! You are each other's launchpad so that you may reach greater and greater heights. And God definitely has a mission for you. You need not seek too hard to find it, because it will find you. Just remain open, pray, and keep loving each other. Your mission shall be revealed to you—step by step, petal by petal, beautifully, mysteriously as spring opens her first rose. (I'm borrowing here from e. e. cummings.)

Marie and Luigi, today I see God holding your hearts in the palms of his hands. Gazing at them, he whispers: "OF ALL MY CREATIONS, BIG AND SMALL, THESE HUMAN HEARTS ARE MY GREATEST. FOR THEIR ABILITY TO OVERCOME

OBSTACLES IS AWE-INSPIRING, THEIR POTENTIAL FOR HEALING, AMAZING! AND THEIR CAPACITY TO LOVE IS UNENDING. THESE FRAGILE AND POWERFUL HUMAN HEARTS ARE MOST BLESSED." Ladies and gentlemen, I wrote those words here in capital letters, because God always speaks in capital letters.

I will close with lines from Scripture and a prayer. The first is Matthew 5, verse 16: "Let your light shine, that they may see your good works and give glory to God who is in heaven." The second is Proverbs 31, verse 10: "He who has found a wife has found a very precious thing." And a prayer:

Dear Lord, please bless this couple. Make their relationship a great and holy adventure. May their joining be a sacred space. May they find rest here, a haven for their souls. Bring them together heart, mind, body, and soul. Guide their way into light. Guide their way into wisdom. Help them grow. May this bond be a channel of healing for themselves, their families, and the world at large. May this marriage now receive your blessing and carry your power. We thank you for the gift of their love. Amen. [Adapted from *Illuminata,* by Marianne Williamson]

Luigi and Marie, God's blessings are with you. Today you walk in grace.

*We followed the **declaration of intent** with this ritual.*

Anointing and Wrapping of the Hands

[Taking the oil from the altar]

Your hands represent giving and receiving. I now anoint them into your new life. May your giving and receiving be everlasting.

[Wrapping their hands with my prayer stole]

The prayer stole symbolizes that God, that which is within you, yet infinitely greater and more loving than yourselves, has joined you together.

Will the fathers of the bride and groom now please come up?

Mr. [Marie's father] and Mr. [Luigi's father], do you bless this union?

Will each of you then place your right hand upon the hands of your children and join me in a moment of silent prayer?

After the fathers had returned to their seats, I supported the couple's hands and offered them this admonition.

As you hold the hands of your beloved, listen to what I am about to say. Above you are the stars, below you is the earth, as time does pass, remember: Like the earth should your love be firm, grounded in your humanity. Like a star should your love be constant, imbued with the light of God. Let the powers of the mind and of the intellect guide you in your marriage, let the strength of your wills bind you together, let the power of love and desire make you happy, and the strength of your dedication make you inseparable.

Vows

Ladies and gentlemen, the vows you are about to hear were written by the bride and groom.

Luigi, please look into your bride's eyes and repeat after me:

I, Luigi, have been blessed with you. Today I ask you, Marie, to be my wife and beloved partner in life. I will always be there for you, shelter and hold your love as the most sacred gift in my life. I will be truthful and honor you. I will be your protector, and care for you always, and stand by you in times of sorrow and joy. I promise you all this, in the presence of God, family, and friends, for all the days of my living life, and if he wills it, through the walls of time, beyond the bounds of eternity.

Marie, please look into your groom's eyes and repeat after me:

I, Marie, have been blessed with you. Today I ask you, Luigi, to be my husband and beloved partner in life, to grow with, love, and cherish. I will be truthful and honor you, stand by you in times of sorrow and joy. I promise you all this, in the presence of God, family, and friends, for all the days of my eternal life.

Blessing and Exchange of Rings

To my explanation of the rings as powerful symbols, I added the words of the poet and mystic Rumi: "Lovers don't finally meet somewhere. They are in each other's souls all along."

Luigi, please take Marie's ring, place it upon her left hand, and repeat after me:

Marie, I give you this ring, a symbol of my abiding love, so pure and faithful. May God encircle our union and bless us. In the hope and prayer to feel this joy forever, I thank God and I thank you. Amen.

Marie, take Luigi's ring, place it upon his left hand, and repeat after me:

Luigi, I give you this ring, a symbol of my vow, love, and devotion. May we walk through life, with the strength and faith we feel today. Forever I thank God and I thank you. Amen.

[Placing my hand over theirs]

This covenant is now sealed in truth and devotion.

Lighting of the Unity Candle

Luigi and Marie, you have committed yourselves to each other through solemn vows. Your life is now one. Together please light the candle symbolizing your sacred union.

From every being there rises a light that reaches straight to heaven. And when two souls are destined to be together and find each other, their streams of light flow together and a single brighter light goes forth from their united being.

[With my hand over their ring hands]

What God has joined together, let no one tear asunder.

After the pronouncement and the kiss, the service concluded with these words.

Closing Blessing

Luigi and Marie, as you go into the world as husband and wife,

We pray that you grow glorious in each other's arms,

We pray that laughter and warmth reign supreme in your home.

We pray that God grant you fine, healthy children, whom you shall cherish, and they you in return.

We pray that you radiate his light, and when eternity beckons, at the end of a life heaped high with love, may the good Lord embrace you with the arms that have nurtured you the whole length of your joy-filled days.

As you walk this journey, Marie and Luigi, know that God's angels walk alongside you, eternally.

Go now with love in your hearts and peace in your souls.

In Nome del Padre, Figlio, e Spirito Santo.

Amen.

Later, Luigi wrote to me, "When you asked for the rings, and said, 'By the grace of God, these rings are hereby blessed,' I felt an enormous sense of relief. This was all that we wanted, a simple acknowledgment that we were good Christians who had never lost their faith."

Chantè and Judah
an African-American, Native American,
Baptist French, Russian Jewish, Sufi, Rastafarian couple
a multicultural spiritual ceremony

"I've started to honor my African roots and Mother Earth," Chantè told me at our first meeting. Chantè was also one small part Native American—and would be, at the time of their marriage ceremony, seven months pregnant. She would invite a large contingent of her mostly Baptist and Born-Again Christian relatives to her wedding, and she wrote, "I want everyone to walk away touched, no matter what race or religion they are. I want our ceremony to signify, as gently and lovingly as possible, the flying out of the nest of our families, to fly together. That we want everyone in attendance to support us with positive energy, each of us as one-half piece of a whole."

Judah's background was quite different. Half French and half Russian Jewish, he said that currently "the most defining characteristic of my family is that we are spread out. We're international!" His mother lived in Paris, his father and brother in California, his married sister in London, and all would be coming to the wedding. Raised as a Sufi for the first ten years of his life, Judah described himself currently as "a worldly mutt melting pot, a white dreadlock Rasta-Sufi, interfaith kind of person." The ceremony he envisioned: "I see it as warm, intimate, and deep, inclusive of all the people there so they feel like they're taking part in something amazing. I want ancient words and proverbs from all cultures, phrases that capture what marriage is, and family. Maybe some precious objects that have meaning for us. I want it to have a kind of ancient feel to it, and definitely some rituals from our cultures."

Can we have, they wondered, expressions of Rasta-Sufi mixed in with Baptist–Native American–African traditions, with a bit of Buddhist feeling as well, and some bow to Russian Jewish and French heritage, plus acknowledgment of the much-wanted baby to come? We did our best! (I think all we left out was some reference to the groom's French and Russian heritage.)

In the outdoor area of the banquet room where the ceremony would take place, Chantè—with the help of the women in her family—had set up a low table that suggested a kind of African-style temple, draped in kente cloth, holding bells, feathers, and incense. There were small bowls of the spices and other ingredients we'd use in one of the rituals. Also on the table was a stick of sage set in a large shell for a Native American smudging ritual; libations and the Jewish kiddush cup; a broom made of twigs beautifully decorated with bells and shells, which would come into play at the end of the ceremony in the African jumping of the broom; and a wrapped glass for the Jewish breaking of the glass. Beautiful African-inspired pillows were on the floor in front of this sumptuous display, and Judah and Chantè would kneel on these during parts of the ceremony.

Here, the wedding of Chantè and Judah.

Procession

Chantè was veiled and remained so throughout the ceremony, until the bride and groom kissed. Her gown, white satin with gold trim, was African inspired. Judah's cummerbund matched his bride's gown, and his blond dreadlocks were sculpted into a crown of sorts. To the reverberating sound of African drumming, Judah walked in, followed by Chantè, who was escorted by her father. What a regal sight they presented!

Opening Words

This very young couple—Judah had just completed college, while Chantè was still attending—had written such impassioned declarations of love about each other, I had to use them in my opening words! Here, in part, is the address.

On behalf of Chantè, Judah, and their families I say, . . . Welcome and blessings upon all here today!

Today we witness the birth of a new family—Judah, Chantè, and the child growing within Chantè's womb. This is the foundation of life, and therefore sacred.

Today we witness the joining of different traditions united in one profound act of love and commitment. This is our hope for the future.

Today we witness the joining of two people who have discovered that love knows no boundaries of skin color, faith, culture, or geography. This is truly the love of God, and may our knees bend in its holy presence!

Before this ceremony, I gave the bride and groom questions that they have answered separately. They have not seen or heard each other's answers until now. Their words are laced throughout this ceremony.

Chantè's words: "Judah showed me God. It was in me—in nature—and in the ability to stop moving and to simply listen. I started to explore and dig up my roots. Judah is so beautiful! He sees beauty in everyone and everything. He's sexy in a manly way. He makes me feel like a woman, a Queen.

He is so passionate, yet humble. So beautiful, yet unknowing. So talented, yet not egotistical. So honest, ready to forgive, even when he shouldn't. A rainbow that shines always. A smile that's always bubbling to the surface. He's bright and lit up. He is pure, good.

"We are a unique couple as different as our colors—black and white—but we meet and mesh and rub off to complement each other in the most amazing silverish gray. We didn't choose each other. We were chosen for one another. The differences in culture and color make our pot all the more tasty."

Judah, you are blessed by Jah—the Rasta name for God—to have someone who loves so much. Take good care of her. Why do marriages take place? Because it is together as husband and wife that bride and groom can best realize the beauty, the glory, the magnificence, the infinite potential that lies within. God's potential. To quote the African Christian Archbishop Desmond Tutu: "We are made for complementarity. I have gifts you do not; and you have gifts that I do not. So we need each other to become fully human."

Now, Judah's words: "We just fit like two pieces in a puzzle. I'm like the white stripes on a zebra and she, the black, and together we are whole. Because of Chantè, I am stronger spiritually. I've come to be more open and thoughtful about my concepts of God and praising him/her.

"I admire Chantè in so many ways. First, her youthful, exuberant energy can light up a whole room. She has some level of pure joy in her that I could feel from the beginning. She is gentle, soft, kind, womanly, radiant, and gorgeous. I also love her maturity and strength that is beyond her age at times. She is amazingly motivated. She knows how to get things done. I know I am loved because she is always going the extra mile for me. She is sooo giving, it's like there is a bottomless well. She reinforces the strength I need.

"I love Chantè beyond what words can describe. I love her because she magnetizes me, everything about her fills up my cup. She is me and I am her and baby is both of us. Our goal is to be happy, stay together lifelong, have beautiful children, and always give back as much as we have received."

Native American Smudging

The bride and groom have requested that we honor and celebrate their spiritual roots. Therefore, we have selected elements from Sufi, Jewish, Christian, Rasta, African-American, and Native American traditions to be blended into one ceremony reflecting their personal beliefs.

We shall open with the Native American tradition of smudging. This is an act of purification, of cleansing. Fire is a great purifier. It is offered to the four corners of the earth. All thoughts, all energies are purified and transformed, from the negative to the positive, from darkness to light, from fear to love, from disharmony to peace.

In honor of and gratitude for the women who gave the bride and groom life, we now invite their mothers to perform this ancient ritual.

Lighting the smudging stick, a tied bundle of sage, I held it briefly to the four corners of the room, then asked each mother to smudge—or wave the stick before, behind, and around—the couple. At the conclusion, Judah and Chantè presented their four parents with flowers, each with a personal note attached.

Reading

In honor of Rasta and Christian traditions, we will now hear a reading that is a combination of two excerpts selected by the bride and groom. The first is from the Great Mercy Proclamation of 1941 by Selassie, the Emperor of Ethiopia; the second portion is taken from the Gospel According to Thomas.

A friend of the couple came forward to read the following statement.

Today is a day on which Ethiopia is stretching her hands to God in joy and thankfulness. . . . Therefore let us rejoice with our hearts . . . in the spirit of Christ. When you make the two one, and when you make the inside as the outside and the outside as the inside and above as below, and when you make the male and female into a single one. . . . When you make an eye in the place of an eye . . . then shall you enter the kingdom.

Pouring of Libations and Blessing over the Wine

In the words of Alice Walker, "To acknowledge our ancestors means we are aware that we did not make ourselves, that the line stretches all the way back, perhaps to God. . . . The grace with which we embrace life, in spite of the pain, the sorrows, is always a measure of what has gone before."

Many cultures pour wine or spirits as blessing. In Jewish tradition it is called the sanctification over the wine, or drinking from the kiddush cup. In African tradition it is known as the pouring of libations. Today we honor and combine these traditions.

I poured the wine—libation—into the kiddush cup, explained its meaning, and followed with an African prayer.

This cup is symbolic of the cup of life. Wine symbolizes all that is good and sweet in life. As you share the one cup of wine, you undertake to share all that the future may bring. All the sweetness life's cup may hold for you, Chantè and Judah, should be sweeter because you drink it together; whatever drops of bitterness it may contain should be less bitter because you share them.

All praise to God Almighty.

Praise to all our ancestors and roots.

God gave his power for the roots of the tree to spread its branches wide.

If man does not know his roots, then he does not know his God.

Let the spirit of God and our ancestors bring us closer to unity.

Chantè and Judah, we ask you now to drink from the cup of mirth and abundance. [Adapted from *Going to the Chapel*, by the editors of *Signature Bride Magazine*]

Celebrant's Address

Chantè had written about an emotional crisis she had endured and emerged from with newfound strength, and I remarked that she had learned one of life's greatest lessons—the lesson of many religions, including that expressed in the Christian crucifixion and resurrection and in the Buddhist image of the lotus emerging pure and undefiled from the mud, whereby pain is transcended and a glorious rebirth occurs. She was that lotus! And again, I used many of the couple's words. Judah had written, "One thing that is special is our laughter. We have so much fun together." Chantè wrote, "We have a no-holds-barred theory on laughter together." What a gift to be blessed with laughter!

Prayers

Placing my hands on the heads of the bride and groom, I offered the following informal prayer.

God has a mission for you, Judah and Chantè. We pray that he/she guide you in that direction. We pray that together you will know many moments of sublime peace. We pray that you will grow glorious in each other's arms. We pray that you shall have a fine healthy child, whom you will love, and that he or she will love you in return. We pray that you will live to know your children's children. May you walk in God's grace with your feet firmly planted on the earth and your arms always reaching up toward the heavens.

May the chariot of your marriage be blessed with golden wings and take you to heights you have never dreamed.

The following marriage blessing, to be read by [friend of the couple], was written by the famous Sufi poet and mystic Rumi. It is called "This Marriage."

May these vows and this marriage be blessed.

May it be sweet milk, this marriage, like wine and halvah . . .

(See page 128 for the complete text.)

Partaking of Herbs and Spices

The bride and groom will now take part in an African wedding tradition in which they will taste various herbs and spices. This act is also reminiscent of the Jewish Passover ritual of partaking of herbs. Judah and Chantè, please kneel.

In marriage you commit to endure all aspects of life together—whether life be bitter as represented by this vinegar . . . or full of sadness, sour like lemon juice . . . or passionate, full of emotion, intense, like hot cayenne pepper . . . or whether peaceful, calm, and smooth like palm oil. We pray for you strength, as represented by these kola nuts. Finally, remember this: Should your love endure all the elements that life brings, only then will your life be truly honey sweet. [Adapted from *Going to the Chapel,* by the editors of *Signature Bride Magazine,* provided by Rev. Valentine]

The bride and groom fed each other, using their fingers, from the bowls containing the ingredients, one by one (the cayenne pepper is intense; water was at hand!) as I explained the significance of each.

Handfasting

*We followed the **declaration of intent,** with the anointing and wrapping of the hands, or the Celtic handfasting (see Chapter 6).*

As you hold the hands of your beloved, listen to what I am about to say. Above you are the stars, below you is the earth; as time does pass, remember: Like the earth should your love be firm, grounded in your humanity. Like a star should your love be constant, imbued with the light of God. Let the powers of the mind and of the intellect guide you in your marriage, let the strength of your wills bind you together, let the power of love and desire make you happy, and the strength of your dedication make you inseparable.

Vows

Before Judah and Chantè said their formal vows, each spoke to the other of his or her love in statements they had written themselves. As Chantè—pregnant, veiled, kneeling before her beloved—read her personal vows, she brought everyone to tears. Here, in part, the couple's words.

[Chantè]

Dear Judah, I'm writing of my love for you, trying to put it into words as best as I can. My world opened up and the sky took me in when I found love in you. Your smile is worth waking up for another day, when I'm down. Your heart is worth listening to, when the drumbeat of mine slows into a solemn, sad rhythm. I pledge to you endless strength that you can count on when you are weak. I'll be music when you can't hear, or your sunshine when you can't see. I'll be your extension of beauty when you go bald, or your perfume when you can't smell. You'll never need to look further than me. I will be your days and nights when you need them filled, your spark of life in the darkness, your hope when you're down-and-out.

I will keep "us" as sacred as the life that God breathed into us. As amazed as that first day we sat together in my kitchen, learning to love as we laughed. Learning to cherish as we stared into the eyes of our destiny. For that moment, I've given up my world—only to find the rainbow at the end of the rainfall. Never stop being my joy, and I will always be your light.

[Judah]

Our rivers join and caress as sweet springs of purity, rhythmically looping and turning to become one flowing body. Our hearts shall be forever beating together in a warm, lifelong embrace like that of two stars dancing through space. In our dance, sometimes I shall lead and sometimes you—through the wild turns and drastic dips and our hearts' beating shall be the music of our love, by which we will be guided for eternity. This is our completion and triumph. Love is not easy. We fought to get here and have earned our love.

I will be next to you in your struggles. I will calm your pain, I will protect you as a shield from harm's way and nurture all your virtuous qualities. I shall never take your love for granted. Our love is destiny.

Blessing and Exchange of Rings

To my standard description of the rings as powerful symbols, I added words from the poet Rumi:

The tender words you have said to one another are stored in the secret heart of Heaven. One day like rain they will fall and spread, and your mystery will grow green over the world.

Celebrant's Words to the Guests

I would like to take a moment to address the families and friends of Chantè and Judah. God has joined this couple together, and they need the support of those they love and cherish most—all of you. As an interfaith, interracial, intercultural couple, Judah and Chantè embody the meaning of respect, tolerance, and understanding. Parents, you are to be congratulated, because it is through your children that Rev. Dr. Martin Luther King's dream is coming true. He had a magnificent dream that one day "all of God's children, black men and white men, Jews and Gentiles, Protestant and Catholics will be able to join hands." He had a blessed dream, that little children would "not be judged by the color of their skin but by the content of their character."

Behold, here today, Martin Luther King's dream! Please see the beauty, the uniqueness of their love. Cherish it and support it. You all have something to offer them. Each of you has your own unique gifts. Please offer your gifts in the spirit of love and unity. As Dr. King stated so eloquently: "Only love can drive out hate. Hate cannot drive out hate. Only love can do that." Let us celebrate this love!

Now will everyone please go inside, to your hearts, and fill yourselves with all your good intentions, your prayers, your hopes and dreams for Judah, Chantè, and their baby for the many years to come. Each prayer is a point of light that goes directly to heaven. Let us send them off with many points of light.

Closing Blessing

Judah and Chantè had selected the Apache Wedding Blessing, which begins "Now you will feel no rain . . ." (See page 128 for the complete text.)

Jumping of the Broom, Breaking of the Glass

We end this ceremony with two delightful traditions—the African-American jumping of the broom and the Jewish breaking of the glass.

Slaves in this country were not permitted to marry, so they would jump a broom as a way to unite, symbolically sweeping away the old and welcoming the new, marking the beginning of making a home together. The ritual was and remains a call of support for the marriage from the entire community. It represents great joy and at the same time serves as a reminder of the past and the pain of slavery.

Similarly, stepping on the glass signifies remembering the past and moving to the future. The couple belong no longer to their parents' houses but to their own. Today, we celebrate the great joy of this marriage, as we also remember the sorrows that exist in the world. We break the glass in the prayer that Judah's and Chantè's marriage will help break down the needless barriers that people create between one another. We break this glass for peace. Judah and Chantè, may your bond of love be as difficult to break as it would be to put back together the pieces of this glass.

It is traditional that an elder place the broom on the ground. Chantè's grandmother will do us the honor. Judah's grandmother, in California, could not be with us today; in her honor, we ask that my hand represent her hand in placing the glass on the ground.

At this point, I asked the bride and groom to face the congregation. I took the twig broom from the altar table and ceremoniously presented it to Chantè's grandmother (a sprite of a woman elegantly donned in a mink stole), who placed it on the ground before them. I then placed the glass on the ground in front of the broom, while giving clear instructions for the couple to: "Jump . . . crush . . . kiss!" Everyone laughed. It was at the couple's specific request that they would jump the broom and simultaneously land on the glass, crushing it with a loud noise. (Admittedly, some of us were a bit concerned about Chantè's jumping in her condition!) Judah would then unveil his bride and sweep her into his arms with a kiss.

Pronouncement

Judah and Chantè, by the great love that has brought you here today, by the vows you have exchanged and the integrity of your commitment, in the presence and mystery of God, in the company of family and friends, it is my honor, and absolute delight, that I now pronounce you husband and wife.

They jumped the broom. Judah crushed the glass under his foot with a distinct crack. *The guests shouted, "Mazel tov!" The bride and groom kissed. And then out they walked to the rousing sound of African drumming. I felt quite certain that Judah's wish had been granted, that all present sensed they had participated in "something amazing!"*

In my work area today hangs a beautiful African angel, a gift from Chantè and Judah, which serves as a constant reminder of them. After a much needed honeymoon in Mexico, Chantè gave birth to a baby boy, Kuane. Another angel!

Sylvia and Fakir
an African-American Christian–Moroccan Muslim couple
a religious ceremony

On a pristine spring day, I met with Sylvia and Fakir in the outdoor garden of their home, where Sylvia had recently planted clusters of crimson flowers in the shape of an enormous heart. During our conversation a hummingbird decided to partake of a flower's nectar, and all our hearts fluttered, as happens when witnessing such beauty. Then something magical occurred: The hummingbird circled, hovering above and just behind our shoulders for well over forty-five minutes. We were in awe! The magic had begun!

Sylvia—a former social worker, now manager of a chic downtown restaurant in New York City—and Fakir—an aspiring actor—would have two ceremonies. Though they had found an imam who would perform a private Islamic ceremony with Fakir's mother present, Sylvia's pastor, a Born-Again Christian, felt that he could not preside over an interfaith union. But they wanted both their families and their traditions honored and celebrated, and came to me to talk about how they might achieve that balance in their ceremony.

In her questionnaire Sylvia wrote, "I envision a romantic, symbolic, heavenly ceremony." Raised in the Protestant faith, "by my mom, who's Born-Again, and my dad, who is Episcopalian," she considered herself now to be very spiritual and all-embracing. Sensitive to the religious and cultural differences between their families, Sylvia had a particular request: "I would like a congregational 'vow' to support us in our marriage, in lieu of my being given away. Allow us to impart to them the infinite possibilities our lives have in store for us; not to be frightened of what it is they don't know, or comprehend." Thus we began to design their ceremony to include Christian, Islamic, Sufi, African, and Moroccan elements—with a touch of Native American—to be witnessed by their 180 guests. These two young people wrote such beautiful words about their love for their parents and for each other that it was not difficult to create the "romantic, heavenly" ceremony they envisioned.

Forever in my mind's eye will be a scene from their wedding rehearsal. After they had finished practicing the recession, Fakir swept Sylvia into his arms, spinning her around and around! Later he told me that he treasured "the paradise she carries in her heart." This is stardust.

> May all creatures be of a blissful heart.
>
> —*Metta Sutta*

On her wedding day, to honor Fakir, his mother, and the rest of the groom's family, Sylvia had the palms of her hands beautifully decorated with henna, as is the Moroccan custom. The ceremony was held a gazebo trimmed with roses that was itself in the garden of a New York banquet facility, near a pond complete with swans and ducklings. The tall, willowy bride wore a princess dress with ballet slippers. The groom was all in white on this summer day, with his long, dark hair loose behind his ears. It had been arranged by mother and daughter that there would be roses, butterflies, and doves, creating a fairy-tale effect, and throughout the wedding Sylvia's mom had the look of contentment and fulfillment that comes from giving a child a dream come true. On the altar we had arranged a pitcher of milk, glasses, and a bowl of dates, which we would use to perform another Moroccan ritual; candles; and roses, a surprise for the couple's mothers.

Here, the marriage ceremony of Sylvia and Fakir.

Procession

To the music of Debussy's Claire de Lune Suite, the bridesmaids—I referred to them as the bride's muses—proceeded down the aisle, releasing butterflies as they walked. The music changed to Stevie Wonder's "Isn't She Lovely?" as the bride was escorted in by her father. When they reached the congregation, Sylvia's mother took her daughter's other arm, and all three processed to Purcell's Trumpet Voluntary.

Opening Words

We opened with an Islamic legend. Then, to my welcome and general remarks on the mystery and magic of this day, I felt it most appropriate to add comments the bride had written to me.

I give you Sylvia's words: "What a unique and blessed union ours is. More than anything, we came together by divine intervention of an entity much greater than all of us. This is an inclusive act, not one which will in any way exclude who we are or what our families have instilled in us. As a matter of fact, we were able to come to this stage of our lives and share such a unique love by virtue of our families, and by what we have been taught and who they'd have us be since we were born. We would like all those in attendance at our wedding to take hold of the overwhelming joy we possess in having found one another."

Will everyone do that now? Will you take hold of this overwhelming joy? Sylvia and Fakir want to share it with you! This is an act ordained by God, blessed by God, and celebrated by his angels—both those in heaven and those on earth, right here today. You are Sylvia and Fakir's angels.

Passing the Sign of Peace

It is in the spirit of this unity that the bride and groom now ask that we pass the sign of peace. For those of you not familiar with this tradition: Kindly extend your right hand to your neighbor in the offering of a handshake. And if you are near someone you love very much and should feel so inspired, a hug or a kiss will do as well!

Reading

I announced that our first reading was from the New Testament, 1 Corinthians, chapter 13; the bride's mother honored us by reading this statement on love.

Honoring of Family Members

We pay tribute to Fakir's deceased grandfather by quoting Fakir's words: "He was a great man, with a lot of happiness. I want to honor him today. He left with the little angels—and I am sure that he watches over me today and that he is happy for what is happening to me."

Here is a portion of my address to the parents of the bride and groom.

In Fakir's words: "I want to thank my parents, and Sylvia's parents, who raised us with nice hearts, and who made us meet and be together on this earth. We were meant to meet, and they helped us to finalize it! I would like to thank all my family for being here today. We will always be a real family, even from far away, even if I can't smile with them or look at them every day. My childhood is present in my memories, and my origins are the base of who I am today. Thank you, Mummy. Thank you, Daddy.

"I would like to tell Sylvia's mother that the prayer she said when Sylvia was born, that a prince would come—her dream becomes a reality. Not because I was a prince to start! I was just a humble gentleman with good intentions, but Sylvia makes me feel like a prince."

To Fakir's family, who have traveled far to be here today—we thank you. We especially honor Fakir's mother. It was through her example that he learned to embody the words of the Hadith, the words of the prophet Muhammad: "Kindness is a mark of faith: and whoever hath not kindness hath not faith." To Fakir's family who are in France and in Northern Africa, especially his father, watching in spirit: We say thank you—shukran ["thank you" in Arabic] and merci. We honor you.

Mr. and Mrs. [Sylvia's parents], your daughter wrote you quite a tribute! She says, "I couldn't be more blessed to have been given the most wonderful parents in the world." Sylvia describes her mother as the most special woman in her life, truly the epitome of a strong, godly, unconditional, supportive, intelligent, and fun-loving being. But perhaps the greatest compliment she gave you is in calling you her best friend. And her father, "the man I most respected and never wanted to let down. He loves me and shows me his love in lots of ways."

Sylvia says, "To live in a Caribbean household is to live a life filled with fun, warm family celebrations, trips to Barbados every year—festivity is key! My parents were there for all the big events of my youth—all the graduations, piano recitals, concerts, and so forth. Culturally, I've had instilled in me a strong sense of pride in who I am and from where I've come."

These are immortal gifts you've given your daughter. Mr. and Mrs. [Sylvia's parents], you have done well. God is most pleased. You embody the words from Matthew 5, verse 16: "Let your light shine, that they may see your good works and give glory to your Father who is in heaven." We honor you. We thank you.

Reading

The bride's brother read the second reading, from Proverbs 31, which begins "A wife of noble character who can find? She is worth far more than rubies." As I told the guests, Fakir had selected the passage in honor of his bride.

Celebrant's Address

Here is a portion of my address to the bride and groom.

As we all participate in something far greater than ourselves, you, Sylvia and Fakir, as an entity, as a married couple, will also help all of us expand heart, mind, and soul. Beyond fear, into love. Beyond doubt, into faith. And beyond separation, into unity. Sylvia, you said it yourself so wonderfully well: "We are living proof that love in its purest form is not selective with regard to religion or culture. If you allow yourself to be touched by the boldness and beauty, you may supersede all of the conditions man has placed on love."

You are speaking here of God's love. It is pure and unconditional. It has no boundaries. The question is: Are you up for the challenge? Will you commit now to always put love first? If you do this then you serve God, for as the apostle John said, God is love. Promise to do this!

Listen to your own beautiful words about each other. Sylvia, this is what Fakir wrote about you: "I met the most beautiful human being, and I never thought this would have happened. She is my destiny, my better half. She changed my life. She gave me hope, confidence in myself. I met her and my life started. She is marvelous, respectful. She has a heart as big as the earth. She is sensible and smart, sweet and magnificent. She is a baby, a child, and a woman at the same time, and she is my queen."

Fakir, when I asked Sylvia to tell me the qualities she most admired in you, she answered with an impressive list. She described you as honest, generous, faithful, fun, intelligent, passionate, real, sexy, and hardworking. When I asked her how you make her feel loved, this is what she said: "With notes, letters of love, helping me unsolicited, small gifts, hugs, kisses just because, respect for my beliefs and opinions."

Keep it up, you two! Don't stop now. Don't stop ever.

Prayer

These are the words of the Hadith, the words of Muhammad: "Shall I not inform you of a better act than fasting, alms, and prayers? Making peace between one another: enmity and malice tear up heaven's rewards by the roots."

God has a mission for you, Sylvia and Fakir. We pray that he guide you in that direction. I envision a man and a woman committed to empowering and uplifting all people. I envision a man and a woman overcoming all obstacles placed before them collectively and individually by the support they provide to one another. I envision a man and a woman joined spiritually, metaphysically, and emotionally, attaining inner peace and true happiness. [Adapted from "My Vision," by Craig Butler]

Sharing of Sweet Milk and a Date

It is a delightful Moroccan tradition that a bride and groom shall drink milk together and share a date. In doing so, they partake of the nourishing sweetness of life. Fakir and Sylvia will now honor this ancient ritual.

Going to the altar, I poured a glass of milk, which Fakir and Sylvia drank. Each then fed the other a bite of the date.

The following blessing was written by the Sufi poet and mystic Rumi:
May these vows and this marriage be blessed.
May it be sweet milk, this marriage, like wine and halvah.
May this marriage offer fruit and shade like the date palm.
(See page 128 for the complete text.)

Blessing from the Fathers and Siblings

After the **declaration of intent** *and the* **anointing and binding of the hands,** *we had a blessing.*

Mr. [bride's father], will you please come forward?

Do you bless this union?

Then kindly place your right hand upon the hands of your children and join me in a silent prayer. The bride and groom have asked that my hand represent Fakir's father's hand in this blessing.

The bride and groom now ask that all their siblings come forward one by one and bestow a personal blessing.

After the family members had offered their good wishes to the couple, I supported the bride's and groom's hands, still loosely wrapped in my prayer stole, and said a brief blessing.

Following the **blessing and exchange of rings,** *Sylvia read aloud a charming poem she had written to her groom, entitled "You, to Me." We proceeded with the* **vows.**

Lighting of the Unity Candle

Will the mothers of the bride and groom kindly join us for the lighting of the unity candle, a Christian tradition? They will light the side candles, symbolic of their giving life to the bride and groom, and Sylvia and Fakir together will light the center candle.

Sylvia and Fakir then presented to each of their mothers a rose with a personal note attached, with a hug and a kiss.

Mothers, in your honor, we offer you this quotation from classical Greek literature, the words of Homer:

It is she, who nourished you
she, out of her treasures.
Beautiful children
beautiful harvests
are achieved from you,
the giving of life itself.
As Sylvia and Fakir lit the center candle:
The following prayer is from the Masai in Tanzania:
Receive this holy fire.
Make your lives like this fire.
A holy life that is seen.
A life of God that is seen. . . .
(See page 219 for the complete text.)

*We concluded the ceremony with the **pronouncement, the kiss,** and my brief address to the guests, asking for their support for this new interfaith, interracial, intercultural couple.*

Reading

These are the words of Kahlil Gibran, from the book *The Prophet,* on marriage. The groom specifically requested this reading, because these words reflect his deepest beliefs.
Fakir and Sylvia:
You were born to be together, and together you shall be forevermore.
You shall be together when the wings of death scatter your days.
(See page 116 for the complete text.)

Sprinkling of Rose Petals

Rose petals represent life's sweetest blessings: beauty, love, romance, poetry, and art. Sylvia and Fakir, as you go into the world as husband and wife, we sprinkle them on your heads. We lay them at your feet.

Go now in peace, with joy and love in your hearts. God's blessings go with you.

Ma'Salaama!

Release of Doves

Doves have long been a spiritual symbol of hope and peace. Our bride and groom will now release doves.

Fakir and Sylvia first released two doves from a heart-shaped basket; after that, forty doves were released. They swooped over the congregation with a great flapping of wings in a V-formation—to the oohs *and* aahs *of the crowd.*

Ladies and gentlemen, it is my privilege to present to you Mr. and Mrs. [bride and groom]! As they leave, please shower them with the rose petals you'll find at the ends of your rows. Shower them with your blessings.

Sylvia and Fakir walked out to a gossamer-covered gazebo, where Berber dancers performed a traditional Moroccan marriage dance—a surprise for the groom arranged by his bride! He was right. She was an angel.

Jacqueline and Kenneth
a Born-Again Christian–Jewish couple
a spiritual ceremony containing Christian and Jewish elements

This is a story of great hope and of a dream. The poet Rumi said, "Where there is ruin, there is treasure." From Jackie's unhappy first marriage came a perfect, radiant child—Macklin. And the crumbling of that "loveless" marriage, as she described it, opened the door for true love to come into Jackie's life.

One night Jackie had a dream, one of those vivid and clear dreams that stay with you. A man whom she didn't know put a key in the palm of her hand, and at that moment and that touch, she fell passionately in love. She woke up still enveloped by the wondrous feeling, and then felt saddened by the fact that she did not have such love in her life. But the dream somehow bolstered her courage, and gave her the strength to separate from her husband.

Jackie later took a job as manager of an executive office building. One day Kenneth stopped by to see a friend and ex-business partner with offices there, who asked him at the end of their visit to drop off a door key with the building manager. Seeing Jacqueline for the first time, Kenneth thought, Wow! Who is that? As for Jackie, when he handed her the key: "I got a jolt! The dream came back to me!" Hearing this story years later, I asked Kenneth if he too had felt the "jolt." He laughed and said, "I *do* remember that she wouldn't let go of my hand! It was definitely a moment when I felt something cosmic was happening."

Within weeks they were inseparable. Though their road was not easy, their love and commitment remained strong. In her questionnaire Jackie wrote, "Kenneth and I have been through so much together, staying together through all our hard times—my divorce, a child custody battle for over two years, moving cross-country twice, unemployment, the death of dearly loved grandparents, trying times with our parents, financial hardships."

What made it all work, she said, was "the willingness to change ourselves and to grow, listening to one another and not giving up on us through all this stuff makes our relationship special and strong. I most appreciate Ken's love for my child. He loves and cares for him as if my son was his."

Kenneth wrote, "I feel in a lot of ways that Macklin and I are as close a father and son as any two nonrelated people can be. Watching him grow inspires me. Raising a child is a special privilege that I treasure dearly."

They were both equally proud of their religious heritages. Jacqueline was raised a Born-Again Christian and attended a Christian high school. Some of her religious beliefs were changing: "I believe God to be my personal savior. One saying I tell myself often is, God will never leave me, nor forsake me. But I am in the process of figuring it out, and I decided it's okay if I don't have it all figured out at this moment."

Kenneth wrote, "I do believe in an eternal being. I was raised in a Conservative Jewish family, went to Hebrew school, had Bar Mitzvah, and was fortunate enough to visit Israel for a full summer to learn more about my heritage. Being in Israel and experiencing things that my ancestors experienced thousands of years ago was a thrill that I have not yet topped. Standing on top of Massadah in Israel and watching the sun rise was a moment I will never forget." Though his parents, he said, always hoped he would marry in the Jewish faith, they had been supportive and accepted Jackie and Macklin into the family with open arms.

Although each was actively involved in his or her beliefs, there was no attempt to convert or impose, only the utmost mutual respect. At a country club near the ocean—"anywhere near the water," she wrote, "is where I love to be"—Jackie and Ken were married in a ceremony that celebrated and honored their differences. Macklin, who at the time was three, was an integral part of the proceedings.

Here, the wedding of Jacqueline and Kenneth.

Opening Words

Here are some of my words of welcome.

There are moments in our lives that we hold so sacred that we see it fitting to conduct ceremonies where we ask God to bless and consecrate the special event. These moments are marked not so much by time but by the heart. Jacqueline and Kenneth have fallen in love so deeply that today they will offer themselves to each other in holy matrimony. Today they will state their vows, in the presence of all of you, their loved ones, and in the presence of God.

Reading

A relative of the couple read the chuppah poem that includes "O my love come dance with me." (See page 183 for the complete text.)

Address to the Couple

I opened my address with the old Jewish legend, that forty days before a child is born, his or her spouse is selected in heaven.

I also told them what impressed me about them as a couple: Jackie's prophetic dream, Kenneth's love and affection for Macklin, their mutual respect for each other, and their enduring ability to work through what life offers. That was, in my opinion, a formula for success.

Readings

Jackie and Kenneth had selected two readings popular with many couples—the passage from Corinthians 1, chapter 13, that begins: "If I speak in the tongues of mortals and of angels, but do not have love . . ." and Shakespeare's 116th sonnet, which begins: "Let me not to the marriage of true minds admit impediments." (See pages 120 and 152 for the complete texts.)

Anointing of Hands

Following the declaration of intent, I anointed the couple's hands with oil, wrapped their hands in my prayer shawl, and offered a silent prayer. We asked young Macklin to come forward and place his hand upon Jackie and Kenneth's hands during the prayer and blessing.

Vows

Here are the beautiful vows Jackie repeated after me [From The Complete Book of Wedding Vows, *by Diane Warner]:*

Kenneth, because of you my heart is at peace. Because of you, I am happy. Because of you, I look forward to the future with joy. Because of you, my world is whole. Because of you, I believe in marriage anew. And because of you, my child is blessed to have you by his side. What a blessing that I met you and that our friendship grew into a love that is eternal. I pledge myself to you this day as your wife and the mother of our children, now and forevermore. May God bless our marriage and our new family.

And Kenneth's vows to his bride:

Jacqueline, as we become one on this our wedding day, we become part of each other. Your feelings become my feelings, your sorrows become my sorrows, your joys become my joys, your worries become my worries, and your child becomes my child. I promise to be a true and faithful husband, always there to comfort you, rejoice with you, and endure all the complexities of life that we will face together as a family in the years to come. My love for you and our son is pure and unshakable, and I hereby commit myself to both of you from this day forth and forevermore.

After my **blessing of the rings,** *Jackie and Ken exchanged ring vows that included the words "With this ring, I give you my heart. I have no greater gift to give." (See page 134 for the complete text by Marianne Williamson.)*

Lighting of the Unity Candle

Now Jackie and Ken, before you take your final vows, I will ask you to light the candle of unity, symbolizing that you are no longer two but one.

"From every human being there rises a light that reaches straight to heaven. And when two souls are destined to be together and find each other, their streams of light flow together, and a single brighter light goes forth from their united being." [by the Ba'al Shem Tov]

Final Vows

The bride and groom in turn answered "I do" to my following questions.

Jackie/Kenneth, do you take this man/woman, Kenneth/Jackie, to be your lawful wedded husband/wife, to have and to hold him/her, to love and to cherish him/her, to nurture and sustain him/her, to be true to him/her through times of darkness as well as light? Do you promise this heart, body, and soul? Do you commit before God to honor this vow all the days of your life?

Closing Blessing

*After the **pronouncement** and **the kiss**, I asked everyone to rise as I offered the following blessing.*

Jackie, Kenneth, and Macklin, the ceremony is done, and now you will begin your life together. We shall call upon four angels to walk with you. To your right is the angel Gabriel, who will be there to give you faith and encouragement. To your left is Michael (in Hebrew, he is called Mikaiel); he shall protect you. Behind you walks Raphael; he shall be there to heal you. And in front of you walks the angel Uriel, whose name means "the Light of God." This angel shall light your path, as you walk hand in hand with Macklin and your future children into your new life together.

Go now in peace. Go now in joy. Amen.

*Kenneth performed **the breaking of the glass**, and family and guests shouted, "Mazel tov!"*

A postscript: Ken and Jackie have since had a second child, Trevor, and are happily living by the ocean—Jackie's sacred spot, where she feels most at peace and inspired.

Epilogue

he world has changed profoundly since I began writing *Joining Hands and Hearts*. The events of September 2001 shook the country from stem to stern. Their reverberations were felt throughout the world.

I live at ground zero in New York City, and witnessed the fall of the mighty towers into the black mushroom cloud. The events that followed were surreal and filled with horror. Tears and acts of selflessness flowed profusely.

Interfaith dialogue is needed now more than ever.

I am proud to have participated in the joining of hands and hearts between Muslims and Christians, Jews and Muslims, Hindus and Christians, Buddhists and Jews, African Americans and Anglo Saxons, Asians and Americans, and many other wonderful combinations. These couples are the Romeo and Juliet stories of our time! Is it so unusual for the incalculable power of love to transcend boundaries of religious dogma, skin color, cultural upbringing, geographical borders or political beliefs? Throughout this book I have said that interfaith, intercultural and interracial unions embody the meaning of respect, tolerance and understanding. We can learn from them. They bring healing and point us towards the way

My effort should never be to undermine another's faith but to make him a better follower of his own faith.

—*Gandhi*

> Every wedding
> where true lovers wed,
> helps on the march
> of universal Love.
>
> —*Herman Melville*

of peace. I have also had the privilege of meeting the grace upon the faces of the children from these mixed marriages. More gifts from the divine. More hope.

I am reminded of a Native American Story in which a grandfather was talking to his grandson about his feelings. He tells the boy: "I feel as if I have two wolves fighting in my heart. One wolf is the vengeful, angry, violent one. The other wolf is the loving, compassionate one." The grandson asks, "Which wolf will win the fight in your heart?" The grandfather answered, "The one I feed."

May love and compassion be our fertile ground. After all, we really are one family, one human race living together on this small sacred earth.

This book is offered in the spirit of peace.

RESOURCES

■

You may contact the following associations for information on interfaith wedding ceremonies. They may help you find a celebrant if you are having difficulty locating a minister, rabbi, or other individual to conduct your service, and provide information on locations in your area.

- American Ethical Union (of the New York Society of Ethical Culture)
    2 West Sixty-fourth St.
    New York, NY 10023
    212-873-6500

- American Humanist Association
    1777 T Street, NW
    Washington, DC 20009-7125
    202-238-9088
    (toll free) 866-486-2647 (866-HUMANISM)
    fax: 202-238-9003

- Association of Interfaith Ministers
    (toll free) 800-275-4809

- Buddhist Churches of America (BCA Headquarters)
    1710 Octavia St.
    San Francisco, CA 94109
    415-776-5600
    fax 415-771-6293

- Quaker Information Center (at Friends Center)
    1501 Cherry St.
    Philadelphia, PA 19102
    215-241-7024
    fax: 215-567-2096

- Rabbinic Center for Research and Counseling
    128 East Dudley Ave.
    Westfield, NJ 07090
    908-233-0419
    fax: 908-233-6459

- Sufi Order International National Headquarters
    P.O. Box 30065
    Seattle, WA 98103
    206-525-6992
    fax: 206-525-7013

- Unitarian-Universalist Association
    25 Beacon St.
    Boston, MA 02108
    617-742-2100

If you wish to order a ketubah for your Jewish-interfaith wedding, here are two companies you might want to contact:

- Caspi Cards & Art
    P.O. Box 220
    Newtonville, MA 02160
    617-964-8888
    800-538-8268

- Good Company
    P.O. Box 3218
    Chicago, IL 60654
    312-913-9193

A FINAL WORD

■

We request and will welcome your interfaith, intercultural, interracial love stories for future editions of *Joining Hands and Hearts*. We will also welcome your interfaith, intercultural wedding ceremonies, especially if they include elements that we did not mention in this edition. If you do decide to share your spirits and your love, we would be most grateful. You may contact us at

www.interfaithweddingceremony.com
www.susannamacomb.com

PERMISSIONS
ACKNOWLEDGMENTS

■

ABOUT THE AUTHORS

■

REVEREND SUSANNA STEFANACHI MACOMB is an ordained, licensed interfaith minister. Her extraordinary ceremonies have earned her an overwhelming number of referrals and features in *Modern Bride, For the Bride,* and *Bridal Guide.* She has appeared on national and local television. Macomb is also an artist whose paintings are of a spiritual nature. She resides in New York with her husband and son.

ANDREA THOMPSON has been a writer on many books, including *Couple Fits: How to Live with the Person You Love,* and *What Do You Want to Do When You Grow Up: Starting the Next Chapter of Your Life.*